Sapphism on Screen

Sapphism on Screen

Lesbian Desire in French and Francophone Cinema

Lucille Cairns

Edinburgh University Press

© Lucille Cairns, 2006

Edinburgh University Press Ltd
22 George Square, Edinburgh

Typeset in 11 on 13pt Ehrhardt
by Servis Filmsetting Limited, Manchester, and
printed and bound in Great Britain by
Antony Rowe Ltd, Chippenham, Wilts

A CIP record for this book is available from the British Library

ISBN-10 0 7486 2165 2 (hardback)
ISBN-13 978 0 7486 2165 1

The right of Lucille Cairns
to be identified as author of this work
has been asserted in accordance with
the Copyright, Designs and Patents Act 1988.

Contents

Acknowledgements

At the institutional level, I wish to thank IRIS (Centre de documentation et d'information) for allowing me access to a number of female-directed films unobtainable in the major French research libraries. On a more personal level, I am indebted to Margaret-Anne Hutton and to Keith Reader for their astute and genuinely invaluable advice on the first and second drafts of the manuscript respectively.

Author's Note

This book occasionally refers to certain comments in a number of my previous publications; in all cases, full references are provided. All translations from French, unless otherwise indicated, are my own.

Illustrations

CHAPTER ONE

Lesbian Desire in Film: Coming to Terms

This monograph investigates the traces and spaces of lesbian desire in a large corpus of films directed by both male and female directors, mainly from France but also from French-speaking parts of Belgium, Canada, Switzerland and Africa (Senegal). The absence of reference to other francophone countries is a correlate of the absence within them, at least so far, of directors who have treated inter-female desire. Spanning the period 1936–2002, the corpus numbers eighty-nine texts. A fair number of these are mainstream films that have achieved high critical acclaim and/or high viewing figures – to cite just a few examples: Henri-Georges Clouzot's *Quai des orfèvres* (1947), Louis Malle's *Milou en mai* (1989), Claude Chabrol's *La Cérémonie* (1995), André Téchiné's *Les Voleurs* (1995) and François Ozon's *Huit femmes* (2001). As such, they have contributed to hegemonic constructions of (female) homosexuality in an episteme wherein sexed and gendered identity, including sexual orientation, has become a pre-eminent factor in the constitution of subjectivity. While such constructions have a French-language specificity and have been produced in distinct socio-political and cultural contexts, the present study will, in its annotated filmography and elsewhere where appropriate, provide points of comparison with relevant anglophone films and their own distinct discursive contexts.

To my knowledge, there are only five book-length studies devoted exclusively to encodings of lesbian desire in cinema: listed chronologically, these are Andrea Weiss's *Vampires and Violets: Lesbians in the Cinema* (1992), Tamsin Wilton's *Immortal, Invisible: Lesbians and the Moving Image* (1995), Clare Whatling's *Screen Dreams: Fantasizing Lesbians in Film* (1997), Shameem Kabir's *Daughters of Desire: Lesbian Representations in Film* (1998) and Patricia White's *UnInvited: Classical Hollywood Cinema and Lesbian Representability* (1999). Yet all of these texts refer largely to anglophone films. Studies which include but are not devoted to lesbianism in film are only slightly more numerous: Richard Dyer's *Now you See It: Studies on*

Lesbian and Gay Film (1990), Judith Roof's *A Lure of Knowledge: Lesbian Sexuality and Theory* (1991), Lynda Hart's *Fatal Women: Lesbian Sexuality and the Mark of Aggression* (1994), Ellis Hanson's *Out Takes: Essays on Queer Theory and Film* (1999), Judith Mayne's *Framed: Lesbians, Feminists and Media Culture* (2000) and Alex Hughes' and James Williams' edited volume *Gender and French Cinema* (2001). In the French-language critical forum, there is an almost complete dearth of sustained attention to lesbian and gay sexuality, and *a fortiori* to lesbian sexuality specifically, in cinema. Bertrand Philbert's *L'Homosexualité à l'écran* (1984), now more than twenty years old, seems to have been followed by a resounding critical silence. Carrie Tarr's and Brigitte Rollet's *Cinema and the Second Sex: Women's Filmmaking in France in the 1980s and 1990s* (2001) is an excellent and groundbreaking study with respect to French women's filmmaking in general, but offers only a two-page section treating lesbianism exclusively.

So, as yet there has been no book-length study dedicated to lesbian desire in French and francophone cinema. My book seeks to fill this gap. It does not aim to provide highly technical cinematic analyses of a psychoanalytic, structuralist or semiotic bent. Crucially, it is *not* primarily a contribution to French cinema scholarship, but rather is a contribution to lesbian/gay/queer cultural studies *within a French-language cinematic context*.

Aside from the obvious,[1] the punning title of this chapter signals my intention to present some of the key terms and underlying concepts which will inform the textual exegeses of the subsequent chapters. Throughout this study every effort will be made to avoid logico-linguistic solecisms like 'lesbian film' or, indeed, 'French/francophone lesbian film'. To anthropomorphise a cultural artefact by ascribing it a human and nationalised sexual identity is patently absurd. However, these solecisms do serve as a useful form of shorthand, and I will occasionally have recourse to them in order to avoid a hypertrophe of admittedly clumsy circumlocutions such as 'lesbian-themed text' or 'lesbian-connoted text'. Evidently, the meanings I ascribe to the word 'lesbian' and its cognate 'lesbianism' need to be transparent from the outset. My definition of these terms has not changed since 2002:

> The sine qua non of lesbianism is, I aver, *erotic* attraction between women. On the whole, then, my study deploys the word 'lesbian' to mean a woman/female human being who may not necessarily have had genital contact with, but whose erotic preference is for, other women/female human beings – at least in the (diegetic or actual) present, for I do not conceptualize sexual preference as a necessarily immutable, and certainly not as a congenital, property. I am thus closer to the constructionist than the essentialist position in the debate that has long raged in discourse on (particularly homo)sexuality.[2] Concomitantly, by 'lesbian-themed text', I designate a text

inscribing sexual (and perhaps also, but not necessarily, affective) attraction between women/female human beings. (Cairns 2002a: 11)

One final point on terminology: the adjective 'gay' will, on the whole, be used to include homosexual women as well as homosexual men.

To go back a step, the reader may ask why this study distances itself from highly psychoanalytic, structuralist or semiotic interpretations. The answer lies in its author's acute reservations about the credibility of canonical film theorisations of 'woman' on screen, particularly in their (arguably outdated) psychoanalytic avatars: the *a priori* masculinised gaze, the oedipally-enslaved rhetorical tropes of fetishism and voyeurism, sadism and narcissism, transvestism and masquerade. Puzzling indeed is the tenacity of this psychoanalytic grip on a post-oedipal family era wherein – at least in Western, postmodern intellectual circles, which, like it or not, constitute *the* circuit of our discursive existence – other factors such as gender, sexual orientation, class, race, physical ability and so on can no longer be ignored as equally compelling factors in spectatorial responses. Yet it would be naïve to ignore such theories, and rather than dismissing them wholesale or else cravenly deferring to them, I will take inspiration from the theoretical magpie Jacques Lacan by occasionally performing strategic raids upon discrete theoretical regimes (without implying acceptance of those regimes in their totality) *where* such raids serve to illuminate the raw material of the filmic text and its audience reception(s). The justification for such a strategy is the conceptual inadequacy of any of these pre-existing theoretical corpuses adequately to account for a previously unexplored territory: that of lesbian-connoted French-language film.

The 'coming to terms' initiated above extends beyond single words such as 'lesbian' and 'lesbianism' to an analysis at the level of the cinematic collocation: it engages with plural terms designating salient discursive nodes that inform more recent and less blinkered discourses on film and sexuality. These include lesbian spectatorship; resisting reading and its various avatars such as reading against the grain, appropriating readings and lesbian interventions; space for the lesbian imagination; the cinematic lesbian continuum; and directorial intentionality versus audience reception.

First, then, what is meant by 'lesbian spectatorship'? In her *Daughters of Desire: Lesbian Representations in Film*, Shameem Kabir rightly states that 'the cinematic apparatus addresses the spectator in definable ways, and the spectator as a social subject receives this address according to our own social and cultural specificities' (Kabir 1998: 184). Her succeeding observation puts the case cogently: 'there is no fixed unitary position of spectatorship, where response is uniform and where subjectivity is stable. We spectate across gender, across race and sexuality, class and culture, age and ability, and our different geopolitical and other positionings result in diverse spectating responses' (Kabir 1998: 185). Tamsin Wilton also privileges the importance of the lesbian spectator's social positioning over psychoanalytic paradigms:

> Arguing for a more complete escape from the Freudian/Lacanian paradigm, my piece suggests that text-deterministic notions of identification are inadequate to account for lesbian viewing pleasure. I propose the notion of the cinematic contract, by which the spectator tacitly agrees to make use of a variety of engagement strategies in order to 'make sense of' the film in question. My suggestion is that such engagement strategies derive less from the unconscious and more from the social location of the spectator, and that hence sociology rather than psychology is the exemplary paradigm for thinking about lesbians and the moving image. (Wilton 1995: 16)

Wilton appositely points to the fundamental schism identified by Jackie Stacey between, on the one hand, 'film studies which generally understand spectatorship as a product of textual address and meaning as being production-led and, on the other, cultural studies which generally understand spectatorship as a process of negotiation between product and consumer and meaning as consumption-led' (Wilton 1995: 145).[3] I concur wholly in Wilton's subsequent reflections:

> It seems clear to me that there is little evidence to suggest that film is in any significant way different from other cultural products. To say that film is polysemic and that its many possible meanings are contingent and, moreover, located at the meniscus between film as product (located within the social and economic relations of production) and viewer as consumer (similarly located within specific social and economic relations of consumption) is only to claim that film is no more and no less intrinsically meaning-full than painting, poetry, novels or any other cultural product. I take for granted here that the sense of a film is made by the spectator – whom we may understand for our purposes as both receptive and engaged, and as bringing to the process of spectating a temporally and culturally specific set of signs, meanings, codes and languages. (Wilton 1995: 145–6)

In the specific context of the present study, that 'sense of a film' made by the spectator can be compliant with dominant modes of spectating – namely, confined to the surface heterosexual meanings – or it can 'resist' those surface meanings. The term 'resisting reading' denotes an interpretive strategy charged with teasing out lesbian traces from ostensibly heteronormative filmic narratives, sequences or images. In so doing, that strategy resists the dominant viewing/reading grain, hence the further term 'reading against the grain', which may, in its turn, be designated by the close synonym 'sub-texting'. The latter term was first coined by Claire Johnston as a strategy serving a counter-cinema resistance to Hollywood practices, but it may be appropriated to indicate the detection, systematic or otherwise, of lesbian potentialities within the images, editing and narratives of mainstream film.[4] As Kabir puts it, the 'position of the lesbian spectator of mainstream film is one where we are usually denied any direct representation of lesbian desire. We have seen that a strategy open to us is to supply a resistant position of spectatorship and read in the desire at the margins of the film. This is to subtext' (Kabir 1998: 185). Resisting readings and subtexting imply lesbian 'interventions' into texts which are at least *prima facie* about straight desire – the act of 'appropriating' for oneself the construction of meaning, even in the face of contrary textual evidence.

This is where I begin to draw the line, to resist intellectually. As Clare Whatling concedes, 'to be sure, in reading lesbian desire into films which offer little narrative opening for the lesbian viewer, one is guilty of committing a certain amount of semantic violence on the text' (Whatling 1997: 58). And as her subtle analysis conveys:

> there is a danger that appropriative reading merely sustains, as it were by default, the reproduction of the status quo . . . does pleasuring in images, despite their foundation in sexism, heterosexism, racism, even in readings that attempt to counter these elements, merely give credence to the oppressor? Who really triumphs here, the text or the audience? (Whatling 1997: 22)

I insist on a *principled* approach to what has variously been termed resisting reading, reading against the grain, subtexting or making lesbian interventions. I unconditionally oppose the doing of semantic violence to a text, filmic or otherwise. As for the 'space for the lesbian imagination', the lesbian spectator in private is obviously free to let her imagination do what it wants with the basic raw materials of the filmic text. However, where there is no textual evidence to support the veracity of these fantasy scenarios, she is *not* authorised to impose them as legitimate public exegeses.

A further note of caution should be sounded: spaces for the lesbian imagination can easily be commercially exploited and recuperated by the homogenising dream-machine of the mainstream screen. Two anglophone examples are *Buffy the Vampire Slayer* and Madonna's *Justify My Love*. *Buffy the Vampire Slayer*, first released as an American movie in 1992, became a highly lucrative television series running from 1997 to 2003. Its producers literally cashed in on the (at least then) lack of American television space for the lesbian imagination. Season five of seven introduced a lesbian dynamic when the witches Willow and Tara fell for each other. Predictably for mainstream drama in which lesbian love is usually doomed, things turned sour: Willow became addicted to magic, Tara turned against her when she realised Willow had been altering her memory, and Tara was eventually killed off. Admittedly, a 'happy' lesbian ending is suggested when, by the end of the seventh and final series, Willow has got over her grief and is now with a young woman called Kennedy. That's OK, then, particularly as all three lesbian characters conform to conventional canons of feminine beauty and can thus also pull in a large heterosexual male audience.

For her part, pop phenomenon Madonna cashed in on the largely untapped queer market with *Justify My Love* (1990). In fairness, it should be acknowledged that during this video performance, straight, queer and lesbian scenarios all get a look in: Madonna gets it on not only with unequivocally masculine men, but with also with one extremely androgynous man whose identification as such (that is, as a man) is by no means immediately obvious, *and* with women, whilst ancillary scenes featuring gender-ambiguous couples and straight buggery (man inside woman) complement the sexual cornucopia. But the 'lesbian' scene is hardly immune from criticism. When, in symmetry with the nominally male desire-object mentioned above, the highly androgynous-looking Amanda Cazalet is on top of Madonna, kissing her slowly and sensuously, they are being viewed by a male voyeur. Thus, potentially dissident desire is framed and contained by the classic male gaze. Independently of *Justify My Love*, Madonna also staged a highly mediatised kiss with pop singer Britney Spears, which contributed to mainstream constructions of 'lipstick' lesbianism as a harmless, titillating and non-threatening form of erotic dalliance. In the French context, the singer Saya also exploited the commercial dearth in spaces for the lesbian imagination in her ostensibly lesbian love-song 'Une femme avec une femme'.[5]

Is commercial exploitation of lesbianism really a cause for complaint? The obverse argument would be that anything that renders more visible, acceptable and even aspirational a hitherto practically invisible and/or stigmatised sexual identity should prompt applause rather than cavil. While I have some sympathy for this argument, the airbrushed quality of these highly packaged lesbian ciphers makes one wonder to what extent the average mainstream viewer will link them to extra-diegetical, real-life lesbians. And there's the rub: lesbian thrills can become aspirational consumer options *if* their protagonists look just like canonically pretty, straight girls. For if they did not, they might alienate the boys – and it is the boys who still, by and large, control every aspect of image-production, be it in film, video or television, from inception, creation, distribution and marketing down to consumption.

Beginning with resisting reading and ending on the possible exploitation of lesbian-encoded spaces in popular media, the foregoing discussion has emphasised the dangers of unfettered voluntarism. A fitting coda to this emphasis is Julia Erhart's warning: '[p]recisely because of the vague way popular, mainstream cinema has always represented lesbianism, writing that decisively claims an ambiguous character or film as "lesbian" lays itself open to charges of voluntarism, that is, to the accusation that it is too interpretation-dependent and not sufficiently empirical' (Erhart, 1997: 93). These dangers notwithstanding, my argument will be that what ultimately makes a film 'lesbian' is not directorial intention but audience reception.[6] Although hardly yet a doxa, this is scarcely a new idea; as Erhart observes, and as I will reiterate in Chapter 4, the value of subtexting or reading against the grain was one of the matters of interest to the editors of the 'Lesbian and Film' section of *Jump Cut*, which appeared in 1981 (Erhart 1997: 86). So what does my position add to the idea? Nothing more and nothing less than the following two conditions. First, the acknowledgement that the same film will not 'be' lesbian for all spectators, since many will receive it differently from a lesbian audience (indeed, a singular ontological status cannot be ascribed to *any* film). Second, an insistence on the need for the variously named lesbian practices of resisting reading, reading against the grain, subtexting, making lesbian interventions or locating spaces for the lesbian imagination to be *principled*: for them not to traduce the integrity of the text, and, when they purport to be generally acceptable exegeses as opposed to products of their author's personal fantasies, for them to be based on palpable textual evidence.

These conditions established, we can begin to talk about lesbianising gaze theory. The convention of the male gaze was first systematically theorised in 1975 by Laura Mulvey's now classic article 'Visual Pleasure and Narrative Cinema', in which she postulated women in cinema as connoting *to-be-looked-at-ness* (Mulvey 1975). Put simply, Mulvey's thesis was that women are the object of the male gaze, consonant with psychoanalytic binaries associating man with the active and woman with the passive, man with desire and woman with lack. Since woman lacked the ability to desire, she could not be the subject of a desiring gaze *a fortiori* because the object of the cinematic gaze was traditionally another woman – and lesbian desire was even more of an absence in classical narrative cinema than was heterosexual female desire. I entirely refute the supposedly ahistorical necessity of this male gaze and instead assert its historical contingency, along with the possibility of female-specific and lesbo-specific scopophilia. When in 1981 Mulvey revisited her argument, in 'Afterthoughts on "Visual Pleasure and Narrative Cinema" inspired by *Duel in the Sun*', she asserted:

> I still stand by my 'Visual Pleasure', but would now like to pursue [the] other two lines of thought. First [the 'women in the audience' issue], whether the female spectator is carried along, as it were by the scruff of the text, or whether her pleasure can be more deep-rooted and complex. Second [the 'melodrama' issue], how the text and its attendant identifications are affected by a *female* character occupying the center of the narrative arena. (Mulvey 1981: 69)

Clearly, Mulvey's second line of thought does not concern us here, since it pertains only to melodrama and to the western, neither of which is germane to our corpus. As for the first line of thought, Mulvey's conclusion is again problematic:

> Three elements can be drawn together: Freud's concept of 'masculinity' in women, the identification triggered by the logic of a narrative grammar, and the ego's desire to phantasize itself in a certain, active, manner. All three suggest that, as desire is given cultural materiality in a text, for women (from childhood onwards) trans-sex identification is a *habit* that very easily becomes *second Nature*. However, this Nature does not sit easily and shifts restlessly in its borrowed transvestite clothes. (Mulvey 1981: 72)

The blindspot in Mulvey's argument is its docile acceptance of Freud's gendered binarisms and of the doxa that desire can only be masculine because only the masculine is active. This reduces the means by which women's viewing pleasure may become 'more deep-rooted and complex' to trans-sex identification. The weakness of Mulvey's second essay lies in its continuing enslavement to a conceptual paradigm in which the feminine and the active are mutually exclusive.

A year later, Mary Ann Doane came very close to Mulvey in arguing that women's viewing pleasure was dependent on female transvestism or masquerade. Doane's new contribution was the postulate of distance. She asserts that '[f]or the female spectator there is a certain over-presence of the image – she is the image' (Doane 1982: 78). As Weiss helpfully summarises:

> [t]his female spectator position lacks sufficient distance from either voyeurism or fetishism, the two forms of looking on which visual pleasure is based, according to contemporary theory. The notion of a feminine 'over-presence'

draws on the Freudian argument that women do not go through the castration scenario which demands the construction of a distance between men and the female image. To simplify a complex argument, Doane finds that the theoretical female spectator's pleasure in the cinema can take the form of masochism in over-identification with the image, or of narcissism in becoming one's own object of desire, or it may be possible, by re-inserting the necessary distance, for the woman's gaze to master the image. This distance can be achieved through two kinds of transformation which Doane identifies as transvestism and masquerade. Female transvestism involves adopting the masculine spectatorial position; female masquerade involves an excess of femininity, the use of femininity as a mask, which simulates the distance necessary for the pleasure of looking. (Weiss 1992: 39)

My question is: *why* should visual pleasure be based on voyeurism or fetishism? It is flagrantly obvious that 'visual pleasure' here is defined in exclusively masculine (heterosexual) terms. According to Doane, one can take pleasure in the cinema as a woman *without* distance, but this means masochism or narcissism; for her, both are antithetical to 'mastering the gaze', which can only be done by inserting distance. What does 'mastering the gaze' mean, other than distancing oneself from its object the better supposedly to dominate it? The circularity of the argument leads to a conceptual impasse outside the restrictive premises of its masculine positioning. More importantly, why should distancing be deemed superior? The very language used – *master*ing – is suspectly over-determined. And even if one provisionally accepts the hypothesis that the pleasure of looking *does* depend on distance from the object of one's gaze, it is still the case that a woman watching a female screen-image may be distant from that image in terms of race, class, physical appearance, ability or disability, and so on. As Weiss goes on to say:

In privileging the Oedipal complex, the psychoanalytic framework polarizes 'difference' along the lines of gender; it denies racial, class and sexual factors which play such significant roles in identity formation. Whether or not one accepts the psychoanalytic model, alone it cannot account for the different cultural positioning of lesbians at once outside of and negotiating within the dominant patriarchal modes of identification. Since the psychoanalytical approach can only see lesbian desire as a function of assuming a masculine heterosexual position, other, nonpsychoanalytic models of identification must be called upon, which can account for the distance that makes possible the pleasure the female image offers the lesbian spectator. (Weiss 1992: 40)

In her last sentence, Weiss herself defers to the dogma that distance from the female image is necessary in order to take pleasure in it. It seems to me obvious that, as literary responses have long shown, and *pace* Doane ('the woman who identifies with a female character must adopt a passive or masochistic position': Doane 1982: 80), pleasure from identification with a diegetic character is by no means necessarily narcissistic and/or masochistic. First, this is because identification is rarely complete, since it is usually with some rather than all aspects of a persona; second, and more to the theoretical point, identification with a person, be they 'real' or on-screen, does not have to be narcissistic because it does not mean seeing oneself in her/him, but rather the opposite – if anything, effacing one's self in a movement of union with another; third, identification with a female image is masochistic only if that female image is passive and subordinated, which is hardly always the case outside the Hollywood cinema, which Mulvey's and Doane's schemas largely invoked. Finally, since I do not agree that distance is necessary for actively desiring visual pleasure, I will not waste time on pondering what strike me, admittedly with the benefit of over twenty years' hindsight, as the strained theoretical conceits of Doane's transvestism and masquerade.

In contrast, one very welcome distance was that taken by Judith Roof vis-à-vis psychoanalytic obscurantism, when she formulated what should have been a truism but was in fact, within that locked grid, an iconoclasm: 'While *gender* is one term, *desire* is another. No gender owns the look; no gender owns desire for woman or for man' (Roof 1991: 50). The celebrated French director Agnès Varda has, however, rightly stressed the need for women to become agentic owners of *their own* gaze:

> La femme ne doit pas être définie par qui la regarde, par le regard des hommes . . . Le premier geste féministe c'est de dire, bon, OK, on me regarde, mais *moi* je regarde . . . Le monde n'est pas défini par comment on me regarde, mais comment *je* regarde.[7]
> [Woman should not be defined by who is looking at her, by the gaze of men. . . . The first step for feminists is to say, right, OK, I'm being looked at, but I too am looking . . . The world isn't defined by how I'm looked at, but how *I* look at the world.]

Varda's stress on the individual woman's gaze ('comment *je* regarde' ['how *I* look at the world']) rather than some essential and collective feminine gaze is vital. Equally, as Caroline Evans and Lorraine Gamman have suggested in an anglophone context, there is no essential model of the so-called lesbian gaze, for individual lesbian spectators 'bring different cultural competences' to lesbian spectating (Evans and Gamman 1995: 35). In a wider, non-heteronormative purview, Ellis Hanson implies the opacity and plurality of what has misleadingly been conceptualised as a single, unified queer gaze:

> Queer theorists have already discovered that the heterocentric and exceedingly rigid structure of the look in Mulvey's analysis – patriarchal masculinity leering at objectified femininity – writes homosexuality out of existence. How do women desire women in and through film? How do men desire men? Is a lesbian gaze a male gaze in drag? What about the gay male identification with the fetishized diva of classic cinema, all those glamorous gestures of Bette Davis and Judy Garland that virtually constitute the contemporary queer rhetoric of camp? (Hanson 1999: 13)

In the same spirit, and much as I applaud the overall quality of the essay in which it is located, I am unable to endorse Valerie Traub's assertion:

> In the context of theorizing a gaze unbounded by rigid gender polarities, the figure of the 'lesbian' is, it seems to me, a privileged site of inquiry. As both subject and object of desire, she embodies the potential desiring modality of all viewing subjects, her body displacing the binary economy enforced by heterosexual ideology. (Traub 1991: 311)

It is true that 'the figure of the "lesbian" ' may be 'a privileged site of inquiry' in that, within a cinematic economy which historically objectivises women, she as a woman can be the traditional object of the gaze yet can also, as a lesbian outside that economy, be the subject of the gaze. However, it is not true that she 'embodies the potential desiring modality of *all* viewing subjects' (my emphasis). Where is the gay male viewing subject in this scenario? Yet despite the need to take account of the gay male gaze, I would be wary of conflating it with a lesbianised gaze in some hypothetical united front against hetero-male scopophila. For all their gayness, gay men are acculturated as *men* first and foremost.[8] A telling example of the dangers of such conflation occurs in Bertrand Philbert's *L'Homosexualité à l'écran* (1984). As its title indicates, this book purports to be a study of homosexuality on screen generally, but in fact concentrates overwhelmingly on cinematic mediations of *male* homosexuality. Curiously, Philbert briefly cites Claude Chabrol's *Marie-Chantal contre Docteur Kha* (1965) in a chapter on lesbianism in cinema. The fact that a gay male author can assume lesbianism on the basis of one woman (Olga) taking off another's (Marie-Chantal's) stockings, with, moreover, venal rather than sexual motives, is revealing. It suggests the influence even on gay men of the hetero-male voyeuristic model of lesbianism. My analysis does not seek to swap one dominant term for another: masculine owner of the gaze for lesbian owner of the gaze. Such absolutes are ontologically untenable, for they presuppose a false homogeneity of the individually and multiply identified members of the crudely designated 'masculine' and 'lesbian' constituencies. If an epithet needs to precede the substantive 'gaze' at all, I would, provisionally and strategically, advance as an agentic (and perhaps utopian) ideal the neologism 'autosexual', which signifies the power of the viewing subject to realise its own sexual desires without imprisoning them within the existing, limited categories of straight, gay, lesbian, bi- or even transsexual.[9]

So far, my reflections have been of a largely transnational nature. What of the specificities of French/francophone cinematic and reception contexts? Virtually the only systematic analysis of lesbian film production in France is Fabienne Worth's article of 1993. Worth rightly situated such production within the context of 'France as the locus of an unshakable modernist ethos in which art is perceived as autonomous and universal, its value being confirmed and maintained by policies that exclude minority cultural expressions' (Worth 1993: 55–6). Although excellent for its time, Worth's article obviously requires some reassessment in the light of certain social, legal and cultural developments in France since 1993. In no particular order of importance, these include the introduction in 1999 of le Pacs (Pacte civil de solidarité: a partnership contract open to gay as well as straight couples, which confers a number of rights relating, inter alia, to taxation, housing and inheritance); the subsequent, growing demands for a bona fide gay marriage (which le Pacs most certainly is not) and for lesbian and gay access to parenthood; partly as cause and partly as effect of the debates provoked by the former three phenomena, a gradual problematisation of the French Republican model, which is supposed to cater for all citizens equally and thus to obviate the need for separate communities, be they based on ethnicity, sexuality or gender; the growing success of the lesbian film festival Cineffable, and the fact that it is now (but only since 2003, its fifteenth year) subsidised by the Mairie de Paris at whose helm has been the out gay mayor Bertrand Delanoë since 2001; and finally, an increase, if not quite a swell, in the number of lesbian/gay/queer-themed films aimed at mainstream French audiences.

All these developments notwithstanding, it is still broadly true that mainstream French cinema privileges depoliticised 'art' and tends to downgrade movies premised on identity politics. Of course there are exceptions, but films treating homosexuality, be it male or female, will often follow a comedic formula (for instance, top hits Gazon maudit of 1995 and Le Placard of 2000). The conceits of invisibility and of spectrality adopted by many scholars to denote the status of lesbian desire in anglophone literature and film such as those of Castle,[10] Fuss (Fuss 1991: 3 and 6), Hart (Hart 1994: ix), Weiss[11] and White (White 1999) could arguably be adjudged even more apt for their French (if not necessarily francophone) counterparts. Yet even if this argument is accepted, the number of films in my corpus – around eighty-nine – is not negligible; and while by no means all foreground lesbian desire, all contain at the very least potent traces of it. Whether or not this is sufficient to justify in a French context Terry Castle's observation that 'one might think of lesbianism as the "repressed idea" at the heart of patriarchal culture' (Castle 1993: 61–2) is a moot point. Less tendentious, perhaps, is the invoking of a cinematic lesbian continuum within French cinema. For readers unfamiliar with this concept, it is worth citing Adrienne Rich's discursive inauguration of it in 1981:

> I mean the term lesbian continuum to include a range – through each woman's life and throughout history – of woman-identified experience; not simply the fact that a woman has had or consciously desired genital experience with another woman. If we expand it to embrace many more forms of primary intensity between and among women, including the sharing of a rich inner life, the bonding against male tyranny, the giving and receiving of practical and political support; if we can also hear in it such associations as marriage resistance . . . we begin to grasp breadths of female history and psychology that have lain out of reach as a consequence of limited, mostly clinical, definitions of 'lesbianism'. (Rich 1980; reproduced 1983: 192)

To my knowledge, Chris Holmlund in 1991 was the first theorist to apply Rich's model of the lesbian continuum to cinematic texts. Whilst the model of the lesbian continuum has obvious flaws, chief among which is its desexualisation of lesbianism, as a model it is no less applicable to cinematic representations of inter-female relationships than it is to such representations in other media. It may well have a special pertinence to French film, for, as we shall see from the sheer length of Chapter 4 below on lesbian liminality, the majority of films in our corpus mediate borderline cases where deep feeling and sensual connection between women may not qualify as *bona fide* lesbianism, but could aptly be located within a Richian lesbian continuum.

The same may not be true for francophone as opposed to French cinema. The proportion of films in the corpus deriving from non-metropolitan France is very small – around nineteen out of eighty-nine, that is, less than twenty-two per cent. (If other francophone films with even a tangentially lesbian-themed dimension have slipped through my questing net, I will be delighted, but surprised.) However, despite this small francophone corpus, within most of the films concerned, particularly those from Belgium and Canada (that is, the majority), the lesbianism of the chief protagonist is in no doubt. Evidently, francophone as opposed to French cinematic and reception contexts cannot be homogenised. The one film from francophone Africa (*Karmen Geï*, 2001) is obviously exceptional, for Senegal is a non-Western, predominantly Muslim country which severely reproves homosexuality. The one film from Switzerland (*Messidor*, 1978) was produced in a small Western country with a very small national cinema and little tradition of sexual politics. Belgium and Canada may be compared favourably with France in both the legal and civic rights granted to lesbians and gays and in the funding of the largely independently made films from these constituencies. First, France lags behind in terms of legal recognition of lesbian and gay partnerships: since 1999 it has had *le Pacs*, but this law confers nowhere near the same rights as marriage. Symptomatically, only one film in the entire corpus of eighty-nine texts conveys aspiration to lesbian marriage. In Catherine Corsini's *La Nouvelle Ève* (1999), Solveig remarks that with the socialists there is hope for the legalisation of gay marriage, and claims she would enter into such a marriage with her partner, Louise. This film's uniqueness in privileging lesbian marriage is matched by its quasi-uniqueness in another respect: bar the obvious exception of the Senegalese *Karmen Geï*, it is one of only two films in the corpus of eighty-nine (the other two being Jean Rollin's *Le Viol du vampire* of 1967 and François Ozon's *Huit femmes* of 2001) to feature a black woman. The obvious inference – that black women are generally more traditionalist even when of non-traditional sexual identification – should not be taken at face value, and demands sociological investigation outside the scope of the present study. Returning to the social fact of France's limitation to *le Pacs*, it is noteworthy that Belgium, despite its enduring Catholic contours, has bettered that by going the whole hog and legalising lesbian and gay marriage (February 2003),[12] as Quebec has since done (March 2004).[13] Second, on the issue of lesbian parenthood, France is again less liberal, explicitly limiting artificial insemination to straight couples,[14] whereas the Belgian state provides artificial insemination for lesbians, and Canada's federal government is about to make it illegal to bar lesbians access to artificial insemination.[15] Second, the official Belgian lesbian and gay film festival held annually in January receives subsidies from the *Communauté française de Belgique* (as does Pinkscreens, the Alternative Gender Festival, albeit on a far smaller scale);[16] and the International Festival of Lesbian & Gay Film in Montreal is also granted a certain amount of financial aid from the city and province.[17]

In conclusion, I shall briefly outline the content of both the corpus and of the chapters to follow. By far the largest proportion of texts within the corpus are feature films, but it also includes documentary films, some shorts and one or two video documentaries. It does not include films made for French television which were not subsequently released in cinemas, for to do so would be to widen too far the scope of my analyses and thus to dilute their critical scrutiny. Second, a good quarter of the films in the overall corpus are based on pre-existing literary texts.[18] Although it is not part of my remit to analyse their adaptation for the sreeen, a few words are in order about the medium specificity, about the cinematographic iconography of lesbianism. What can be achieved by the medium of film as opposed to the medium of literature? Or, to put it another way, what can a director do visually on the screen that cannot be done verbally on the page? One obvious difference between the two forms is that images conjured up by a written text are constituted cumulatively, word after word, whereas a filmic image presents all its constituents instantly and simultaneously, and may well be accompanied by a soundtrack. Kabir's observations are eminently worth citing:

> To move from a verbal text to a visual screen medium involves a necessary modification of materials, a reshaping of them according to the demands of different media. The first rule is compression (Peary and Shatzkin, 1977: 5–6).[19] With the aim of refiguring a large text into economically functional visual units, entire sequences and characters are left out, the timeframe can change, the plot can be altered and dialogue is often condensed in key places. These are established conventions in the compression of literary texts into workable screen versions, so the omission of lesbian desire can be achieved easily for the purposes of cutting down the larger scope of a novel into a smaller screen version. (Kabir 1998: 113–14)

Suffice it to say that 'the omission of lesbian desire' may well have occurred in other French/francophone films based on literary texts, but that no such films are treated here, for self-evident reasons. The point is worth making if only to flag up the varying gradations of censorship to which the lesbian subject may have been subject; but that is another story (a brief introduction to which is made in Chapter 5).

Finally, a few words about the structure of this study. This first chapter has attempted to introduce the topic and to situate it theoretically and culturally. Chapters 2 and 3 will examine the two most predominant lesbian paradigms immanent in the corpus: criminality and pathology (although it should be noted that there may be synchronicity of the two within a single film). Chapter 4 will examine borderline inscriptions of lesbianism: lesbian liminality. Chapter 5 will focus on more apparently lesbo-affirmative *mises en scènes* of lesbian desire, but not without problematising them where necessary. The concluding chapter will provide a chronological and synthesising overview, tracing shifts in French-language cinematic mediations of lesbianism over the twentieth and early twenty-first centuries, and identifying any national specificities (metropolitan French, French Belgian, French Canadian, French Swiss, French African). Within each chapter and within each chapter's discrete sub-sections, discussion of the films will be conducted in largely chronological order, a methodology designed to reveal any significant representational evolutions. Where appropriate, however, chronological structuring may be subordinated to an initial, conceptually-driven organisation.

Notes

1. Namely, parodic resignation faced with an unpalatable reality: here, the presence since at least the 1930s of lesbian desire in French, if not in francophone, film.
2. Edward Stein provides a helpful and accessible definition of the terms 'essentialism' and 'constructionism' in the context of sexual orientation: 'Essentialists hold that a person's sexual orientation is a culture-independent, objective and intrinsic property while social constructionists think it is culture-dependent, relational and, perhaps, not objective' (Stein 1992: 325).
3. Wilton's reference is to Stacey 1994.
4. Johnston 1976: 217.
5. Lyrics written by José Cano; French adaptation by Pierre Grosz.
6. But see Holmlund 1991: 148, 161.
7. Interview with Varda in Marie Mandy's documentary film on women film directors' approaches to desire, *Filmer le désir (voyage à travers le cinéma des femmes)* (2001).
8. Castle's parenthetical comment in the following is noteworthy: '[b]y its very nature (and in this respect it differs significantly from male homosexuality) lesbianism poses an ineluctable challenge to the political, economic, and sexual authority of men over women' (Castle 1993: 62).
9. The term 'autosexual' was coined by a teenaged girl attracted to her own sex in the unattributed English documentary screened during the 12.00–14.00 showing at Le Trianon during the 2003 'Quand les Lesbiennes se font du cinéma' Cineffable festival.
10. 'The lesbian remains a kind of "ghost effect" in the cinema world of modern life: elusive, vaporous, difficult to spot – even when she is there, in plain view, mortal and magnificent, at the center of the screen . . . Why is it so difficult to see the lesbian – even when she is there, quite plainly, in front of us? In part because she has been "ghosted" – or made to seem invisible – by culture itself. It would be putting it mildly to say that the lesbian represents a threat to patriarchal protocol: Western civilization has for centuries been haunted by a fear of "women without men" – of women indifferent or resistant to male desire' (Castle 1993: 2 and 4–5).

11. 'Lesbian images in the cinema have been and continue to be virtually invisible. Hollywood cinema, especially, needs to repress lesbianism in order to give free rein to its endless variations on heterosexual romance. Each lesbian image that has managed to surface – the lesbian vampire, the sadistic or neurotic repressed woman, the pre-oedipal 'mother/daughter' lesbian relationship, the lesbian as sexual challenge or titillation to men – has helped determine the boundaries of possible representation, and has insured the invisibility of many other kinds of lesbian images. And yet, this invisibility can foster visibility as well. Each instance of invisibility seems to leave a trace, if only a trace of its absence or repression, which is also a kind of image. These faint traces and coded signs are especially visible to lesbian spectators. Lesbians, moreover, have looked to the cinema, and especially to these traces and signs, to create ways of being lesbian, to form and affirm their identity as individuals and as a group' (Weiss 1992: 1).

12. '[L]e texte accorde aux couples homosexuels les mêmes droits qu'aux couples hétérosexuels, qu'il s'agisse des droits sociaux, fiscaux ou de ceux liés au patrimoine et à l'héritage. Idem en cas de divorce. Seules exceptions: l'adoption et la filiation. Ainsi dans le cas d'un couple lesbien, la mère biologique sera considérée comme l'unique parent de l'enfant. Le texte prévoit, en outre, qu'un couple homosexuel ne pourra pas adopter d'enfant' ('Infos: Revue de Presse', *Lesbia Magazine*, April 2003, p. 17). ['The law grants homosexual and heterosexual couples the same rights, be they social, fiscal or linked to inheritance. The same applies in the case of divorce. The only exceptions are adoption and filiation. So in the case of a lesbian couple, the biological mother will be considered as the child's sole parent. In addition, the law does not allow a homosexual couple to adopt children.']

13. Just as this book was being completed, the whole of Canada looked set to legalise lesbian and gay marriage if the Senate ratified the bill approved on 28 June 2005 by the Ottawa House of Commons. Nine of the thirteen Canadian provinces and territories had already authorised lesbian and gay marriage.

14. Article L 152–2 of the Code de Santé Publique stipulates that AMP (assistance médicale à la procréation [medically assisted procreation]) is available only to a man and a woman who are either married or can prove that they have lived together as a couple for at least two years. It thus excludes single people, lesbian and gay couples, and even a couple formed by a gay man and a lesbian woman both of whom want a child, since this type of couple cannot (usually) offer proof of two years' cohabitation. For further information, see 'Rapport n°1407 sur l'application de la loi de bioéthique du 29/7/94' by Alain Claeys et Claude Huriet.

15. 'Ottawa – Le gouvernement fédéral s'apprête à écrire noir sur blanc dans ses lois qu'il est illégal d'empêcher les lesbiennes d'avoir recours aux nouvelles techniques de reproduction, y compris l'insémination artificielle' (Hélène Buzzetti, 'Feu vert aux lesbiennes pour l'insémination artificielle', *Le Devoir*, 24 April 2003). ['Ottawa: The federal government is getting ready to make it

absolutely clear that it is illegal to prevent lesbians from having recourse to new techniques of reproduction, including artificial insemination.']

16. Marie Vermeiren, in private correspondence with the author, 15 December 2003.

17. I am grateful to Durham Modern Languages Series for permission to reproduce here certain comments on lesbian and gay rights in France, Belgium and Canada from my chapter in Günther and Michallat (eds) 2006.

18. Corpus: Limur, Jean de, *La Garçonne* (1936), Audry, Jacqueline, *Olivia* (1951), Audry, Jacqueline, *Huis clos* (1954), Henri-Georges Clouzot, *Les Diaboliques* (1954), Audry, Jacqueline, *La Garçonne* (1957), Albicocco, Jean-Gabriel, *La Fille aux yeux d'or* (1961), Franju, Georges, *Thérèse Desqueyroux* (1962), Rivette, Jacques, *Suzanne Simonin, La Religieuse de Diderot* (1965), Buñuel, Luis, *Belle de Jour* (1967), Casaril, Guy, *Emilienne et Nicole* (1970), Casaril, Guy, *Le Rempart des Béguines* (1972), Kaplan, Nelly, *Néa* (1976), Baratier, Jacques, *L'Araignée de satin* (1984), Fleury, Joy, *Tristesse et beauté* (1985), Granier-Deferre, Pierre, *Cours privé* (1987), Lipinska, Christine, *Le Cahier volé* (1992), Chabrol, Claude, *La Cérémonie* (1995), Akerman, Chantal, *La Captive* (2000), Despentes, Virginie, *Baise-moi* (2000), Ozon, François, *Huit femmes* (2002).

19. Peary and Shatzkin 1977: 'Introduction'.

CHAPTER TWO

Bad Girls: Criminality

As was signposted in Chapter 1, Chapters 2 and 3 will examine the two most salient lesbian paradigms (even, it is arguable, archetypes) in the corpus of eighty-nine films spanning the period 1936–2002. My temporal treatment of these two paradigms – first criminality, then pathology – broadly refers to the Foucauldian genealogy of discourses on homosexuality generally (for which read *male* homosexuality: amongst Foucault's many strong points, gender-sensitivity was conspicuous by its absence).[1] This genealogy posits a discursive shift 'from sin to sickness'. Whilst sin and criminality are, of course, not conceptually identical, they are sufficiently proximate to justify invoking the Foucauldian model: both denote the transgression of a law, be it divine or man-made, and both have connotations of evil. In a largely post-religious Western context, sin/vice no longer has the currency it once enjoyed as a category of behaviour and mind-set, but cultural links, whether conscious or unconscious, still exist between lesbianism, aggression and criminality. Lynda Hart puts the case fulgently:

> I argue that one ghost in the machine of heterosexual patriarchy is the lesbian who shadows the entrance into representation of women's aggression. . . . the shadow of the lesbian is laminated to the representation of women's violence . . . indeed it is the lesbian's absent presence that both permits women's aggression to enter the specular field and defuses the full force of its threat. . . . If desire inevitably confirms masculinity, so does crime. Masculinity is as much verified by active desire as it is by aggression. The question that initiated this study concerned what the latter had to tell us about the former. Pursuing this question, I came to see that these two discourses were not discrete. On the contrary, the desiring subject as confirmation of masculinity to some extent depends on the presupposition that women cannot perform acts of aggression. Historically inscribed both as 'not-woman' and as violent, the lesbian occupies an ambivalent position in this Symbolic Order. She 'comes in handy' as a criminal, but she is also something of a Trojan horse. She operates within this system as a *necessary*

placeholder to rein in and provide closure to a heterosexual imperative, but she also functions to expose that little bit of the *Real* that the Symbolic must exclude. (Hart 1994: ix–x)

According to Hart, then, the sign 'lesbian' is both the harbinger of women's aggression generally and a category to which heterosexual patriarchy can consign any woman who displays aggression, the better to strip her of her identity as a 'real' woman (something which lesbians are deemed not to be). Whilst it will always be possible to find filmic examples of aggressive heterosexual women and of non-aggressive gay women, Hart's argument is seductive as a general theory, and it is certainly the case that in the present corpus, a fair number of lesbian-identifed or lesbian-connoted female characters also exhibit aggressive and/or violent characteristics. Technically, or maybe merely lexically, problems may be posed by the post-religious tendency to explain many if not all forms of aggression and violence in terms of the culprit's individual psycho-pathology. For the sake of clarity, I shall attempt to keep the two paradigms conceptually discrete, whilst acknowledging from the outset that there may on occasion be synchronicity of the two within a single film.

Another form of law-breaking consists in violating so-called natural laws, and the figure of the lesbian as denatured woman is also prominent in French, as in other national, cinemas. The 'animalistic lesbian body' is one of the three major lesbian stereotypes delineated by Barbara Creed as perceived threats to patriarchal regimes:

> There are at least three stereotypes of the lesbian body which are so threatening they cannot easily be applied to the body of the non-lesbian. These stereotypes are: the lesbian body as active and masculinized; *the animalistic lesbian body*; the narcissistic lesbian body. Born from a deep-seated fear of female sexuality, these stereotypes refer explicitly to the lesbian body, and arise from the nature of the threat lesbianism offers to patriarchal heterosexual culture. (Creed 1995: 88; my emphasis)

This chapter, then, will identify and analyse instances in French and francophone films where lesbian desire is laminated to – and, in most cases, assimilated to – one or more of the categories mentioned in this brief introduction, which all coalesce under the broad sign of 'criminality': sin (breaching of religious prohibitions), vice (affronts to religious and/or social – usually bourgeois – morality), aggression, violence, bestiality. The danger represented by the lesbian figure may be physical or, though less commonly, merely a violation of the Symbolic (gendered) Order in which straight male supremacy inheres.

In only one film within the corpus is the expression of lesbian desire explicitly figured as breaching religious prohibitions: Jacques Rivette's *Suzanne Simonin, La Religieuse de Diderot* (completed in 1965 but not granted general release in France until 1967 because of censorship).[2] When the conscripted young nun Suzanne guilelessly tells her confessor about the Mother Superior Mme de Chelles's sexual advances on her, he orders her to avoid all contact with the woman and to recognise in her face that of Satan; this is the most obvious, and the most literal, diabolisation of lesbian desire in the entire corpus. Lesbian desire as contiguous with vice in the sense of an affront to bourgeois morality which is uncontaminated by violence or aggression is rare in the corpus: the only obvious instance is Luis Buñuel's *Belle de Jour* (1967). Using discontinuity editing, Buñuel traces the psycho-sexual trajectory of Séverine (played by Catherine Deneuve), a conventionally beautiful, bored young bourgeois wife who becomes intrigued by prostitution and begins working in a high-class brothel, run by the sophisticated Anaïs. Anaïs, transgressor of surface bourgeois morality by virtue of her role as brothel-keeper (needless to say, many of her clients are members of that same sanctimonious bourgeoisie), asks Séverine to kiss her on the lips, then herself takes the initiative, from which a startled Séverine recoils. As in many films in the corpus, the lesbian-connoted character fits conventional canons of feminine beauty (see Chapter 6), which may well be an index to the prioritising of perceived French male spectatorial demand: although short-haired, she is not in the least bit butch. On the other hand, she has the seductive self-assurance and 'phallic' authority associated with masculinity. As her adventures at the brothel multiply, including such extremes as sado-masochism and even necrophilia, Séverine's sexual and personal confidence increases . . . in symmetry with which her lesbian experience recedes into the background. Yet when she resigns from the brothel, in inverted symmetry with their first meeting it is she who tries to kiss Anaïs on the lips, and Anaïs who resists. Anaïs's resistance has a different basis, however: piqued jealousy about Marcel, the man she knows Séverine desires and thinks she is leaving prostitution for, and the sense of disempowerment which this masculine upstaging creates.

Belle de Jour stands out through its atypicality. What of the plethora of films laminating lesbian desire to aggression and/or criminality? First, we need to establish precisely who or what is targeted. Physical violence in a lesbian couple which is non-shamefully closeted, either to themselves or to others, is extremely rare in the corpus: in fact, only one instance of it has been found. This is probably less to do with generally positive takes on lesbian relations and more with the dearth of films mediating non-closeted lesbian couples. In Sylvie Ballyot's *Alice* (2002), the eponymous character gets annoyed at what she sees as her girlfriend Elsa's intrusiveness, and initially picks a verbal fight; the viewer registers Elsa's rising and understandable irritation, and correlatively, Alice's rising, hitherto repressed anger (a repression which the discontinuity editing traces back to childhood abuse by a male cousin, compounded by incestuous frustration centring on her newly married sister's non-availability). We next witness a scene of over-determined violence: a mutual slapping-match in which Elsa seems to be simulating real combat as a means to purge Alice's aggression. The sequence is filmed in slow motion, with blurred lens focus increasing the sense of unreality, of quasi-simulacrum: a form of acting-out in relation to Alice's childhood traumas, in which the victim assumes agency against a fantasised aggressor, with the latter role being assumed with inchoate instinct by Elsa.

Eventually, her aggression spent, Alice weeps, and Elsa embraces her. Cut to the bedroom, where the camera lens focuses on Elsa's hand upon Alice's body. The red and black tinges to the images, combined with the cross-cutting to the scene of childhood rape by her male cousin (conveyed through a grey, grainy textured, slow-motion sequence, with full sordid visual details as the lens centres on his sperm on her child's belly), confer a disturbing parallel on the two objectively opposed sex-scenes, a vacillation which is presumably meant to evoke Alice's own difficulty in separating the two. Yet the film does narratively convey her eventual success in doing so. The woman-on-woman violence is thus given an aetiology in circumstances external to the inter-female relationship – the childhood sexual abuse by an exploitative male, and, more problematically, the incestuous fixation upon her sister. Whilst the latter skirts dangerously close to a conflation of lesbian desire with early dysfunctional familial relations, the overall tenor of this film desists from essentialising Alice's violence as an intrinsic property of lesbian desire.

Instances of lesbian desire as somehow (and the 'how' does vary considerably, as we shall see) intrinsically linked to violence and/or crime are far more numerous. Discussion of these films will be conducted in chronological order, a methodology sustained throughout this book with a view to identifying in its concluding chapter any significant representational evolutions.

A rather camp classic, Jacques Deval's *Club de femmes* (1936) is set in a young women's hostel, the Cité Femina, which offers material comfort and 'moral security' for all young women working in Paris and categorically bans men. Alice, a nineteen-year-old medical student, is unequivocally represented as being secretly smitten by the rather dizzy blonde Juliette. A coded antecedent to what becomes patent is Alice's appreciative gaze, conveyed in close-up shot, lingering on Juliette's feminine curves as she emerges from the swimming pool. In the second sequence bringing the two young women together in the frame, the soundtrack immediately conveys Alice's intense attraction to Juliette through its heightening of emotion. In the third sequence centre-staging the two women, Alice's strong feelings for Juliette are again encoded by the soundtrack (stereotypically romantic), by their spatial relationships within the frame – Alice leaning close over Juliette, almost touching her, ostensibly to check her spelling – and also by their encryption within the poem which Alice has chosen for the dictation exercise (her cover for close contact with Juliette being that of spelling tutor). The poem in question is 'L'Invitation au voyage' by Baudelaire, one of the most famous male writers to have depicted lesbian desire, in his *Les Fleurs du mal*.[3]

The dramatic dénouement is triggered by a sobbing Juliette's confession to Alice that the receptionist Hélène had lured her into a meeting with a man she thought would offer her a respectable job, but who merely exploited her sexual naïvety. Alice's jealous anguish boils over into a literally homicidal drive for revenge on Hélène – interestingly, *not* for the male culprit – whose drink she fatally poisons. Alice effectively confesses by handing the empty poison bottle back to its owner, the dyke-encoded house doctor, Gabrielle Aubry. This second, and much more oblique, lesbian encryption has functioned via Gabrielle's strictly tailored suits, her masculine manner in holding cigarettes and her generally gratified gaze over her captive female audience. Gabrielle covers up Alice's crime to the police by mendaciously certifying that Hélène died of a brain haemorrhage, but severely remonstrates with Alice in private. Eventually, she sends her away to nurse at a leper colony; note the use of leprosy as a metonym for homosexuality as a form of plague or illness, and the convergence of leprosy and homosexuality in the figure of the pariah.[4] One opacity remains: whether Gabrielle has fully understood Alice's motives, and if so, how, for nothing is asked or said in the diegesis. Gabrielle the protodyke is thus an ambivalent figure, at once showing solidarity with a fellow lesbian by protecting her from the full consequences of her crime, but, on the other hand, banishing her to a quasi-penitential environment. She is awarded the *Légion d'honneur* at the end of the film – which, within our specific optic, provides something of a hermeneutic impasse: is Gabrielle thus honoured *despite* her implied lesbianism, or is the latter an unproblematic component of her overall honourable identity? More negatively, is it unproblematic only because apparently non-active and clandestine?

Eighteen years later, in her adaptation of Sartre's 1944 play *Huis clos*, Jacqueline Audry was the fourth French director to bring to celluloid a criminal lesbian character. Inès's status as criminal is not exceptional: axiomatically, all three characters are in hell for wrong-doing. In her case, the criminal deed was a *crime de passion*: murder of her cousin for taking Florence, the woman she loved. Interestingly, it is Inès who is the least negatively portrayed in that she is the only one of the three with enough courage to admit that they are in hell. She is the least steeped in bad faith; in fact, if anything, she displays remarkable honesty and self-consistency, however unappealing the majority may find her feminine atypicality (hatred of children as well as men: 'Un enfant – quelle horreur!' ['a child – how horrible!']). Far from being hidden, her status on earth as a 'cursed' woman (the 'femme damnée' of the original referring obviously to Baudelaire's [in]famous designation of the lesbian) is self-proclaimed. And while one of her last remarks, apropos the straight couple Garcia and Estelle, now about to fornicate – 'C'est vous les plus forts' ['*You're* the ones with the most power'] – may evince despair about homosexual love, it also reflects lucidity about her subject-positioning within her particular historical context.

Homicidal violence in a lesbian-encoded character was less mitigated in Jean-Gabriel Albicocco's *La Fille aux yeux d'or* (1961). A modern adaptation of one of Balzac's short stories in *L'Histoire des treize* (1834), Albicocco's film is set in contemporary (1960s) Paris, and Balzac's aristocrat Henri de Marsay has become a fashion photographer, aided and abetted in both his professional and seductive enterprises by his business (and, previously, it is implied, sexual) partner Eléonore. An arrogant womaniser who treats women as objects of his perverse pleasures, he eventually falls for 'la fille aux yeux d'or' ['the girl with the golden eyes'], whose real name is never revealed. The truth which emerges towards the end of the film is that she is in fact emotionally, and it would appear sexually, in thrall to Eléonore. Eléonore eventually imprisons the girl with the golden eyes, tries to wean her off Henri, then, when faced with the girl's enduring heterosexual love, stabs her fatally from behind whilst maintaining an amorous embrace. Her love for the girl compared to her previous love for Henri is both more acute and more deadly: an excess that can only lead, in its possessive intensity, to destruction of its object. In short, a criminal passion with traces of pathology, depending on one's moral and jurisprudential position.

Two years later, the concatenation of lesbian desire and criminal violence is consummate in Nico Papatakis's *Les Abysses* (1963), which is based very obviously in all but name on the infamous case of the Papin sisters:[5] the initial intertexts refer to the shocking incident of 1933, and the film is prefaced by a photographic still showing the Papin sisters after their arrest. Papatakis's film has a visually and aurally gothic texture, and the acting is highly stylised, as Edwards and Reader have remarked; I would go further by dubbing it operatically histrionic. The day-to-day relationship between the older, tougher sister Michèle and the younger Marie-Louise is sado-masochistic (see Chapter 3), but includes mutually erotico-amorous moments (for discussion of its incestuous nature, see Chapter 3 also): early on in the film, a medium close-up shot frames them locked in feverish embrace, hands fluttering manically over each other's bodies, as they emit almost bestial moans – on the one hand, for all the world like ardent lovers, but on the other, conjuring up the animalistic spectre of classic lesbian mythopoeia. If Edwards and Reader are right, and I believe they are, in aver-ring that what 'ultimately drives the sisters to murder is not so much the fact that they lose the smallholding . . . but the fact that Elisabeth, reconciled with her husband, threatens to have the sisters put in a convent where they would be separated',[6] then lesbian love is clearly being posited as the matrix of murderous violence; again, by virtue of its maleficent intensity.

This model of lesbian love segues into Claude Chabrol's *Les Biches* (1968), where it is blended with that of narcissism/fusion (and, symbol-ically, with that of animality: the does of the title are the two women). Rich, elegant Frédérique patronises a penniless female artist whom she nick-names 'Why' (in echo of the response given when the artist is asked her name, but also symbolising the epistemological enigma formed by lesbian desire in this film); after an initial period of mistrust on Why's part, the two women are erotically drawn to each other and share an idyll that is medi-ated as enchanted, but childlike and ephemeral. When Why sleeps with Paul and Frédérique steals Paul for herself, Why merely asks if she can stay in Frédérique's home while the couple go to Paris for two weeks, insisting that she's not at all angry. But her facial expression is inscrutable, and she surreptitiously follows them to Paris, finally asking Frédérique if she can stay, declaring that she loves them both. Frédérique replies that she finds Why's love loathsome. Why ripostes that she too wanted to get rid of one of them, but we are left ignorant as to which one, Frédérique or Paul. Why proceeds to monologue, coming up behind Frédérique, caressing her and then, in a dramatic dénouement, suddenly stabbing her, thus activating an intertextual link with Albicocco's *La Fille aux yeux d'or*. The stabbing over, her monologue continues, embodying the narcissistic/fusional model of lesbianism presaged earlier (see Chapter 3). When Paul's phone-call inter-rupts her dramatic soliloquy, she appropriates Frédérique's identity fully, pretending she *is* her; thus ends the film. This is both a criminalising and a pathologising representation of lesbianism: Why's attraction to Frédérique is at once narcissistic, murderous and even cannibalistic, in the sense of incorporating radically the object of one's desire.[7]

While retaining the triangular structure of *La Fille aux yeux d'or* and *Les Biches*, Guy Casaril's *Emilienne et Nicole* (1970) signals a change of tenor to the more prurient and salacious. In Casaril's quasi-soft porn movie, the trio is formed by a married couple, Claude and Emilienne, and a younger woman, Nouky, who desires them both at varying valencies. When Claude and Emilienne go to a small island to repair their marriage after Nouky's inroads, the initial euphoria of their reunion is heavily compromised by the discovery of a lesboerotic community featured as sinister and cult-like, indeed witchlike, with connotations of virginal sacrifices (cf. the vampire movie *Les Lèvres rouges*, discussed below). During a visually and aurally gothic storm (Casaril is nothing if not given to cinematographic hyperbole), Claude and Emilienne seek refuge in a somewhat improbable home for sailors' widows. Equally improbably, all the women are blonde and dressed in white, and, in a neat reversal of (hetero-)normative visual codes, stare at the straight couple as if they were the aberrance. Emilienne sneaks away from a sleeping Claude and goes back to the home, where he sees her, through a window-frame, being kissed and stimulated by the blonde white-clad women, who take turns to grope her, prompting an orgasmic response from Emilienne; eventually she faints and is carried onto a bed where the women feast on her body in a *mise en scène* suggestive of vampirism and diabolical possession. In the top left-hand corner of the screen, the older woman of the home keeps a watchful eye over them, conferring a benign matriarchal authorisation to the proceedings.

However, the power of these women over Emilienne, represented as almost supernatural and certainly with hints of black magic, is not allowed to cast its spell for too long and, true to generic conventions, Claude soon reasserts male supremacy. When Emilienne rejects him and taunts him verbally by claiming he gets pleasure from seeing her 'roll in the dirt' (a suspect judgement on lesboeroticism, but an apt indictment of his voyeurism) and, more interestingly, orders him to keep his hands off her, mocking any hope he might have of taking the place of a woman, he forces himself on her sexually. Terry Castle's statement on lesbians and witches ('the witchcraft connection could be counted on to add an invidious aura of diabolism to any scene of female-female desire' [Castle 1993: 62]) may well be true of other films, but with *Emilienne et Nicole*, that diabolism can only be sustained through spectatorial acknowledgement of and willing engagement in high kitsch. Aware that I may be accused of anachronism, of neglecting what now seem like the jejune reception contexts of early 1970s soft porn French cinema, I offer a resolutely twenty-first-century reading, which can never be as innocent.

Nelly Kaplan's *Néa* (1976) also features supernatural and witch-like elements in the eerily agentic complicity between teenager Sibylle and her 'familiar', Cumes the cat. Depiction thereof tilts the film temporarily out of its otherwise realistic framework towards the fantastical. Here, though, the connotations of witchcraft are positive and feminist-derived – intelligence, power, independence from patriarchy – and are more explicitly foregrounded by the precocious young teenager in defence of her mother against her male supremacist and heterosexist father. The complicity with the cat is also sensual and productive of its own erotic viewing pleasures. The cat's licking itself prompts Sibylle to masturbate; and it is the cat's preternaturally loud purring that leads her to discover her mother in bed with her sister-in-law, Sibylle's aunt Judith. Surprisingly for such an early film – only some three years into the 'sexual liberation' period following May 1968 – the lesbian sub-plot ends happily, with the mother leaving her husband at her daughter's behest for her true love, Judith (note the oracular powers connoted by Sibylle's name).

Altogether more grim is Joy Fleury's *Tristesse et beauté* (1985). The film's centre of gravity is the love borne by Prudence, a talented young sculptress, for the older, established artist Léa, and, more importantly in narrative terms, Prudence's determination to avenge Léa for the suffering inflicted by her lover Hugo's rejection twenty years ago. Prudence's hatred for Hugo is left in no doubt: 'Je le *hais*' ['I *hate* him']. Ostensibly referring to her sculptural technique but in reality to her attitude towards Hugo, Léa entreats her: 'résiste à ta violence' ['don't give in to your violence'], in response to Prudence's having daubed on a canvass 'Je vous vengerai d'Hugo' ['I'll get you revenge on Hugo']; later, that canvas becomes a painting expressing the violence of Prudence's feelings through its harsh line-work and colours. Prudence engineers vengeance on Hugo in two ways: the more minor is by having sex with him, then suddenly screaming out 'Léa!', before asserting that she could have strangled him; the more major stratagem is to get Hugo's son Martin to fall hopelessly in love with her and thus to become her victim. Meaning is never fixed in this film, and the ambiguity increases the complexity of any interpretation one might hazard, but the obvious inference is that Prudence in fact intends Martin to die, and maybe herself too as collateral damage, when she takes him out on a boat, distracts him with her winsome body and the boat ends up crashing against a large rock. In the ensuing wreckage, Martin's body is never found, while she survives – although her own survival could not have been guaranteed. Léa gently strokes the face of the rescued but still unconscious Prudence, who gradually awakens to her touch. The screen is then suffused with sombre blue, which fades and gives way to the credits, signalling the end of an extremely enigmatic narrative in which lesbian desire has been conveyed as literally murderous in its jealous and protective passion.

Equally sinister, if far more oblique in its encoding of lesbian desire, Diane Kurys's *À la folie* (1993) also construes, once more, an infernal triangle. (The trope of the trio is discussed more fully in Chapter 4.) In an interesting if unintentional prolepsis of Ballyot's *Alice* (2002), the two main female protagonists are named Alice and Elsa, and, in Kurys's film, they are sisters. In contrast, in Ballyot's film the eponymous Alice will be simultaneously in love with girlfriend Elsa and haunted by an incestuous love for her own sister, Manon. Phonetically, the proper name Manon equates to 'ma non': 'my no', perhaps alluding to the prohibition of Alice's desire for her sister, much as in the same Symbolic Order the 'non du Père' prohibits all desire exceeding the oedipal gridlock. In *À la folie*, even though Alice has a boyfriend (Franck), Elsa suggests that she and Alice go off together and declares that she can not live without her. This is the one scene where an unequivocally erotic gesture is made, as Elsa repeatedly kisses Alice on the lips. But Elsa's sorority is dominated by the motifs of manipulation and exploitation. She in fact treats Alice appallingly, wrecking her artist's[8] studio, conniving with Franck in Alice's imprisonment, and then submitting her to physical degradation and mental torture (Alice is tied to a radiator and forced to listen to Elsa and Franck having noisy sex). As Thierry Jousse asserts, this is an 'histoire mi-réaliste, mi-fantastique, qui navigue entre sororité, homosexualité féminine et théâtre de la cruauté' (Jousse 1994: 68–9) ['half-realist, half-fantastical story, moving between sisterhood, female homosexuality, and the theatre of cruelty']. And in the context of our discussion here, the linking of female homosexuality with cruelty is not, one suspects, ideologically innocent.

Claude Chabrol's *La Cérémonie* (1995) also provides a somewhat dubious space for the lesbian imagination. The obvious downside is that any lesbian desire perceived in this film is heavily compromised by the issue of the women's complicity in bloody murder (preceded by implication of a criminal past in both cases: infanticide for Jeanne, parricide for Sophie). Chabrol's film, like that of Papatakis mentioned above, ineluctably evokes the infamous case of the Papin sisters. Whilst Chabrol himself has denied any direct inspiration by the case, affirming instead his film's basis in Ruth Rendell's novel *A Judgement in Stone* of 1963, in the free play of signification formed by the textual field such intertextual echoes are clear. The two women, Sophie the illiterate maid and Jeanne the defiant postal worker, are not sisters but do become extremely close, and ultimately together massacre the family to whom Sophie has been servant (and whose patriarchal head had disapproved of Jeanne). Further, when they lie on a bed tickling each other, their laughter takes on a vaguely subhuman tone

1. *La Cérémonie* (1995): Sophie and Jenne's defiant intimacy heralds worse forms of connivance (see Chapter 2). France 3 Cinema/The Kobal Collection

like that of crazed birds, hinting at the animalistic lesbian body mentioned by Creed (see above).

The latent signs of lesbian desire between Sophie and Jeanne have been well documented by Joël Argote (Argote 2002). I would merely add that the operation of these signs is highly discreet, and would invoke the metaphor of sapphic semaphore to describe the process: only those 'in the know', namely the resisting lesbian viewer, are likely to intercept and decode signs which to others may appear senseless, if foxy, flailings. In what do these signs consist? In an extreme close-up doubling as a point-of-view shot from Sophie's perspective, the camera lingers on Jeanne's hands – the privileged sign of the lesbian phallus, as I have argued in relation to lesbian literary imagery (Cairns 2002c). Sophie's facial expression at this point is inscrutable. Does it signify longing? Desire? Desire *for* Jeanne, or *to be* Jeanne: that is, literate, confident, robust? Later, Sophie again stares at Jeanne, this time sensuously, while eating the birthday meal prepared for her by the latter. Later still, a full shot shows them sitting watching television in Sophie's room, their arms round each other's shoulders. A tender kiss between the two women is again accompanied by lingering eye-contact. And finally, after their savage murders, and just before leaving, Jeanne kisses Sophie one last time, lingeringly, skirting her lips, smiling enigmatically.

Three of the few mainstream critics to have intercepted at least
flickerings of the sapphic semaphore in this now canonical film are Judith
Mayne, and Rachel Edwards and Keith Reader. In her admirably powerful
chapter on *La Cérémonie*, Mayne comments insightfully on the interweav-
ing of crime and lesbian attraction, and the, precisely, flickering presence
of both in the film before its bloody finale:

> The connection between criminality and lesbian attraction is made force-
> fully yet indirectly, for the revelation of the respective crimes of the two
> women functions as a kind of flirtation. The repetition of the phrase 'On n'a
> rien prouvé!' (They didn't prove anything!) suggests that their crimes, like
> lesbianism in its stereotypical forms, are both there and not there, present
> and absent at once. (Mayne 2000: 33)

However, while Edwards' and Reader's general analysis of the film is consummate, I do contest their take on the question of lesbian desire. They
astutely locate an erotic current between the two women: 'When Jeanne
invites Sophie to stay with her when she leaves the family, she does so kneel-
ing on her bed with her legs slightly apart. There is only one bed in her small
deux pièces (two-roomed flat) and the implication is clear.' But their ensuing
comment – 'However, their sexuality is not presented as a mature sexuality,
but instead as a childish sexuality reminiscent of the relationship existing
between the two teenage girls in *Heavenly Creatures*, before it becomes a
fully-fledged affair' – reflects the blindspots common in designations of
lesbian sexuality: the failure to see beyond Freudian-derived edicts that
because it is non-heterosexual and non-reproductive, it is therefore sympto-
matic of arrested development – in a (Edwards' and Reader's) word, 'childish'. Further, Edwards' and Reader's argumentative sleight-of-hand –

> Sophie stands on one side and leans on her rifle (she is therefore still invested
> with a penis) and Jeanne, without her gun, approaches her like a woman in a
> saloon going up to her mate. She leans against her and brushes the hair from
> her face as the Don sings 'Lasciati almen veder, mio bell'amore!' ['At least let
> me see you, my beloved'], highlighting the fact that the act is a sexually
> charged one, but now it signifies heterosexuality and difference rather than
> homosexuality and sameness which was characteristic of the women's rela-
> tionship before the murders. (Edwards and Reader 2001: 104–12)

– is seductive, but in fact ignores the fact that gender-play, or gender-
bending – here, mimicry of a straight couple – does not necessarily negate
the lesboerotic properties of the dynamic between them. For the principled
resisting spectator (see Chapter 1), then, there is more than enough textual

evidence to support a lesbian sub-texting of *La Cérémonie*. The problem
with the film lies elsewhere: in the fact that lesbian desire is located
between a couple of women encoded as pretty much gratuitously vicious
(their motives for murder remain opaque, other than resentment of their
socio-economic marginalisation vis-à-vis their privileged bourgeois target
family), and likely only to alienate the spectator.

François Ozon's *Regarde la mer* (1998) also yokes covert lesboeroticism to
vicious murder, but differs from *La Cérémonie* in that only one of the
women is thus tainted by criminality, and also in that, like Chabrol's *Les
Biches*, it conjugates criminality and narcissism. Wife and mother Sasha lets
vagrant Tatiana camp in the grounds of her country home and becomes
fatally fascinated by the uncouth young woman. A point-of-view shot from
Tatiana's perspective suggests her sensuous appreciation of Sasha's scantily clad body stretched out tantalisingly on the beach. Tatiana herself is
framed in a vulture-like position relative to Sasha. After Tatiana has pitched
her tent in the garden, Sasha is shown staring at her through the window;
her vision is itself framed by the window-frame, which suggests directorial
emphasis on the object (Tatiana) and nature (desirous) of her vision. She
goes beyond the bare minimum of civility by asking Tatiana to dinner. That
night, when Tatiana is back in her tent, Sasha is again shown staring at her
through the window, and this time she masturbates directly after the gazing.
The montage here cannot help but suggest some kind of lesboerotic arousal
on Sasha's part. Similarly, when Tatiana leaves the beach saying she is
bored, a slighted Sasha goes off into the woods and lets a male stranger
perform cunnilingus on her, which would appear to be some kind of
metonym for lesbian sex. The following morning, preparing to serve break-
fast to Tatiana, she chooses her clothes with obvious seductive intent,
donning a skimpy red dress with plunging neckline. She also sneaks a look
at Tatiana's diary, which *inter alia* has a page manically covered with dupli-
cations of a female name (another possible index to lesbian desire/obses-
sion). And when Tatiana massages Sasha's shoulders, a close-up shot
conveys her intent gaze resting on Sasha's back and her sensual caressing of
the other woman's arms.

Finally, in a scene depicting Tatiana staring at Sasha's naked body as she
lies sleeping with her baby, the obsessive nature of Tatiana's gaze is conveyed via a combination of a long-held shot and a disorienting blue filter.
She then undresses and appears to be getting into bed with Sasha, but this
remains unconfirmed due to the abrupt cut to a new scene in which Sasha's
husband Paul arrives home to find his house deserted. In a scene of mounting tension Paul searches for his wife and daughter, finally opening the zip
of the tent in the garden to the horrifying sight of a woman's decomposing

body. The horror of the scene is intensified both aurally, by the soundtrack of flies buzzing, and visually, by the husband's gagging gesture. The blue filter of the earlier shot depicting mother and daughter now gives way to red, as the camera focuses on the bound figure, head covered in a black plastic bag and pubic area shaved and sewn up – a visual intratextual allusion to an earlier expression of Tatiana's preoccupation with tearing of the genitalia in childbirth, and to an apparently gratuitous shot of her gazing at raw red meat in a supermarket just after close physical proximity with Sasha. Once more the camera sets the viewer up. Our assumption that the victim is Tatiana, and, correlatively, that the woman in the next and final sequence is Sasha (she wears Sasha's red dress and holds the baby in her arms) is dramatically undercut as the camera eventually reveals the woman in the red dress to be Tatiana. The stomach-churning inference is that the mutilated victim must be Sasha, and her mutilat*or* Tatiana. Ozon thus connotes without directly denoting lesbian desire, and in one of the two women concerned it is mediated as a literally fatal force, which many a viewer would qualify not just as criminal but as truly evil.

In *Les Filles ne savent pas nager* (2000), Anne-Sophie Birot also defers revelation of an immanent violence in lesbian desire to the sobering finale of her film. Teenagers Gwen (a close homonym of the French word 'gouine', meaning 'dyke') and Lise have been close friends since early childhood, spending summer holidays together every year. The film traces the build-up to Lise's arrival, their joy at finally being reunited, and the transformation of both their relationship and, ultimately, their lives, due to Lise's jealous love for Gwen. Lise's discovery that Gwen has been sleeping with boys triggers a precursor to the physical violence that is to prove literally fatal by the end of the film; here, it is limited to her smashing a bottle. But in the literally fatal dénouement it escalates beyond all control. Spurned by Gwen, Lise locks herself in her bedroom, sobbing, and starts packing her bags. Gwen's father tries to comfort her in a paternal manner by minimising the row, but soon finds himself – truly shockingly – kissing her. He quickly comes to his senses and pulls away, saying 'C'est ridicule' ['It's ridiculous'], that she's just 'une petite fille' ['a little girl']. Lise is not so easily daunted: she goes after him, tries to embrace him, struggles when he gently rebuffs her and finally pushes him down the stairs, at the foot of which he lies immobile, and, as is rapidly confirmed, dead. What is never confirmed is whether Lise's act of murder is involuntary. (For further analysis of her motives, see Chapter 3.) Voluntary or not, it is, in legal terms, undeniably criminal.

Catherine Corsini's *La Répétition* (2000) is relatively low-key in its yoking of lesbian desire to violence, which takes a largely verbal or potential form; the film's main line of attack on lesbianism will consist in pathologising (see Chapter 3).[9] When Louise attempts to caress her neck from behind, Nathalie slaps her brutally and shouts, 'Tu dégages!' ['Get lost!']. Louise is next seen self-harming, in a sense acting out without actualising her previous suicide attempt prompted by jealous possessiveness of Nathalie, but clearly extremely distraught with blood on her hand; and we may ponder the lesbo-specificity of this bodily part, along with her mutilation of it. When Nathalie later falls seriously ill and an ambulance crew arrive at the house, Louise refuses to answer the door bell, despite a frightened Nathalie's pleas, and even turns off the light so that the crew will think there is nobody there. Shrouded in darkness, Louise is seen weeping. How is the viewer meant to interpret this? It is clearly not simple desire for revenge that causes her to put Nathalie's life at risk, as some of the French reviewers imply. Is it, in fact, more a desire to destroy that which she desires and loves but cannot possess? Finally, the ambulance crew enter, though it is unclear whether they break in or Louise has relented and let them in; Nathalie survives, but no thanks to her female desirer.

Chronologically, the third film in the corpus inspired by or invoking the case of the Papin sisters, Jean-Pierre Denis's *Les Blessures assassines* (2000), is unique among the three in tracing a familial aetiology of the violence wreaked by the two outwardly quiet young women: a broken family, a distant mother, an elder sister who, after being sexually abused by their father, has taken the veil and cut off contact, and a consequent determination never to be parted from each other. Christine is violently possessive of her younger sister Léa, trying to prevent her from seeing their mother and becoming furious at the mother's allusion to Léa eventually marrying; the director uses her internal monologue to reveal her fear of losing Léa as she had lost her other two sisters, Emilia and Isabelle. The incestuous nature of their relationship, which is soon made explicit, will be discussed in Chapter 3, and further scenes of eroticism between them will be analysed in Chapter 5; for our purposes in this chapter, let us turn to the yoking of lesbian desire and criminality.

What immediately precedes the appalling and very graphically conveyed murder may well have had some causal role in that murder. For one privileged evening, the sisters anticipate freedom in the absence of their employers to indulge their desires. They play oral games with food in bed, hungrily kiss each other's breasts, the sexual tempo increases . . . when suddenly Madame and Mademoiselle return unexpectedly early, curtailing their brief sexual idyll, throwing them into a panic born from fear of censure and separation. As *Les Inrockuptibles* observes, 'c'est la découverte éblouissante du plaisir et la peur panique d'être découvertes, donc à nouveau séparées, qui explique le passage à l'acte et la complicité meurtrière des sœurs-amantes'[10] ['it's the dazzling discovery of pleasure and the terror of being discovered, and thus separated again, which explains what pushed the sister-lovers to murder and also their murderous complicity'].

In the foregoing discussion, what may shock readers most is the figure of the lesbian as murderer, be it actual or potential, of her female desire-object. Unsurprisingly, such scenarios are rare, being confined to Albicocco's *La Fille aux yeux d'or*, Chabrol's *Les Biches* and Corsini's *La Répétition* (Louise as *potentially* fatal to Nathalie). Mainstream reception of Albicocco's *La Fille aux yeux d'or* offers no elucidation of this paradox: Henry Chapier of the left-wing *Combat*, for instance, maintains a puzzling silence on the ultimate murder, and appears anxious to provide a fully sanitised reading of the film which borders on the ingenuous:

> À aucun moment la passion de Mme de Sanreal pour la *Fille aux yeux d'or* ne comporte d'éléments choquants: jamais le film n'effleure les méandres de la psycho-pathologie sexuelle . . . Et lorsque, les yeux émerveillés par la beauté des images, l'esprit se ressaisit, on n'en sait que plus gré à J.-G. Albicocco d'avoir manié avec délicatesse un sujet aussi dangereux à porter à l'écran.[11]
> [Never once does Mme de Sanreal's passion for *The Girl With the Golden Eyes* include any shocking elements; never does the film even come close to the ramblings of psychosexual pathology. . . . And when, having been filled with wonder by the beauty of the images, we pull ourselves together, we are all the more grateful to J.-G. Albicocco for having handled so delicately a subject so dangerous for the screen.]

Corsini goes to the other extreme in overdetermining a hermeneutics of pathology, qualifying the relationship between her two female protagonists in *La Répétition* as 'une amitié névrotique, obsessionnelle 'à la vie *à la mort*' telle que l'on peut la vivre dans la fièvre de l'adolescence . . .'[12] ['a neurotic, obsessional friendship for life until death, the sort that you have in the excitement of your teen years . . .'].

Reflecting largely unconscious cultural anxieties, far more widespread are filmic mediations of lesbians as representing death to men, be it literal (physical murder) or symbolic (castration, which as Shameem Kabir (1998: 50) reminds us, is in a wider sense a 'decisive metaphor' for all loss) (Metz 1983: 69). By far the most predominant site for this kind of configuration is the vampire genre, which will be considered in more detail towards the end of this chapter. Before that, I would like briefly to consider two films falling outside that genre but none the less feeding similar anxieties: Henri-Georges

2. Lesbianism as criminality: in *Les Diaboliques* (1954), Nicole and Christina plot to kill.
Filmsonor/The Kobal Collection/Mirkine

Clouzot's *Les Diaboliques* (1954) and, from Switzerland, Alain Tanner's *Messidor* (1978).

It has quite rightly been claimed that the lesbian content of Clouzot's *Les Diaboliques* (1954) consists only in 'sous-entendus':

> Tout est dans les sous-entendus: Nicole, cheveux courts, costaude, et énergique, Christina, cheveux longs, plus chétive et soumise. Les regards échangés, certains tremblements dans la voix de Christina, leur dégoût pour Michel . . . Clouzot n'explicite pas mais le vrai couple du film, est bien Nicole et Christina.[13]
> [Everything is implicit: Nicole with her short hair, sturdy and energetic, Christina with her long hair, more frail and submissive. The looks that are exchanged, certain waverings in Christina's voice, their disgust for Michel . . . Clouzot doesn't make it obvious but the real couple in the film is obviously Nicole and Christina.]

Those 'sous-entendus' are, however, very voluble for any resisting lesbian spectator, as Susan Hayward's artful analysis makes clear (for further exegesis, see Chapter 4). Nicole (played by Simone Signoret, something of a lesbian icon)[14] and Christina grow ever more complicit in their growing hatred for Michel, Christina's bullying husband (who publicly humiliates and privately rapes her) and Nicole's brutal lover (who gives her a black eye on at least one occasion). Unlike Michel, Nicole shows solicitous concern for Christina's fragile health, and condemns Michel as 'infecte' ['foul'] when he has publicly forced his wife to eat inedible food. When in the car together, alluding to their respective positions vis-à-vis Michel (wife and mistress) and to the mutual resentment these would normally prompt, Christina comments that Nicole must have been tempted to kill her at some point, to which Nicole replies 'Moi pas, mais lui . . .' ['Me, no; but him . . .']: a highly ambiguous utterance which could conceivably be read as suggesting Nicole has felt murderous towards Michel because of his abuse of Christina. When they are plotting to poison him, a two-shot frame shows Nicole gripping Christina's arm tightly, ostensibly to stiffen her resolve, but perhaps also translating inchoate desire. Clouzot's film allows, *inter alia*, at least two interpretations: that women oppressed by men may connive to eliminate their oppressor by whatever means, including murder; and, more disturbingly, that women open to the allure of other women may easily become hom[me-]icidal.

Alain Tanner's *Messidor* (1978) is also open to either of these interpretations. It has been described as a '[l]esbian 'road' movie'.[15] In certain obvious ways, it anticipates both *Thelma and Louise* (1991) and *Baise-moi* (2000) in its focus on two women on the road whose abusive treatment by men fosters an intimate bond between them. With respect to *Thelma and Louise*, there is the same killing/assault (whether the male victim dies or not remains unconfirmed in *Messidor*) by one of the women of the other's sexual assailant: Marie protects Jeanne by attacking the would-be rapist with a stone's blow to his head. After this traumatic experience, a medium close-up shot of them in adjacent hotel-beds portends intimacies to come, with Jeanne's assertion, 'On s'emmerde bien toutes les deux . . .' ['We get on pretty damned well together . . .'], receiving Marie's full assent. And with respect to *Baise-moi*, other parallels include the fact these two women become wanted criminals who constantly defer parting: the refrain of 'Je reste avec toi?' ['Shall I stay with you?'] resembles Manu's 'Je propose qu'on reste ensemble' ['I suggest we stay together']. Hart's canny analysis of the anglophone films *Thelma and Louise* and *Mortal Thoughts* could in certain respects be applied to *Messidor* (with the exception of the reference to critical responses):

> *Thelma and Louise* and *Mortal Thoughts* [are] among the recent proliferation of 'killer women' films that have captured the imagination of a mass audience.

These two films represent women acting together in retaliation against the dominant culture's gender expectations. Summoned through negation both within these films' 'content' and extradiegetically in critical responses to them is a history of identification between the female outlaw and the lesbian. These representations carry within them, and work overtime to disavow, the unconscious weight of a culture that has made the lesbian and the female criminal synonymous by displacing women's aggression onto the sexual deviant. (Hart 1994: xii)

However, there are also marked dissonances between *Messidor* and these various intertexts. First, the crimes of the two women in the Swiss film are far less serious – defence against a rapist, stealing a gun with which they do not quite know what to do, stealing food to survive – and involve no gratuitous violence, in contrast with *Baise-moi* particularly. Second, whereas the lesbian content of *Thelma and Louise* and *Baise-moi* is only latent, in *Messidor* it is, if not central to the narrative economy, certainly manifest. Third, against the conventions of the typical female road- or revenge-movie, neither of the two women dies; rather, the film ends with their arrest. Finally, it initially seems that the only distinct national traits marking *Messidor* out as a specifically Swiss film are superficial (the alpine landscape, the roadsigns and the mixture of languages used: here, mainly French and German), and it could be argued that the film partakes of a French/francophone/even 'European art-house' philosophical tradition alien to both the anglophone road-movies and to the much more recent and self-consciously 'in-your-face' *Baise-moi*. *Messidor* is ultimately more about an existential quest, a form of revolution (hence the title: Messidor is a summer month in the French Revolutionary calendar), which includes but is not limited to a transgressing of sexual norms. Emerging from rural isolation into an urban space, Marie intimates metaphysical alienation in asking what all these people are doing, where they're going; Jeanne had earlier speculated on time, space and emptiness. A strong sense of life's banality and absurdity is conveyed; the only certain thing is their growing need for food and the presence of the other – a vital and embodied presence that is minatory only to men who threaten them.

Finally, we come to the most obvious paradigm of lesbianism as violent, criminal, even hom[m]icidal: the lesbian vampire. The lesbian vampire is a(n in)famously tenacious trope that has already prompted a relatively ample body of critical commentary. Andrea Weiss's early comments were apt:

outside of male pornography, the lesbian vampire is the most persistent lesbian image in the history of the cinema. . . . The association of vampirism with lesbianism is far-reaching and long-lived. As Richard Dyer has pointed out, the literary images of each are closely related and often described in the same morbid language. . . . The connection between lesbians and vampires has not been restricted to the horror genre, but resonates throughout much of the existing cultural representations of lesbianism. (Weiss 1992: 84–5)

A more positive spin on the lesbian vampire-figure was later provided by Ellis Hanson's essay on 'lesbians who bite', in which he questions 'the pre-occupation of lesbian and feminist film criticism with negative stereotypes and the patriarchal gaze by offering an appreciation of lesbian vampire films as a genre that foregrounds female visual pleasure' (Hanson 1991: 16).

As I look at lesbian vampire films, I am no longer struck by their misogyny, but quite the opposite. They do not always follow the predictable track-and-kill tradition of the vampire genre, and lesbian desire often functions as a destabilizing, even derailing force in the paranoid narrative that seeks to demonize and contain it. Some of the more complicated examples of the genre present a number of entertaining and intriguing possibilities for lesbian and feminist fantasy. (Hanson 1991: 184)

Most recently, Clare Whatling has summed matters up consummately:

Despite a long history of homophobic representation . . . the vampire continues to straddle a number of discourses, both anti-lesbian and lesbian-appropriative. The heady combination of desire and repulsion, fascination and abjection, illustrates the double-bind between cultural oppression and sexual fantasy. (Whatling 1997: 93)

Appropriation of what was originally a lesbophobic configuration operates, one hopes self-consciously, on questionable political terrain, which celebrates the supremacy of fantasy and the powers of voluntarism to transform objectively dubious textual materials into satisfying private pleasures. The dubiety of these materials consists, *inter alia*, in connotations of parasiticism and of contamination. The story goes that, once bitten and sucked by a vampire, you become 'one of them'; many a representative of the moral right's family values would impute the same contaminatory venom to lesbians and gays. In the context of AIDS, it is a myth that has already been deployed to tragic effect in efforts to hasten the decimation of gays. Yet whilst technically it meshes with the darkest variants on the narcissistic/fusional model of lesbianism, it is clearly also susceptible of a celebratory reading. All of the films examined below exemplify apparent lesbophobia, yet most are recuperable to this more celebratory type of reading. However, proselytism is perhaps the most disturbing of the potential blindspots within lesbian appropriations, and it will become clear in the following commentary that the primary, mainstream interpretations of this corpus should not be ignored. The result could well be a sapphic solipsism which would only serve further to disenfranchise lesbians in the material world.

While Jacques Baratier's *L'Araignée de satin* (1984) is not a vampire movie *per se*, it does contain some choice magpie pickings from the genre. Set in an early twentieth-century girls' boarding school, it is a heavily stylised horror film in kitschly gothic mode, with stilted, theatrical dialogue and an anachronistically flickering quality. One of its gothic features is the deathly pallor and implicitly vampiric tendencies of its chief protagonist, Solange, an older pupil. Conjugated with these vampiric tendencies are marked lesboerotic leanings. An early sequence forms a voyeuristic, erotically charged objectification of young girls on the part of a joint female gaze as Solange and the headmistress leaf through a photo album of schoolgirls favoured by the headmistress: 'elles sont toutes si belles, si parfaites' ['they're all so beautiful, so perfect']. At the sight of a very young, probably prepubescent girl, Solange utters, 'Tu exagères . . . T'es vraiment diabolique' ['That's a bit much . . . You're really devilish'] – a remonstration which, for all its playful complicity, may well taint the headmistress and her particular sexual preferences with a very real diabolic charge for the mainstream spectator, particularly within contemporary interpretive communities more than sensititised to the perils of paedophilia. (A later sequence supports this imputation of diabolism when Solange, having heard that a priest has submitted the lesbo-susceptible schoolgirl Lucienne to the 'pénitence' ['penance'], proclaims, 'C'est tout le contraire de ce que nous aimons' ['It's the exact opposite of all that we hold dear']. Thus a series of interlinked binary oppositions is inscribed between good and bad, holy and evil, chastising of female sensuality and tactile pleasure between women.) The soundtrack of haunting, menacing music augments the disquieting effect of the dialogue between the two women as they engage in scopophilic erethism centring on the young female body. The elder entertains two competing discourses: 'Que de futurs monsters . . . Quel plaisir de les sentir près de soi, de les caresser!' ['What future monsters . . . And what pleasure in feeling them close to one, in stroking them!'], whilst the younger alludes to the eroticisation of power imbalance: 'Qu'elles sont obéissantes!' ['How obedient they are!'], a trope taken up by the elder in her expression of pleasure at the girls crying, her comforting them and her pleasure in seeing them suffer. This discursively-loaded sequence ends upon sexualised commerce between the older and younger woman, with the former kissing the latter, who has lowered herself onto the sofa. The concluding frame sets the viewer up to perceive the headmistress as vampiric: seen from behind, this female figure with flame-red hair (icon of sinful sensuality as well as symbol of blood) goes for the blonde woman's mouth. The taint of lesboerotic diabolism intensifies when Solange takes 'innocent' schoolgirl Lucienne to an island castle, which was formerly the site of pagan worship – fetishism, black magic and even human sacrifices, all of which heresies could be conflated with homosexuality in the religiously fundamentalist purview which Baratier courts and exploits.

Lesboeroticism is also harnessed to disturbing violence. In a troubling juxtaposition, Solange's narrative of her rape by an unknown man on a train is accompanied by visual mediation of her own quasi-rape of Lucienne. She aggressively tears off the girl's slip just as she recounts the train crashing – a patent symbol of her orgasm at the hands of the male rapist, whom she claims to have loved. As she evokes the memory she is voraciously kissing Lucienne, and the camera suggests, without actually visibilising, lesbian genital sex through the couple's head and shoulder movements. The camera's gaze fixes upon Solange's grip of Lucienne's hand as she brings her to climax: we see only her hand in the left-hand side of the frame, with Lucienne's shoulders, head and orgasmic facial expression dominating the rest. Whilst the most libertarian of lesbo-appropriative spectators could justifiably argue that Solange's gaze is lesbo-specific and thus transcends the superficially reproving framework of the film at large, it is at the very least problematic that Solange is narrating orgasm with a male rapist as she brings Lucienne to orgasm. The police inspector finally rolled in to effect the heteronormatively sanitising dénouement insinuates that Solange has been guilty of a number of crimes: amongst these, which include drug-taking, theft and, most seriously, murder of two schoolgirls, figures lesbian love: 'les amours interdites' ['forbidden loves']. Notable in this finale is the coalition of hegemonic institutions in condemning the chief lesbian character: Church, medicine, police.

Now to the real lesbian-vampiric McCoy: the films of Harry Kümel and, more particularly, of Jean Rollin. A co-production between Belgium, France and West Germany, with some funding from the US, Kümel's *Les Lèvres rouges* (1971; originally entitled *Le Rouge aux lèvres*) came out in both French and English versions. Whilst visually restrained in comparison with Rollin's *œuvre*, it features a central lesbian character whose powers of seduction, murderous destruction and contamination of hitherto 'normal' women tap into primeval male paranoia.

With strains of Sheridan Le Fanu's *Carmilla* (Kümel denies any direct influence, but admits that he had seen *Blood and Roses* which was based on

3. *Les Lèvres rouges* (1971): cult actress Delphine Seyrig, here a vampire countess, possesses Valérie from behind (see Chapter 2). Showking/Roxy/Snc/The Kobal Collection

it, and avers, 'Of course, it's so evident that women vampires should be lesbian. . .'),[16] the plot of *Les Lèvres rouges* revolves around the sinister powers of an ageless Hungarian countess, Elisabeth Bathory (played by Delphine Seyrig, a cult actress for French and francophone lesbian audiences), who, aided and abetted by her Goth female 'companion' Ilona, manipulates and ultimately rends asunder the newly married couple Valérie and Stefan. While Elisabeth strategically deploys her sexual magnetism to beguile Stefan, she is clearly after his wife alone. On first sighting the couple at the vast, deserted Ostend hotel in which they are staying, she remarks to Ilona on Valérie's beautiful skin and lips, prompting a jealous response. This scene, during which Elisabeth strokes Ilona's hair, is tinged ominously with red. The serial murders of beautiful young women reported in Ostend within the diegesis are never directly attributed to Elisabeth, but the viewer is induced to assign her mysterious signature to them. In each case, the girl has been found with a gaping neck wound but no blood, suggesting a vampiric vacuum-cleaning job. Elisabeth and Stefan libidinously evoke the legend of Elisabeth's ancestor, also a countess who, hundreds of years earlier, had tortured 800 young virgins and bathed in their blood, which she believed to be the elixir of youth. She was finally condemned to be walled up in her room and her accomplices were executed. Yet she appears to have transcended death, or else to have been reincarnated in her ageless descendant, Elisabeth.

When Valérie attempts to run away after Stefan's vicious assault, Elisabeth persuades her to stay via a blend of verbal charm and beguiling tactility. She asks Valérie to give her her hand, and the camera shows the two linked hands – a prominent motif in lesbian literary imagery, as remarked above – in close-up, followed by Elisabeth's kissing Valérie's hand and leaving a lipstick imprint which resembles blood. Sexual politics subvert the traditionally male-dominated ideo/visuolect of the vampire movie as Elisabeth exposes the charade that Valérie's marriage to Stefan is, insisting that he dreams of making his wife a slave, as all men dream of making all women. Returning to the hotel, they find Stefan and Ilona together naked; Valérie's resistance soon crumbles, as we see in an extreme close-up shot of Elisabeth kissing her sensuously on the lips, Valérie looking hypnotised, and the camera focusing on Elisabeth's deep red lips and langorous yet sultry eyes. A dramatic zoom-out next shows Elisabeth enclosing Valérie in a black cape, looking like a predatory bat – a stock prop in the vampire genre. A later red-saturated shot shows a silent, slow-motion sequence of Elisabeth apparently kissing Valérie's exposed neck, but from her query as to whether it hurt, we infer that she had in fact been vampirizing Valérie. The dimension of sexual politics again emerges in the mortal combat between Elisabeth and Stefan over Valérie. He declares with transparently sexist logic that he is a man and Valérie is his, and promptly begins to beat his 'possession'; Elisabeth comes to Valérie's defence and the two women kill him. Elisabeth's inchoate utterance 'The blood' is succeeded by Valérie sucking the blood of her dead husband.

The sequence forming the narrative climax of the film shows Valérie driving and Elisabeth urging her to go ever faster – so that she will not be exposed to sunrise and her vampiric status thus confirmed. Valérie is now competely and passionately in thrall to Elisabeth, panting 'Soon, the border, the other side . . . Oh Elisabeth, you forever![17] Your hand, your hand', and reaching round as if to kiss Elisabeth's hand. Her words operate on a figurative as well as a literal level: Valérie is crossing not only into a different national territory but also into a different sexual, amorous, indeed ontological territory. Elisabeth, for her part, breathes huskily, 'My love my love, my only one there's so much left of life still to taste . . .' (her pun on life-blood to taste providing unintentional humour) and their two faces are shown in close-up, Valérie looking orgasmic in front of the wheel, Elisabeth behind her. The music increases the dramatic tension, and, inevitably, they crash. Propelled through the window-screen, Elisabeth is (melo)dramatically impaled on a tree branch, and goes up in flames. This climax is succeeded by the intertitle 'A few months later . . .' and by a short, enigmatic sequence showing Valérie flanked by a new man and child, giving us to believe through her coded words that she has become the new Elisabeth . . . Thus Kümel melds the narcissistic/fusional model with the dangerous/death-to-man model of lesbianism (more of which below).

If Kümel's lesbian-vampire movie shocks the spectator, the only way in which s/he could derive any viewing pleasures from Jean Rollin's numerous products within the genre is to read very strenuously indeed against the grain, viewing them as artefacts of camp excess, as Andrea Weiss intimates:

> Jean Rollin directed a series of surrealist French horror films, including *Le Viol du vampire* (1967), *La Vampire nue* (1969), *Le Frisson des vampires* (1970), and *Vierges et vampires* (1971), all of which sacrificed narrative coherence for shocking sado-masochistic lesbian images. Rollin's iconography features leather and metal chains, spikes protruding from women's breasts, scenes of gang rape, and vampires reduced to drinking from their own veins. Such jarring imagery departs significantly from that of the typical, more romantic lesbian vampire film, which has certain fairly consistent characteristics: Gothic themes and imagery, large empty castles and dark, romantic landscapes, and the arrival, early in the film, of a mysterious, aristocratic figure. With a few exceptions, these horror films were made on very small budgets, with extremely low production values. Their low budget often gives them an exaggerated, camp quality, which for viewers today is often their redeeming feature. They were originally shown in second-rate commercial movie houses or in drive-in theaters, and now a number of them have been resurrected on the home video market. (Weiss 1991: 85)

I largely concur in Weiss's overview but would, perhaps pedantically, make two corrections: first, *La Vampire nue* contains no 'sado-masochistic lesbian images'; second, Rollin's lesbian-vampire films do in fact frequently feature 'Gothic themes and imagery, large empty castles and dark, romantic landscapes', and thus do not depart quite so significantly as Weiss suggests from the 'typical, more romantic lesbian vampire film'.

The first of his offerings, *Le Viol du vampire* (1967), ostentatiously self-classifies as a 'mélodrame', and includes a full complement of gothic music – organs, violins, jarring discordant notes; gothic imagery (castles, brooding skies); disorienting camera angles; and disturbing use of lighting and darkness. For our purposes, only Part Two is of relevance: here, the malevolent 'reine des vampires' appears, and the action is dominated by male-initiated efforts to conquer her. Surrounded by devoted female vampires, she is the classic lesbian-encoded s/m dominatrix: of androgynous amazonian physique, clad in fetish items such as black leathers, straps, studs and so on.

At one point she flings a woman down onto a bed and covers her prey's body with her own: a vampiric gesture which also figures as a sexual gesture. Similarly, in the grand finale of film, she is seen vampirising a sacrificial young woman, but her gesture looks for all the world like passionate kissing. Finally, she is killed off: within the self-consciously Manichaean codes of Rollin's *œuvre*, this is a triumph of good over unquestionable evil. Might we none the less question the political significance and effects of casting Jacqueline Sieger, of Afro-Carribean appearance, as this incarnation of evil? To view this as an alignment of one persecuted minority with another is perhaps to credit Rollin with a little too much subtlety within his historical context: in the France of 1967, black rights and lesbian and gay liberation were not yet on the political or cultural agenda.

In *Le Frisson des vampires* of 1970, the deathly white vampire Isolde caresses the hair of a naked Yse, uncovers her breasts (eliciting an aroused smile), massages her shoulders, nipples and waist then, with the sound-track indicating rising erotic tension, takes her to a graveyard where she makes her drink blood and starts kissing her again. During this treatment, the camera figures Yse's body in red-saturated colours, connoting both her arousal and her damnation, confirmed by her swooning. Later, Yse refuses to sleep with her new husband for the second night running, and goes to bed alone. In a supreme example of camp excess, she is startled by the sudden apparition of a naked Isolde behind her bed, arms raised above her in predatory fashion, cape stretched out like a bat, accompanied by a thunderclap on the soundtrack. She kisses Yse on the lips, then vampirises her. Isolde is unambiguously on the side of evil within the crude codes of the vampire genre: she is an s/m, malevolent lesbian vampire, sporting breast-studs, violently killing a woman who caresses her by biting her nipples viciously. But eventually she falls from the pedestal of dominatrix into the pit of victim, getting her due comeuppance within the heterosexist super-structure of the genre, for, somewhat implausibly, she is overpowered and raped by the two male *châtelains* (lords of the castle) who had previously seemed to respect her powers. This reflects a common proviso of male sub-mission fantasies: that ultimate control be vested in the male, including his prerogative to invert the contrived power imbalance.

Vierges et vampires, also known as *Requiem pour un vampire* (1971), repre-sents a nadir in Rollin's lesbian-connoted vampire movies. It contains a shockingly bloody pre-sequence before the credits, and several discomfiting scenes of straight-oriented soft porn s/m, in which the victim is female and visibly not masochistic in any contractual sense at all: she is merely, and abjectly, a victim. The lesbian element of the film is exceedingly slight, and contains no imputation of evil – but this is precisely because the two women in question, Michèle and Marie (in fact, supposedly schoolgirls, and often dressed titillatingly as such, but physically very precocious), are utterly disempowered, infantilised and victimised in a cringe factor that goes off the scale at least of this author's usual monitor. The only interesting, but inchoate and unexplained factor here is that, at the start of action, these two supposed schoolgirls are on the run after shooting from a man's car, dousing the driver with petrol and setting him alight (cf. *Baise-moi*, *Messidor*). The film's narrative development offers no elucidation of their eminently criminal action, or of its motivation. The two appear to have no route plan and survive by stealing food, until they stumble into an old castle, which turns out to be the lair of the last vampire ever. One scene shows them naked in bed caressing each other. The angle resembles very much that of a similar shot in *Le Frisson des vampires*: a high-angle shot encompassing a diagonal line formed by the bodies of two naked, caressing women, heads at the top right-hand side, feet at bottom left-hand side. In both films, an impression of enclosure and stasis is conveyed by such framing. The soundtrack is, for the first time in *Vierges et vampires*, peaceful, suggesting an ephemeral lesbian enclave within this demonic diegesis. Most striking of all about this couple is the fact that they do not exchange a word until fifty-two minutes into the film, which suggests either mute complicity or sub-humanity.

Their initial tenderness is sharply inverted towards the end of the film when Michèle, desperate to extract information on the whereabouts of the male intruder who she believes will destroy them all, whips a chained Marie. The flagellation is filmed in what seems painfully, in the second-degree sense of the word, like real time, and the camera sadistically lingers on the increasingly bloody weals inflicted, while the soundtrack conveys Marie's pain through her screams. Michèle the torturer somewhat incongruously cries out through her tears, 'I love you as much as you love me. We ran away together, and I'll always love you' – an uneasy conjunction of desire and sadistic torture. Finally, she gives up and kisses the still chained Michèle on the lips, imploring forgiveness, insisting she had to do it because she did not want to die. As in *Le Frisson des vampires*, the tenuous agency of the lesbian couple, along with any suggestion of female solidarity, is duly vanquished: the whipping has taken place at the behest of the female noviciate vampires in thrall to their male master. One of these, Erica, second-in-command to the 'maître' [master], is androgynously dressed, and gets pleasure from various un-p.c. lesbian-connoted activities: watching female victims being raped by henchmen, sensuously stroking women's hair before ravenously biting them, and biting women's breasts. Her generic imperviousness to human suffering constitutes her as evil, but of signal importance is the fact that she in no way contests the male supremacy of the diegesis.

Not atypically for the lesbian vampire genre, Rollin's *Fascination* (1979) also has elements of soft porn, with frequent gratuitous shots of women's breasts and positioning of women as objects of a male gaze. What distinguishes this film from Rollin's previous forays into the genre is that the male interloper within the lesbian-connoted relations is neither a vampire nor ultimately victorious. In this case, the diegetic gaze objectifying women belongs to the thief Marc, who initially holds the two female protagonists Elisabeth and Eva hostage in their château; within the wider generic conventions of production and consumption, the gaze being activated is that of the voyeuristic male viewer. Beyond these sexually-specific elements, the classic iconography and acoustics of the vampire movie are wheeled out – women sucking blood from their victims, lips snarling in pre-bite mode, gothic music, thunder claps, baying hounds.

At an early point in the film Elisabeth and Eva are framed kissing each other on the lips with playful eroticism. Shortly afterwards we have the same visual scenario, but the soundtrack now accompanying it, presumably intended to evoke an experience of emotional intimacy as well as sexual pleasure, in fact strikes a somewhat weak chord which is not dissonant with normative conceptions of lesbian sex as lacking a hard erotic edge (see comments on Kristeva, Chapter 3). However, there is also narrative development, for in this sequence they slowly undress each other, embrace, caress each other's arms, shoulders, back and buttocks. There is no suggestion of genital sex, of course: this is sanitised, soft-core sapphism.

Their candyfloss cavorting is succeeded by much more hard-edged treatment of the iconically masculine Marc. First Eva bites his neck, to dramatic non-diegetic music, then shortly afterwards is captured striking a seductive pose and stripping to her underwear for him. The narrative oscillates between confirming the lesbian bond and putting it under potential erasure. Eva seduces Marc, they have sex and Elisabeth is tempted to shoot first them, then herself; but Eva later caresses her shoulder, protesting that she had sex only to ensure he stayed the night – as we ultimately discover, for the purposes of sucking his life-blood once their secret female society of 'women of good background' has assembled at midnight. Eva is also forced to have sex with another male thief, but she resourcefully stabs him to death midway through his attempted rape. For good measure, she also decapitates two of the other male thieves with an enormous scythe (figure of Death), then kills the one female thief, but declines to decapitate her. The obvious castration symbol reinforces the notion of woman as dangerous to man. If this is so of women generally, it is *a fortiori* true of lesbian women. One might even go as far as to say that in this film, as in many other lesbian vampire films, and even though the victims are not *always* male, lesbianism is both a metaphor and metonymy for death to men.

In the grand bloodbath of a finale, Elisabeth shoots Eva, who croaks, 'Pourquoi as-tu fait ça? J'étais ton amie' ['Why did you do that? I was your [girl]friend']. Other women from the infernal gathering appear and start biting Eva like a pack of hounds, and the camera dwells pruriently in close-up shots on their blood-stained lips. Just before shooting Marc, Elisabeth retorts to his question 'Tu m'aimes, n'est-ce pas?' ['You love me, don't you?'] with a confused, 'J'aimais Eva. Je l'ai tuée' ['I loved Eva. I killed her'], then adds 'Je crois que je ne t'ai jamais aimé . . . Ce que j'aimais en toi, c'était . . .' ['I don't think I ever loved you . . . What I loved in you was . . .'], the final ellipsis leaving the viewer to fill in the gap with the obvious 'ton sang' ['your blood']. Finally, Elisabeth lies to Hélène, the third obviously lesbian-vampire figure (who had also played the dominatrix role with Marc, verbally seducing then biting him) that Marc had killed Eva so she killed him in revenge. Hélène, uninterested in the moral niceties of the slaughter, says that Elisabeth is beautiful with blood on her lips; they kiss on the lips, the frame of their kiss freezes and the film ends.

In this narrative hotchpotch it is difficult to discern any overriding logic. What is clear is that lesbians are associated with death to men (and sometimes to women), and that the advent of a male seducer in a lesbian couple may well spell death also to the lesbian who falls prey to his charms – at the avenging hands of her usurped lesbian lover. Whatever the case, that lesbians spell trouble is the obvious message for the implied viewer, who may none the less get a voyeuristic kick from watching simulations of lesbian sex.

Three years later Rollin released *La Morte vivante* (1982), to date his last exploit within the lesbian-vampire genre. Catherine, supposedly dead for over two years, awakens in her coffin and proceeds to gouge out the eyes of the hapless man who has uncovered her. Through flashback, we are privy to a scene between her and her friend Hélène when the two were prepubescent girls. Catherine had then sworn eternal love for Hélène, and the two had made a blood pact: if one were to die, the other would follow her into death. Back in the diegetic present, Hélène is astounded to find the beloved friend she thought was dead not merely (if ambiguously: cf. title) alive, but also covered in the blood of her victims. She asks Catherine why she had not told her she was alive, remonstrating that she should have been told: 'on aurait dû savoir que je t'aimerais toujours, même . . . différente . . .' ['they should have known that I'd love you for always, even if you were . . . different . . .'], the last line generating some humour, albeit presumably unintended. Remembering their childhood blood pact, Hélène cuts her arm and lets Catherine suck the blood – to which Catherine reacts with an almost orgasmic expression.

Thus begins a gory tale where the two women are placed outside any kind of moral framework. Hélène is convinced that Catherine needs fresh human blood to thrive, so lures an unsuspecting stranger – significantly, a woman – to the château, where Catherine vampirises her. The scene hovers on the border between the visually horrific and the downright comic in its sanguinary hypertrophe and its parodic ascription of eroticised ecstasy to Catherine as she sucks the woman's blood. Catherine's assertion to Barbara, a female photographer, that she will love Hélène forever and will never be separated from her is problematised when, in reaction to Hélène wishing to take her away, she accuses Hélène of wanting to draw her back into the world of the living, whereas she had been quite comfortable in the crypt surrounded by corpses: 'C'est moi qui fais charnier, c'est moi qui ai vidé ces corps de leur sang pour qu'il coule dans le mien' ['I'm the one who created this mass grave, who drained these bodies of their blood so that it would flow in my own']. She then begs Hélène to kill her. Is this a metaphor for lesbian love as murderous of individual identity, or as pathological to the death – or just the sensationalist, screwball fantasies of a voyeuristic male director?

Perhaps the most (ominously) pregnant line of the whole film is when Catherine tells Hélène 'Je suis *ta* mort' ['I am *your* death'] (my emphasis), then vampirises her to death, even biting chunks out of her neck. The thunderclaps of the soundtrack, the cross-cutting of the camera from the murder to close-ups of blood on the paving stones then back to Catherine's bloodsucking, all combine to provide a bathetically melodramatic dénouement. Significantly, Catherine also bites off Hélène's thumb – a synecdoche for the hand, which is highly salient in lesbian iconography/semiotics.

This is a salutary warning indeed against the dangers of sapphic solipsism. Private fantasies and private pleasures are all very well, but what do we gain by ignoring the very direst of implications: that lesbian desire may be recuperated by heterosexist film directors and depicted as murderous of its lesbian object? We may qualify this either as delirious lesbophobia or as innocuous camp excess; but if we wish to function in a wider Symbolic Order, we should not ignore its *nox*ious social effects on constructions of ourselves which can never be entirely *ours*. For all appears to proceed in a teleological line, and the lesbian vampiric destroyer of lesbianism is but the logical conclusion, albeit taken to fantastical and (male?-)fantasised excess, of the criminal model of lesbianism with which this chapter began.

In the foregoing study of films constructing the figure lesbian as criminal (be it through her sin/vice or her aggression/violence), three interrelated topoi have emerged: triangular relationships involving two women and a man; revenge or at the very least aggressive reaction against men; and death. The corpus of films treated in this chapter numbers twenty-five; of these, nineteen (seventy-six per cent) were made by men, and only six (twenty-four per cent) by women. Whilst it is, of course, true that male directors outnumber female directors generally in French/francophone cinema, as in other national cinemas, the forthcoming chapters will bear witness to a broad correlation – with some exceptions – between, on the one hand, male-directed films and a more or less problematising vision of lesbianism, and, on the other hand, female directors and a broadly more upbeat take.

Why, though, this nexus of triangularity, revenge and death? In one sense, its presence in a chapter devoted to mediations of lesbianism as criminality is hardly surprising. A lesbian is by definition an outlaw vis-à-vis the gendered structures of the phallocentric Symbolic Order; she it is who disrupts the logic of that order, indeed does violence to it. To put it another way, with recourse to a Wittigian ideolect, lesbians are not women in that they are not defined by their (subservient) relation to men; yet they refuse to go away and may well make criminal raids on the male-owned goods represented by proper (that is, heterosexual) women. Alternatively, they may aggressively, potentially fatally, resist the attempts of a man – or indeed a woman, namely their female desire-object – to disrupt a lesboerotic dyad. The association of the lesbian figure with death reflects fantasmatic fears on the part of hetero-patriarchy about her ability to emasculate, plunder the goods of or eliminate – and thus impose death on – what should, within the Symbolic Order, be the central, all-powerful term: the male/masculine. These fears, largely unconscious and culturally embedded, are translated into diegetic realities, and the economy of the film narrative works towards elimination of the threat which the figure lesbian is perceived to represent. The lesbian vampire is a hypostatised version of this general association of the lesbian with death: she consummately embodies the contaminatory powers imputed to lesbianism generally (it can be catching, according to popular mythology), and gives hyperbolic form to the murderous powers invested in lesbians by a paranoid collective (usually masculinised) imaginary.

Notes

1. Some feminist readers have objected to the masculinist bias in Foucault's model; and at least one male reader has cautioned thus:

   the ethical problem of self-stylization is based on a physiological order, and not a scientific principle or a theory of the 'subject', and hence cannot be considered independently of one's own sex. Foucault himself did not retreat into a theoretical gender-neutral position, convinced that there is an isomorphism between the elaboration of an aesthetics and ethics of existence and the sex of an individual. The consequence of this is the problematization of a virile ethos (appearing, especially to women, one-sided and misogynous). (Nilson 1998: 136)

In fairness, Foucault did acknowledge that there would also have been close monosexual relationships between women; but, as Herman Nilson points out, '[t]here were hardly any testimonies at all to these relationships, let alone from the women themselves' (Nilson 1988: 137).

2. Due to an outcry from the Catholic Church, Rivette's flm, originally entitled simply *La Religieuse*, was first banned to under-eighteens in March 1966, then to all viewing publics. It received only one screening, at the Festival de Cannes. After a virulent polemic and an anti-censor movement, the film finally received its 'visa d'exploitation' (distribution number) on 6 July 1967, under the enforced new title of *Suzanne Simonin, La Religieuse de Diderot* (which was presumably intended to distance nuns in general from the perceived perversion of the one particular lesbian nun in Diderot's text).
3. Charles Baudelaire, *Les Fleurs du mal* (Paris: Poulet-Malassis, 1857).
4. Keith Reader has observed in private correspondence with the author that 'leper colonies in 1930s French cinema were sometimes used (as in Léon Poirier's highly successful biopic of the Abbé Foucauld, *L'Appel du silence*) as metonyms for self-sacrifice (helping to rescue the benighted natives etc.)'. Whilst I am grateful for this wider cultural reference, and half-excited by the notion that *Club de femmes* might conceivably suggest a sub-textual ennoblement to Alice's exile to a leper colony, the notion of a lesbian out to educate 'the natives' in the 1930s is, alas, at best a retrospective interpretation that would probably have horrified the director. Yet in the free play of meaning authorised by postmodernist critique, it has its hermeneutical place – more of which, below (in Chapter 4).
5. For an excellent study of this case, see Edwards and Reader 2001. In brief, the two Papin sisters were involved in an incestuous relationship, and ultimately killed their employer 'Madame' and her daughter in a slaughter so viciously bloody that it has continued to fascinate the French public imagination as well as the French intelligentsia since its occurrence in 1933.
6. Edwards and Reader 2001: 100–1.
7. For a fuller investigation of triangular relationships, see Chapter 4.
8. It will have become apparent that the conjunction of the artist and the figure 'lesbian' is something of a leitmotif in the corpus. For further analysis, see Chapter 5.
9. I am grateful to Durham Modern Languages Series for permission to reproduce here certain comments on *La Répétition* from my chapter in Günther and Michallat (eds) 2006.
10. 'Sœurs Papin, films frères', *Les Inrockuptibles*, 21 November 2000.
11. Henry Chapier, 'La Fille aux yeux d'or', *Combat*, 23 August 1961.

12. Brigitte Baudin, 'Catherine Corsini: l'amitié trop forte', *Le Figaro*, 22 August 2001; my emphasis.
13. David Lebois 'Bleu, blanc, rose', jeudi sur Canal Jimmy (Télévision), Têtu.com, (Media-G) le 13/06/03.
14 As Susan Hayward asserts, Signoret 'plays with the fixity of gender identity. And it is in this way that she appeals to both sexes' (Hayward 1995: 70). And Judith Mayne's comment is intriguing: 'One might say that Signoret's persona is inverted in *Les Diaboliques*, but one could also argue that a hint of inversion was already present in her persona, that *it excudes a sexuality so excessive that it is never quite convincingly contained within a heterosexual framework*' (Mayne 2000: 46; my emphasis).
15. 'Gay and Lesbian Film/Videography (Annotated)', *Quarterly Review of Film and Video*, vol. 15, no. 1 (1993), p. 110.
16. Interview with Kümel on the DVD version of *Les Lèvres rouges*.
17. Cf. Tony Scott's *The Hunger* (US, 1983), in which Deneuve tells Sarandon, 'You are a part of me now. I cannot let you go . . . You will begin to love me as I do you. Forever. Forever and ever.'

CHAPTER THREE

Mad Girls: Pathology

In terms of discursive chronology, Chapter 2 investigated the first of the two most salient lesbian paradigms in the corpus: criminality and pathology. Criminality was historically conceptualised as sin or vice, but in the context of religious decline I have interpreted it more widely to encompass transgression of man-made and 'natural' as well as putatively divine laws. The present chapter will examine the second of those two dominant paradigms: pathology, or lesbianism, as sickness. (Transgression of 'natural' laws differs from pathology in that sickness is involuntary, transgression intentional.) The discursive shift from condemning lesbians[1] as sinful to certifying them as ill was largely prompted by the birth of sexology in the second half of the nineteenth century, then of psychoanalysis at the start of the twentieth. In the twenty-first century, psychoanalytic dogma still holds astonishing sway in critical practices, and it is certainly at the origin of most contemporary models – be they clinical or more widely cultural – of lesbianism outside those affirmative models elaborated by lesbians themselves in the post-1968 period. The chief avatar of this pathologising paradigm in French and francophone cinema is narcissistic fusion, which, as a quest ultimately for the self, can also be expressed as indifferentiation, doubling and psychosexual immaturity. In saying 'can also be expressed as', I do not wish to imply an exact equivalence of these four highly proximate but discrete phenomena (further qualification is provided below). All of these models intersect to some extent with the second most prominent variant of the pathologising paradigm of lesbianism: the mother–daughter model, which posits lesbianism as an anaclitic quest for the lost mother, and thus as a regression to the realm of the Imaginary, entailing exclusion from the Symbolic Order and, according to Kristeva, psychosis in the adult lesbian-identified woman. Whilst the bulk of this chapter will concentrate on these two dominant schemata, it will begin by scrutinising some less precisely defined variants on the pathologising model thrown up by the corpus (treating them chronologically within each sub-set where there is more than one instance of the variant in question).

Despite a promising start given the period in which it was produced, Michel Wichard's *Le Quatrième sexe* of 1961 ultimately constructs and ridicules the lesbian as freakish aberration of nature, with echoes of Richard Krafft-Ebing, Radclyffe Hall and other prophets of lesbo-ontological doom. It traces the psychosexual trajectory of Sand, a rich American painter in Paris,[2] from lesboeroticism to virtually parodic heteronormativity. Sand is self-confident and dresses in sexily androgynous mode, attracting attention from both women and men. It is the latter desire category that finally triumphs, under the (egregiously) mysterious pull of the classic suffering-but-macho artist figure Michel. When Caroline, who will later become sexually involved with Sand, asks who she is, Michel replies snidely that Sand is 'the fourth sex'[3] – a denigratory model reiterated when he haughtily sets himself above Sand's girlfriends: 'I'm the first sex, not the fourth'. The grand finale represents a caricatural summum of various heteronormativising discourses when Sand declares to Paul apropos her earlier quarrel with Michel:

> Do you know what a lesbian's like? She's sort of not masculine and not feminine – just the fourth sex. That caused our fight. I'm afraid I was wrong. . . . I felt so filthy, so freakish, when he said that. Suddenly everything seemed distasteful. The only thing left to do was to get back. How stupid! If only Michel knew how sorry I am about Caroline! I was so mixed up for so long. Michel made me normal. He made me a woman!

Even more invidiously than theorisations of lesbians as men trapped in women's bodies (the foundational model being the *Zwischenstufen* theory),[4] this utterance evacuates the lesbian of both masculinity and femininity, thereby reducing her to non-human status.

Predictably, Michel relents, and the film ends with them about to kiss. What Barbara Creed says of two non-French-language classics, *Calamity Jane* (US, 1953) and *Queen Christina* (US, 1933) could well be applied to Wichard's lesbophobic pamphlet:

> Freud's narrative of woman's sexual journey from clitorial pubescence into mature vaginal bliss is a bit like the transformation fairy tales in which the ugly duckling matures into a beautiful swan and marries the handsome cygnet. Literary and filmic narratives replay this scenario of female fulfilment through the figure of the tomboy. The tomboy's journey is astonishingly similar to that of the clitoris. During the early stage, the tomboy/clitoris

behaves like a 'little man' enjoying boy's games, pursuing active sports, refusing to wear dresses or engage in feminine pursuits; on crossing into woman-
hood the youthful adventurer relinquishes her earlier tomfoolery, gives up
boyish adventures, dons feminine clothes, grows her hair long and sets out to
capture a man whose job it is to 'tame' her as if she were a wild animal.

We see this narrative played out in *Calamity Jane* where the heroine (Doris
Day) relinquishes her men's clothing, foul language, guns and horses for a
dress, feminine demeanour, sweet talk and a man. She also gives up the
woman, Alice, with whom she has set up house and whom she clearly
loves. . . . *Queen Christina* depicts the lesbian queen (Greta Garbo) in the first
part of the narrative wearing men's clothes and long riding boots, striding
about the palace accompanied by two great danes and muttering to her
manservant that all men are fools and she will never marry. Predictably, she
falls in love, throws off her mannish trappings, gives up the Lady Ebba and
redirects her erotic desires towards the Spanish ambassador, one of the
'fools' she vowed she would never marry. (Creed 1995: 95)

Caroline alone resists the heteronormative imperative: the only erotic attraction she evinces is for Sand, and her response to Paul's ardent attentions is
tepid. Otherwise, this is the most blatantly lesbophobic film in the corpus.
The only principled resisting reading envisageable would have to posit an
underlying irony in the film's systemic lesbophobia. When Sand tells Smith,
a male friend who not so secretly desires her, that she had almost enjoyed
being slapped by Michel, that when he kissed her she was 'on fire' and that
she's really 'fallen' for him; that yes, she has no artistic talent, so she'll 'cook
all day and throw the paints away', Smith's aghast words – 'Please say it's a
joke!' – perhaps provide a space for critique of the normativising operation
being launched. But it is a highly exiguous space, to say the least.

Twenty-eight years later, Louis Malle's *Milou en mai* (1989) over-
determined spectatorial conceptions of the figure 'lesbian' as less than
healthy by over-writing on it the category of disability. The first apparition – and the term is used advisedly – of the lesbian figure Claire, Milou's
niece, is of a ghostly white, almost ethereal figure highlighted eerily against
the twilight setting. She is thus immediately encoded as essentially
different from the rest of the physically robust (albeit morally corrupt)
family members. This impression of sickliness is consolidated by the fact
that she walks with a limp (having been disabled as a child during a car
accident which killed her parents). This is something of a caricature: one
can already hear the quip that were she black, the stereotype would be
complete – female, lesbian, crippled, ethnically marginalized . . .

Finally, in Olivier Assayas's *Irma Vep* of 1996, Zoé's 'sickness' of (recre-
ational) drug dependency seems to function as a metonym for her sexual

attraction to women. The lesbian space conceded in this film is, again, somewhat slight. It consists in the unilateral sexual attraction felt by wardrobe mistress Zoé – blonde, feminine-encoded, but also quite spiky in appearance – for the classically beautiful leading actress, Maggie. A brief summary of the film's lesbian sub-plot may throw some exegetical light on it. Zoé is bisexual according to one of her so-called friends, Mireille, with whom she goes into ecstasies about Maggie's sexy black latex outfit for the movie,[5] saying, 'Elle est bien, elle est vachement bien' ['She's nice, she's damned nice']. Maïté, second-in-command to the movie's director René, spreads rumours that Zoé has slept with Maggie, then warns Maggie off Zoé; Maggie, though not really turned on by Zoé, defends her by saying she's a nice girl, that, OK, she likes girls but that's no big deal, right (this big-hearted liberal concession illustrating containment theories of homosexuality). Maïté, however, makes the more serious charge that Zoé is a drug-dealer. While a later sequence shows Zoé herself taking drugs, it is never confirmed that she sells them. This sequence follows Maggie's departure from a rave to which Zoé had taken her: a despondent Zoé does a hit to face the night alone. Yet the very allegation that she deals in drugs rather than just taking them herself figuratively insinuates the contaminatory operations of the gay subject. Dina Sherzer's approving statement appears wide of the mark: 'Assayas displays lesbian desire and sexual attraction with simplicity. His characters talk overtly about their feelings, do not hide their sexual orientation, and are comfortable with their sexuality' (Sherzer 2001: 236). My own *un*comfortable question is: why does the one character exhibiting unequivocal lesboerotic tendencies, as opposed to aspirationally hip but basically straight-identified characters, have to be associated with drug dependency and criminal behaviour?

A more distinct form of pathology, sado-masochism, is imbricated in lesboerotic relations mediated by five films in the corpus, to be discussed below. In the short history of its classification, s/m has been classically viewed as a masculine stronghold. Both Krafft-Ebing and Freud posited sadism in men as stemming from the distortion of the aggressive element in the male sexual instinct. Masochism in men, on the other hand, was viewed as far more of a perversion, inimical to the fundamentally active and often aggressive nature of male sexuality. Whilst it also came to be thought that sadism and masochism could be combined in one human subject, their conjoint operation between two individuals has remained under-theorised. Further, both Krafft-Ebing and Freud assumed that masochism was so inherent to female sexuality that it would be difficult to distinguish it as a separate inclination. In 1967, Gilles Deleuze proposed a new theorisation of at least masochism in *Présentation de Sacher Masoch*. He recognised that in the conventional heterosexual s/m scenario:

> si la femme-bourreau dans le masochisme ne peut pas être sadique, c'est pré-cisément parce qu'elle est *dans* le masochisme, élément réalisé du phantasme masochiste: elle appartient au masochisme. Non pas au sens où elle aurait les mêmes goûts que sa victime, mais parce qu'elle a ce 'sadisme' qu'on en trouve jamais chez le sadique, et qui est comme le double ou la réflexion du masochisme. On en dira autant du sadisme . . . (Deleuze 1967: 37)
> [the woman torturer of masochism cannot be sadistic precisely because she is *in* the masochistic situation, she is an integral part of it, a realisation of the masochistic fantasy. She belongs in the masochistic world, not in the sense that she has the same tastes as her victim, but because her 'sadism' is of a kind never found in the sadist; it is as if it were the double or the reflection of masochism. The same is true of sadism . . .]

But precisely in the present corpus we could not be further from the conventional heterosexual s/m scenario, and certain key concepts articulated by Deleuze may be strategically deployed to analyse specifically lesboerotic instances of s/m in the aforementioned five films. None of the cases of masochism to be considered below equates to algolagnia, which is a rather more straightforward predilection for pain without any need for domination, submission or humiliation. In an intriguingly named article, 'Girls on a Wired Screen: Cavani's Cinema and Lesbian s/m' (1995), the French-Canadian critic Chantal Nadeau usefully summarises these key Deleuzian concepts: sadism connotes institutionality and political control whereas masochism relies on contract and individuality.

> Deleuze's revision of Sacher-Masoch's *Venus in Furs* (1989) – the classic novel which gave masochism its name – constitutes a 'treatise of politics' in which masochistic sexual practices are revealed as deeply dependent on contract. And because s/m sex is strongly dependent on expectations, consensus and reciprocal pleasure, the desire manifested by the masochist does not express a lack but a very physical and contractual involvement through post-ponement and delay. . . . According to Deleuze, this opposition between individual and institution is one of the statements that distinguishes sadism and masochism as two different organizations and structural (narrative) contexts. Indeed, both imply power and relations of control, but the representations and the practical realizations specific to each system cannot be settled in the same space. Sadism is strongly connoted by the institutional aspect, as masochism appeals to the notion of contract. The former directly refers to the political aspect of control (in the sense of policies on sexual behaviour), the latter to the individual dimension of the sex games. Sadism is then

sketched as a conspiracy – often a group against an individual – as masochism is seen as the perfect expression of personal fantasy – one individual abandoning himself/herself to the will of the other, a will totally delimited by the limits of the abandoned. One then could be read as the sexualization of control, and the other as the liberation of the sexual imagination. One evokes the repressed, the other the free spirit. (Nadeau 1995: 214–17)

Deleuze's model is certainly consonant in some respects with the sado-masochistic relationship between the two sisters in Nico Papatakis's *Les Abysses* (1963). The older, sadistic Michèle is dominant almost by 'institutional' virtue of the familial seniority, which tacitly authorises her controlling behaviour, whilst the younger, Marie-Louise, is submissive as if through a tacit contract respecting the privileges attached to that seniority within the institution of the family. Let us recall Deleuze's emphasis on the contractual basis of the masochistic relation: for him, (love) relationships must be ruled by contracts which formalise and verbalise them. Yet these power relations between the sisters obtain in their everyday interactions rather than in the erotic dynamic between them; in the latter, there is more reciprocity, as Edwards and Reader imply:

> When they go out to the chicken coop to collect eggs for the crêpes they snuggle together in the straw which recalls the clichéd image of lovers in a haystack. Here the balance of power is shared: at first Michèle assumes the dominant role as Marie-Louise rests her head upon her shoulder; then they switch positions and Marie-Laure lends her shoulder to Michèle. (Edwards and Reader 2001: 100)

However, a more complex enactment of masochism is to be found in their boss's daughter, Elisabeth, the third nodal point in the lesboerotic configuration. As the left-wing newspaper *Libération* noted, 'Le personnage est curieux: c'est une jeune bourgeoise chrétienne et progressiste, un peu mystérieuse, assez masochiste et un peu lesbienne aussi puisqu'elle est visiblement attirée par la plus jeune des deux bonnes: Marie-Louise'[6] ['The character is curious: she's a young bourgeois woman, Christian and progressive, a little mysterious, rather masochistic, and with lesbian leanings too since she is obviously attracted by the younger of the two maids, Marie-Louise']. Elisabeth caresses Marie-Louise's fingers erotically whilst fixing her with an intense gaze, and masochistically submits to the insults and blows rained upon her by both her desire-object and by Michèle. Elisabeth's masochism is infused with Christian strains of martyrdom which would indeed view gratification signally in terms of postponement and delay (see

Nadeau above), that is, in a heavenly afterlife. Here in her earthly life, les-boerotic pulsion needs must be sublimated. She is ill rewarded for her pains, being butchered to death.

In Luis Buñuel's *Belle de Jour* (1967), the chief protagonist's name, Séverine, evokes Séverin, the masochist in Sacher-Masoch's *Venus à la fourrure* (1870), and Séverine in *Belle de jour* certainly has a marked predilection for masochism. When the film begins, her erotic life is limited to fantasies about her adoring but boring husband Pierre (with whom she remains frigid) treating her as a sexual object, having her tied up, whipped and gang-raped. Later on, after assuming a double life (prostitute 'de jour' [by day'], middle-class wife at night), she also fantasises about being tied up and having excrement thrown at her as she is insulted: an eroticisation of degradation. In reality, she rejects Pierre's sexual overtures, wanting only his company in bed, which prompts the semi-tender, semi-resigned query, 'Tu ne grandiras donc jamais?' ['Are you never going to grow up, then?']. His question reveals an infantilising view of his wife, and indeed, her experimentation with high-class prostitution could well be dismissed as a bourgeois, spoilt brat's whim. In this reductive optic, the one les-boerotic element to the film – high-class brothel-owner Anaïs's attempted seduction of her – could equally easily be dismissed as just one harmless vicissitude involved in gratifying this whim. Certainly, the masochism is strictly heterosexualised in Séverine's fantasies, as later in her 'profes-sional' practices; and it is not irrelevant that it is the scenes involving such heterosexualised masochism which have the greatest visual impact of all in Buñuel's film.

Guy Casaril's *Le Rempart des Béguines* (1972) is structurally similar to *Les Abysses* in that the sadistic partner's seniority provides an institutional basis for her sadism in the lesboerotic relationship. Fifteen-year-old Hélène falls in love with Tamara, her father's new, thirty-eight-year-old lover. Tamara soon becomes a dominatrix both in and out of bed. When Hélène fails to meet her demand that the father be informed of their acquaintance, Tamara slaps her violently. Hélène rushes off shouting that she will never see Tamara again, but returns in the very next scene, where Tamara orders her to get on her knees and apologise. An incredulous Hélène cries out, 'Mais je t'aime' ['But I love you!'], is brutally thrown out by Tamara, crumples into sobs and is finally let in again by Tamara, who adamantly pursues her sadistic line of conduct, thrusting Hélène's head under the cold tap, forcing her onto her knees and extracting the apology she had originally demanded. Her demands satisfied, she kisses Hélène and rips off her clothes passionately; her kissing becomes devouring, she smiles triumphantly, and we witness a frenzied clasping of hands, shoulders (and, we are encouraged to deduce, areas below the waist). The ensuing sex-scene is accompanied by a highly evocative soundtrack.

Yet Hélène, true to the conventions of the female-slanted *Bildungsroman* on which Casaril's film is based,[7] eventually transcends her adolescent sub-servience. She comes to reject the pleasures of postponement and delay in a realistic operation of risk assessment, finally, though not without immense distress, freeing herself from the domination of a woman who has, for her part, ceased to enact the desirable role of proudly indomitable dominatrix, and in so doing has lost her erotic sway. For Tamara, craving social acceptance and material security, decides to accept Hélène's father's proposal of marriage. Hélène strives to sabotage the impending marriage and domestication of her erotic idol, protesting that Tamara will lose her independence and become utterly banal; a large part of what had initially attracted her had been Tamara's perceived freedom from convention. When Tamara makes conciliatory advances, Hélène, although visibly aroused, resists; when Tamara says she has changed, Hélène retorts that it is she who has changed; before, if she (Hélène) had resisted, Tamara would have created a violent scene. Tamara grabs her hair, but Hélène defiantly points out that she cannot create such scenes now she's about to become domesticated (that is, married, recuperated by the dominant order). Thus the sado-masochistic dynamic is neutralised and their love-affair corres-pondingly asphyxiated. The film ends with Hélène sobbing after the mar-riage ceremony, which breaks the Deleuzian contract on which Hélène's masochism had been based. However, for those intent on reading Hélène's love for Tamara as anaclisis – an unconscious quest for the mother-figure (whom she lost early on in life) – one other aspect of Deleuze's *Présentation de Sacher-Masoch* is a gift: Deleuze's presentation of masochism as a 'staging of degradation which enables the subject to eliminate the paternal superego and achieve union with the mother' (Reader 2005: 130).

The Deleuzian model of s/m provides no analytic fulcrum for the rela-tionship between Claire and Marie-Laure in Louis Malle's *Milou en mai* (1989). (For discussion of the second, if more tenuously sado-masochistic current that unexpectedly develops between Claire and male lorry driver Grimaldi, see Chapter 4 below.) The dynamic between the women is one of master–slave, or at least an attempt on Claire's part to master the younger Marie-Laure. This attempt manifests itself in two ways. The first works allusively via the visual codes of bondage: through the eyes of Milou's little granddaughter Françoise, who sneaks into the young women's bedroom, we see that Marie-Laure's arms have been bound to the bedstead. Second, we witness Claire's public displays of sexual jealousy: when Marie-Laure flirts with a male lawyer, Claire pulls her away and slaps her; and when Marie-Laure succumbs to the charms of Pierre-Alain, a younger member of the family fired up with revolutionary fervour, Claire's manic piano-playing and venomous stares speak volumes. Ultimately, Claire's bid for domination fails; but this is at least partly contingent on the directorial over-writing of her lesbian desire by another category of marginality, namely, disability (she is severely lame) and her consequent construction as always already disempowered.

Le Figaro was quick to remark of Diane Kurys's *À la folie* (1994) that '[l]es rapports entre les deux sœurs sont très sado-maso!' In the newspaper's interview with Kurys, the director at once infantilises and pathologises the dynamic between sisters Alice and Elsa:

> Aimer à la folie, c'est aimer trop et pas bien. Ces jeux idiots, s'attacher au radiateur, se faire mal, on y a joué cent fois quand on était mômes. Alice et Elsa ne sont pas sorties de l'enfance et le jeu auquel elles se livrent n'est dangereux que parce qu'elles sont devenues adultes. Enfants, elles étaient cruelles. Adultes, on appelle ça de la perversité.[8]
> [To be madly in love is to love too much and to love badly. We've all played those stupid games of tying each other up and hurting each other hundreds of times as kids. Alice and Elsa have not emerged from childhood and the game they play is only dangerous because now they are adults. As children, they were cruel. As adults, that sort of behaviour is called depravity.]

To dismiss sado-masochistic interaction between two women as silly childish games is of course the director's prerogative, but it does smack of (hetero) sexist condescension and leads to a political and theoretical impasse. Why would a woman (here, Elsa) who clearly has a very intense attachment to her sister (here, Alice) treat that sister so brutally (see Chapter 2 above)? And why does the mistreated sister so passively accept her victimisation? To reduce these complex behaviour patterns to mere juvenile games is intellectually myopic. It is also highly significant that Kurys's failure even to allude to the lesboerotic current in *À la folie* partly reproduces what I would bluntly designate as her bad faith in denying the same in her earlier *Coup de foudre*, which despite that denial has become a cult 'lesbian' movie (see Chapter 4 below). With respect to *À la folie*, the Deleuzian model ceases to apply, and I would contend that Elsa's sadism is, rather, a counter-formation prompted by anxiety about Alice's successfully accomplished differentiation. As for Alice's masochism, it is perhaps better viewed as an extreme and ultimately self-endangering passivity forming the residue of, precisely, a highly fusional relationship with her sister in childhood. I am aware that, in myself invoking this infantilising and fusional model in the context of lesboeroticism, I may appear to be reinforcing the very stereotype which I will contest below; but I can only work with the raw material of the film, and accept no responsibility for its disempowering nature vis-à-vis lesbian subjectivity.

Infantilisation is another variant on the generally pathologising construction of lesbian desire under scrutiny in this chapter, and whilst in our corpus it is rare in unadorned form, it does merit brief attention, not least because of its frequent embeddedness in the two more dominant avatars for later discussion: fusion and mother–daughter regression. In Guy Casaril's *Emilienne et Nicole* (1970), Emilienne and Claude's marital bond is exploded by the art student Nouky, who begins as Claude's mistress and ends up sexually involved with his wife too. Nouky is depicted unsympathetically as a simultaneously manipulative, callous and infantilised woman, and the fact that it is she who initiates the older Emilienne into the pleasures of lesboeroticism is at once a paradox and a 'logical' correlative of heteronormative theories equating lesbian desire with immaturity. However, when Nouky is distressed, to 'comfort' her Claude starts kissing her on the lips, his eye-contact with Emilienne suggesting that this is a joint, almost parental project; Emilienne starts to kiss Nouky's nipples, erotic temperatures rise and soon all three are having sex with one another. Casaril's film here approximates to Chabrol's *Les Biches* in the structuring of a younger woman within a female–male–female trio as the oedipal child of the older straight couple. Sixteen years on, in Geneviève Lefebvre's *Le Jupon rouge* (1986), Bacha refers to her close 'friend' Manuela's passion for Claude in similarly minimising terms: 'c'est plus de ton âge, ces histoires' ['you should have outgrown that kind of business'], and even indulges in not-so-oblique anti-Semitism (Manuela's female lover Claude is Jewish): 'Tu espères quoi avec cette gamine, l'arrivée du Messie?' ['What are you hoping for from that kid, the coming of the Messiah?']. Although the slur is quite clearly a function of her jealousy, it also reflects a common myth about lesbianism which has gained credibility due to vulgarised Freudian equations of homosexuality in general with arrested psychosexual development.

Apropos vulgarised notions, what of neurosis, as in general instability, and lesbianism as a component of it? This is what Pierre Granier-Deferre's *Cours privé* (1987) appears to present. Schoolteacher Jeanne has in the past been sexually involved with a schoolgirl not much younger than herself, Agnès, who defiantly unveils her ample breasts to Jeanne while changing for PE and gets slapped for her efforts, but also elicits an undeniably erotic response. When Agnès phones her at home, Jeanne cradles the receiver between her breasts. Jeanne is next framed in the bath caressing her breasts and belly, then placing her hand on her groin. The montage here is significant, with the auto-stimulation of the second scene standing in metonymic relation to the arousal by Agnès in the first. So far, so good; at least there has been no overt pathologisation. But Jeanne goes on to tell a young male colleague that as a young teenager she had been molested by a male stranger, and later confesses that her supposed boyfriend Dominique is pure fiction (the choice of the androgynous name Dominique in itself suggesting strong equivocations about heterosexuality). Do these details contribute to an aetiology of sexual dysfunction of which the lesboerotic component is a 'natural' part? After visiting Agnès – and again the sequencing is significant – she is framed naked in bed, entertaining lesboerotic fantasies in which one of the protagonists is Agnès. The camera then provides the image of a quasi-orgy in which Jeanne had participated with some older pupils, caught by a photo of her and Agnès in erotic commerce. At this mental image, which turns out to represent a memory, Jeanne throws a lamp at the wall, and the cause of her violence remains ambiguous – distress, fear, arousal, or a mixture of all three? For the first time non-diegetic music accompanies the images, the piano enhancing the emotional impact of her recalled caresses and gazes, and Agnès's blissful smile in return. The very low-key lighting here creates an oneiric, slightly ghostly atmosphere, again implying a certain pathology or unwholesomeness.

Towards the end of the film, Jeanne expresses her sense of inability to sustain or even begin a relationship with anyone. This statement is supported by her interaction with her male colleague Laurent: after they have had sex she tells him she had hated his smell, his desires, his actions; he leaves; she sobs. The portrait of psychosexual dysfunction is complete, its lesbian element in due and proper place. Only Agnès seems to have felt anything like healthy lesbian desire, and even this gets perverted into bitterness and despair. The constitutive heteronormativity of the film's economy is underscored by director Granier-Deferre's claim that Jeanne's refusal of heterosexual relations constitutes her 'real' pathology:

> 'Jeanne', poursuit le metteur en scène, 'est une jeune femme qui semble ne pas avoir de problème dans la vie. En réalité, elle en a un qui est dramatique, c'est de refuser les relations avec les hommes. Lorsque Ketti [her boss] lui fait une cour pressante, et même trouve un moyen de la piéger, elle devient d'une violence inouïe qui débouche sur la mort.'[9]
> ['Jeanne', the director goes on, 'is a young woman who seems to have no problems in life. In reality, she has a dramatic one, which is her refusal of relationships with men. When Ketti woos her insistently, and even finds a way of trapping her, she becomes so violent that it leads to death.']

After this adumbration of more minor variants on the pathologising model, the focus will now turn to the first of its two more dominant avatars:

lesbian desire as consisting in fusion, rather than desire for a differentiated other; or, similarly but not identically, in a quest for the same and thus, ultimately, for the self. Before analysing instances of this model in the primary texts, I will briefly present some of its most influential theoretical articulations. Direct reference will be made to my deliberations on the subject in *Lesbian Desire in Post-1968 French Literature* (2002) and in 'Identity or Difference? The Ontology of Lesbianism in Contemporary French Realist Fiction' (2002): since, to my knowledge, none of the major theoreticians addressed in these two pieces has inflected her position by further published work, my own position in relation to them remains broadly unchanged. What has changed, however, is my use of the epithet 'narcissistic' and its cognates. Narcissism is essentially attraction to the self. By a semantic slippage, it has often been conflated with attraction to the same. That conflation is not entirely to be dismissed, for in falling in love with himself, Narcissus refused difference, and refusal of difference is synoymous with indifferentiation. But refusal of difference is *not* wholly synoymous with *fusion*, because attraction to the same involves only one term, and for fusion to occur two terms axiomatically need to exist at least prior to the fusion.

Because my present study, unlike those of 2002 cited above, centres on cinema rather than literature, I will begin this brief recapitulation by citing additional, highly pertinent material. Barbara Creed helpfully draws attention to specifically visual mediations of lesbianism as narcissism:

> *Fin de siècle* art depicted the lesbian in a number of bizarre stereotypes . . .
> In painting, lesbian contact between women was portrayed as an inevitable
> extension of their narcissistic desires. Women were frequently depicted as if
> mirror-images of each other: identical faces, hair, clothes. They were usually
> shown as locked in a close embrace as in Fernand Khnopff's *The Kiss* (1997),
> Edmond Aman-Jean's *In The Theatre Box* (1898) and Pablo Picasso's *The
> Friends* (1903). . . . With the advent of the cinema, stereotypes of the lesbian,
> which draw so heavily on the visual, were represented in increasing variety.
> (Creed 1995: 86–7)

Amongst the 'stereotypes of the lesbian' which Creed goes on to list we find, predictably, the 'narcissistic double'. The phenomenon was not, of course, limited to visual representations: Creed also observes that '[t]urn-of-the-century medical writers pointed to the supposed connection between masturbation in women, narcissism and lesbianism' (Creed 1995: 100). And with the advent of Freudian psychoanalysis, the more specific connection between lesbianism and narcissism was, with time, to acquire the status of a scientific truth as opposed to the mere hypothesis that it is. Derived from Freud's opposition of identification and desire, and his tenet that desire was the preserve of men, psychoanalytic dogma posits lesbianism as based on identification with the same rather than desire for a differentiated other. This dogma, indeed doxa, is endorsed to varying degrees by a number of renowned contemporary female theorists from whom one might have expected more of a critical grip.

In *Histoires d'amour*, Julia Kristeva posits 'les amours lesbiennes' ['lesbian loves'] as comprising 'la plage délicieuse d'une libido neutralisée, tamisée, *dépourvue du tranchant érotique de la sexualité masculine'* (my emphasis) ['the delightful arena of a neutralised, filtered libido, *devoid of the erotic cutting edge of masculine sexuality'*]. So, an immediate attenuation of the erotic force of lesbian desire; but worse is to come. Considering the temerity of lesbian love's aspiration to 's'ériger en absolu d'un rapport à deux' ['to set itself up as absolute of a mutual relationship'], she predicts dissolution of differentiated subjecthood and a resulting form of psychosis:

> . . . éclate le non-rapport qu'il est. Deux voies s'ouvrent ensuite. Ou bien, elles reprennent, plus farouches encore, la manie érotique avec les ravages du jeu 'maître-esclave'. Ou bien, et souvent en conséquence, la mort explose dans la paix qu'on croyait avoir absorbée. Mort par broyage dans ce ventre auparavant si protecteur, cajoleur et neutralisant. Mort de n'être qu'un *on*: identité perdue, dissolution léthale de la psychose, angoisse des frontières perdues, appel suicidaire du fond. (Kristeva 1983: 80–1)
>
> [. . . the non-relationship that it is bursts into view. – Two paths are then open. Either they take up again, yet more fiercely, the erotic mania along with the havoc of the 'master–slave' game. Or else, and often as a consequence, death breaks into the peace one thought one had taken in. A grinding death in that belly that had previously been so protective, coaxing and neutralizing. Death from being merely a some one: lost identity, lethal dissolution of psychosis, anguish on account of lost boundaries, suicidal call of the deep.]

Unlike Kristeva, Luce Irigaray stops short of imputing psychosis to the adult lesbian woman, but she too essentially configures lesbian relations as based on identification rather than desire for a differentiated other. In the now classic 'Quand nos lèvres se parlent' (Irigaray 1977), Irigaray blurs ontological distinction between the two female lovers, chiefly by use of the compound pronoun 'tu/je' ['you'/'I'] and by statements such as 'Quand tu dis je t'aime … tu dis je m'aime' (206) ['When you say I love you … you're saying I love myself'], 'Tu te/me retrouves autant que tu te/me confies' (206) ['You find yourself/me again as much as you confide in yourself/me']. Her denial of this blurring – 'Elles ne se distinguent pas. Ce qui ne signifie pas qu'elles se confondent' (p. 209) ['They are not distinct, which does not mean that they are blurred'] – receives no authentification.

Judith Butler's position is altogether more nuanced: she concedes the possible *coexistence* of identification and desire, which is a rather more sensible approach to certain – if not all – lesbian relations (as to other kinds of relations), and argues that to view these categories as mutually exclusive plays into the hands of heterocracy. She also wishes to 'focus attention on yet a different construal of that scenario, namely, that "wanting to be" and "wanting to have" can operate to differentiate mutually exclusive positionalities internal to lesbian erotic exchange' (Butler 1991: 26). Most cogently of all the four major thinkers considered here, Teresa de Lauretis recognises that 'desire itself, with its movement between subject and object, between the self and the other, is founded on difference – the difference and separateness of one from the other … desire is a tension toward the other(s), a drive towards something or someone outside the self' (Lauretis 1994: 229 and 234).

The foregoing is intended as a rough theoretical map within which consideration of the filmic texts can be situated. Patently, this particular cartographer has not adopted a neutral stance. This is because I believe the identity model of lesbianism to be desexualising, disempowering, degrading, but, most importantly of all, in most cases plain erroneous: desexualising because it suggests that lesbians merely want to meld with one another rather than make love to/have sex with (according to your own ideolect) each other; disempowering because this reduces lesbians to the level of the pre-Symbolic infant seeking a lost fusion with a mother-figure; noxious because in its extreme form (Kristevan) it imputes psychosis and, by implication, even abjection to lesbians: abjection Kristeva defines as the horror of not recognising the boundaries between self and other (Kristeva 1980), and, inversely, not recognising the boundaries between self and other is precisely how she characterises lesbianism. Following de Lauretis, I contend that the identity model of lesbianism ignores the fact that the very presence of desire necessarily posits a distinction, a gap, between the desiring subject and the desired object. If the latter two were one, desire would not exist, since desire is predicated on lack: here I go along with Lacan. Yet most basic of all is a point I have made previously: '[o]n the material level, female sexual organs may well be the only physical similarity between two lesbian lovers. And beyond bodily morphology, differences rather than similarities abound with respect to multiple aspects of identity: class, ethnicity, age, political allegiances, educational achievement, and so on' (Cairns 2002b: 158). (The same is, of course, true of gay male relationships, but since the fusional model is generally restricted to female homosexual relations, this is not a statement that requires urgent articulation.)[10] Notwithstanding my personal rejection of the model, readers can now at least, map in hand, place the numerous filmic mediations of lesbianism as (sometimes but not always narcissistic) fusion within a theoretical context.

Temporally, the first instantiation of the model is Georges Franju's *Thérèse Desqueyroux* (1962), based on François Mauriac's 1927 novel of the same title. Disturbed when the object of her (unavowed) desire Anne writes to her about a new boyfriend, Thérèse looks at a mirror – specular symbol *par excellence*, visually embodying the narcissistic model – and cries out, 'Et moi alors, moi!' ['And me, what about me!'] On a simple level, her polysemic utterance could just convey mere pique at being excluded (what about me?), but it could also suggest both a sense of possessiveness (I own you) and fusion (what of I as you in this relationship of yours with another?). Through voice-over, her inner words reinforce the model: 'Si nous ne possédions rien d'autre en commun, que nous ayons au moins cela: la solitude, et surtout, surtout pas l'amour. Pas l'amour pour Anne. Pas l'amour!'[11] ['If we were to have nothing else in common, let us at least have that: solitude, and not, above all not love. Not love for Anne. Not love!'] The implication that difference between them will threaten their intimacy implies in its turn that their intimacy inheres in their *lack* of difference.

Claude Chabrol's *Les Biches* (1968) also gives strong visual embodiment to a model of lesbianism as mimesis, but here it is arguable that the (not necessarily conscious) drive is less towards fusion with the initially desired woman and more towards replacing or substituting for her. This model is most prominent in triangular figurations where the male third term invades and often destroys the lesboerotic dyad – thus reflecting male 'revenge' fantasies stemming from their decentring as the locus of all desire. First, Why contrives her image exactly in that of her desire-object Frédérique, donning Frédérique's clothes, hairstyle and style of make-up, even painting on an identical beauty-spot. When, towards the end of the film, Why has stabbed Frédérique, her monologue encapsulates consummately the arguably fusional, arguably substitutional model of lesbianism presaged earlier. She asks the dead Frédérique if she had not noticed how 'on se ressemblait' ['we resembled each other'], how 'on a la même peau, les mêmes cheveux, la même bouche, la même expression parfois, les mêmes goûts ...' ['we have the same skin, the same hair, the same mouth, sometimes the same expression, the same tastes ...'], and, more enigmatically, 'Comment peux-tu me reprocher de t'aimer, d'aimer Paul, puisque toi-même ...' ['How can you reproach me for loving you, for loving Paul, when you yourself ...']. The conundrum – does Why mean she could not help loving Paul because even Frédérique did, or, precisely, *because* Frédérique did, and they are one? – is never resolved, for the phone interrupts her soliloquy. Hearing that it's Paul (first her boyfriend, then purloined by Frédérique), she appropriates

Frédérique's identity fully, pretending she *is* her. Critics were quick to make the sanctioned link: lesbo-striated *mimétisme* equals madness. The Catholic newspaper *La Croix* refers to Why's descent into madness through over-identification with her desire-object:

> Son rejet par le couple, et particulièrement par Frédérique, ébranlera cette petite chatte fragile, la conduisant bientôt à la *folie*. Elle commencera par copier Frédérique, lui empruntant ses affaires, se maquillant comme elle, s'imaginant trouver sa force dans l'imitation de ses apparences.[12]
> [Her rejection by the couple, and particularly by Frédérique, will shake up this fragile little creature, soon leading her into madness. She will start by copying Frédérique, borrowing her things, making herself up like her, imagining that she is coming into her own by imitating these outwards appearances.]

The respected literary journal *Les Lettres françaises* concurs, but strikes a less predictable note by acknowledging Chabrol's reduction of the male figure to a mere instrument of revenge or possession within the primary relationship between the two women.

> [Why] s'empare, en imagination, du bonheur dont l'accès lui est interdit. Transfert qui mène à la folie, de même que l'épreuve de force entre les deux femmes – l'homme n'étant de toute façon qu'un instrument de revanche ou de possession – ne peut conduire inéluctablement qu'à la destruction et à la mort.[13]
> [In her imagination, [Why] seizes the happiness that is forbidden to her. It is a transference that leads to madness, just as the battle between the two women – the man being in any case a mere instrument of revenge or possession – can only lead, ineluctably, to destruction and death.]

In a lesbian utopia Paul might never have threatened the primary relationship, but in the socially realistic framework of enduring hetero-patriarchy which the film constructs, the threat rings true.

That threat also resonates throughout Henri Calef's *Féminin-Féminin* (1973). There are two lesbian foci in this film. The first promises but never delivers. It centres on the relationship between Françoise (played by Marie-France Pisier, possibly the most lesbo-friendly of all famous French actresses if the number of films featuring lesbianism in which she has acted is anything to go by) and her mother-in-law Cécile, who has an unusual predilection for watching her daughter-in-law having sex with her son, Georges. Indeed, one of the opening scenes is of Cécile watching the two copulating through a pair of binoculars, which literally shape the frame of the spectator's perception. Cécile again arrogates for herself the masculine-defined position of voyeur when she stares at the two in their bedroom having sex. Constructed as a strong, independent career woman, she also flirts verbally with Françoise, provoking her to anger and then saying, 'Vous êtes encore plus belle lorsque vous vous mettez en colère' ['You're even more beautiful when you get angry']. Françoise responds by saying that she's lived in Cécile's home for a year and still feels she doesn't know her, finding her simultaneously 'fuyante et présente ... parfois trop présente' ['elusive and yet present ... sometimes too present'] – a paradoxical blend of distance and intrusiveness, the latter consisting in Cécile's voyeurism; Françoise adds that when she and George are having sex, she sometimes feels Cécile is watching them behind the door: 'J'ai beau regarder, je ne vous aperçois pas, mais je vous sens' ['However much I look, I don't see you, but I feel you there']. The exchange, conveyed through shot-reverse-shot, casts Cécile, as remarked above, in the classical masculine position of voyeur and destabilises the trope of lesbianism as fusional/osmotic. Yet while the classic male voyeur derives pleasure from his masterful position, Cécile is visibly distressed during a subsequent sequence when she hears sounds of sexual arousal coming from the conjugal bedroom. Her staring at the camera with a face-pack rendering her ghostly white draws the viewer's attention to her spectrality when deprived of the scopic (she can hear but not see their sexual intercourse).

The second lesbian focus is on the doomed relationship which Françoise initiates by leaving her husband to set up a new life with Marie-Hélène. Initially, both the image-track (idyllic vignettes of hair-stroking, feeding each other, little attentions between the two women) as well as the exalted soundtrack foster an impression of a bliss at once domestic and utopic: utopic because exterior to acceptable partnership structures of early 1970s France. While it might be argued that the very excess of their initial bliss bodes ill, the lesbian-identified viewer may none the less take a certain, albeit fleeting pleasure in the self-sufficient happiness which the two women obviously share . . . if but ephemerally. A disorienting close-up of the two women's faces in bed is saturated by ominously dark-purple hues, with equally inauspicious music on the accompanying soundtrack. Marie-Hélène is about to rise from an intimate position, but Françoise strokes her and she falls back onto the bed. Is this meant narratively to presage Marie-Hélène's impending 'fall' from a lesbian idyll that is becoming claustrophobic? Stifling fusion is strongly evinced by Marie-Hélène's ex, Jacques, who accuses Françoise of having 'séquestrée' ['locked away'] Marie-Hélène, but the confinement-impulse is seen to be bilateral rather than unilateral in Marie-Hélène's comment to Françoise, 'je n'aime pas quand tu sors' ['I don't like it when you go out']. It is also reiterated by Marie-Hélène's disinclination to travel to beautiful places now she is living with Françoise: 'Ma vie n'a jamais été aussi remplie depuis que nous vivons seules … Je n'ai pas envie de bouger' ['My life has never been so full since we've been living on our own together . . . I don't want to go out']. When she launches into a panegyric on their happiness together, Françoise becomes alarmed, cautioning thus (again, note the motif of excess): 'notre exaltation est effrayante: elle risque de tout brûler, de tout détruire' ['our elation is frightening: it could burn everything, destroy everything']. And this, inexplicably, seems to be the maieutic prompt for Marie-Hélène's change of mind: the crystallisation in language of the notion that lesbian happiness is somehow doomed to die, incompatible as it is with normal functioning within the Symbolic social order, and prohibitive of contact outwith the utopian space ('Je n'ai pas envie de bouger'). For soon after this Marie-Hélène succumbs to the pleadings of her ex, Jacques, and leaves Françoise. Françoise's eventual response – suicide – is another chestnut in mainstream encodings of frustrated lesbian desire, with as (in)famous inauguration Ovid's corruption of the Sapphic legend. In Ovid's 'version', Sappho, the lesbian poetess, is transformed into a suicide who drowns herself because her male lover Phaon has abandoned her.

Capitulation to the straight imperative also ultimately characterises Léonard Keigel's *Une Femme, un jour* (1974). As in *Thérèse Desqueyroux*, the narcissistic model of inter-female love is implied through the trope of specularity. In one sequence, Nicky's desiring gaze becomes that of the camera as she, and we the spectator, watch her desire-object Caroline undressing in a clothes shop. Less progressive than this female appropriation of the scopic prerogative normally devolved to men, however, is the framing of the two women in a mirror-image: while the viewer might well concur in Nicky's 'Regarde-nous: comme nous sommes belles' ['Look at us: how beautiful we are'], the implication of lesbian narcissism is ineluctable.

In Jacques Rivette's *Céline et Julie vont en bateau* (1974) it is less ineluctable, but only because the very existence of lesbian desire itself is far less firmly established. Desire between the eponymous female characters is never made explicit. Only once is physical intimacy between them visualised, when Julie kisses Céline tenderly, just brushing past her lips, then puts her arms round Céline's shoulders. What *is* clear about Céline and Julie's relationship is a profound closeness, complicity and periodic fusion of identities. The (con)fusion-of-identity motif is developed when Céline, taking a phone-call from Julie's childhood sweetheart, pretends to *be* Julie and even goes to meet him with her hair styled like Julie's; he, comically, exclaims that nothing has changed. The trope recurs when Julie in her turn assumes Céline's identity, dressing like her and replacing her on

4. The old chestnut of lesbianism as narcissism is somewhat strained in *Céline et Julie vont en bateau* (1974) (see Chapter 3). Les Films Du Losange/The Kobal Collection

stage as a magician. The French press quickly picked up on this (con)fusion of identities, and to this extent it is perhaps surprising that no inferences were made about a lesboerotic subtext to the film. *Télérama* even qualified their closeness as osmosis and this osmosis as forming the very basis of the film: 'cette osmose entre Céline et Julie est la base du film. Les deux personnages sont permutables. C'est pourquoi, à certains moments, l'une devient l'autre. Ces deux personnages sont peut-être les deux faces d'un même personnage'[14] ['This osmosis between Céline and Julie is the basis of the film. The two characters can be switched around. This is why, at some points, one becomes the other. These two characters are perhaps the two sides of a single character']. *Le Monde* echoes this perception of the two women's ontological imbrication: 'Céline et Julie vont devenir amies. Mieux qu'amies: complices. Mieux que complices: inter-changeables. À la fin du film, on ne sait plus très bien qui est Céline et qui est Julie'[15] ['Céline and Julie will become friends. Better than friends: complicit. Better than complicit: interchangeable. At the end of the film, we no longer really know who is Céline and who is Julie']. The represent-ation of potentially lesbianisable intimacy depends upon endorsement of the hackneyed fusional model of lesbianism, yet the film may still yield considerable viewing pleasures by virtue of its very ludicity, along with the aesthetic appeal of its two chief protagonists: both women are young and attractive.

As in *Thérèse Desqueyroux* and *Une Femme, un jour* (1974), Jacques Baratier's *L'Araignée de satin* (1984) deploys specular imagery to suggest a narcissistic bent to the erotic charge between schoolgirls Solange and Lucienne. The film includes an oneiric dance sequence in which the girls' images are reflected and then merged. They face each other, bodies almost touching; Solange tells Lucienne to raise her slip, which exposes her buttocks, then to look at herself in the mirror. As with previous lesboerotic scenes in this movie, the finale evokes quasi-cannibalism – the ultimate form of incorporation and obliteration of subject boundaries: Solange seems to be on the verge of eating Lucienne, then puts her hand up to the girl's mouth, tremulously, and finally rips off Lucienne's slip to reveal the girl's breasts. The charge of narcissism is, however, fairly innocuous compared with the pathologising and prurient implications of *Le Monde*'s parallels between the film's opening scenes and early twentieth-century psychiatry's circus-like abuse of women: 'Vers la même époque [les années folles], le psychiatre Gaétan Gatian de Clérambault faisait, chaque semaine, des présentations de malades à l'infirmerie du Dépôt. Les "sujets" étaient généralement des femmes surprises à voler des coupons de soie dans les magasins, vols qui traduisaient leurs obsessions érotiques'[16] ['Around the same period (the Roaring Twenties), every week the psychiatrist Gaétan Gatian de Clérambault would present invalids at the Infirmerie du Dépôt. The "subjects" were usually women caught stealing silk remnants/rolls from shops, thefts which betrayed their erotic obsessions'].

On a less grimly clinical note, the French-Canadian director Léa Pool's *La Femme de l'hôtel* (1984) also brushes with the fusional model of lesboerotic desire. Andréa, who at the start of the film is encoded as heterosexual (seen with her male partner), is trying to make a film about a distraught singer/actress who suffers a crisis of confidence and existential breakdown. At the Montreal hotel where she is staying for the shooting of the film, Andréa becomes fascinated with Estelle, a real-life woman who increasingly begins to shape Andréa's conception of her filmic protagonist. Slowly, the two women build up an intimacy based on a shared elaboration of the film character's story. Voice-over conveys Andréa imagining telling Estelle things she would not dare tell her in reality, and expressing a deep, almost compulsive interest in her; when the image-track shows Andréa in tears, her emotional investment in the relationship with Estelle is reiterated. Estelle later suggests imbrication of their individual identities by referring to the fictional character's story as 'une histoire qui aurait pu si facilement être la mienne ou la tienne' ['a story that could so easily have been mine or yours']. This in itself is neither negative nor pathologising; what *is* is Estelle's eventual accusation that Andréa has used her as an instrument for creation and the proximate imputation made by one reviewer of morbid annexation and incorporation: 'Andréa, la cinéaste, dit dans le film que tous les créateurs sont des voleurs. Estelle, la femme mystérieuse et dépressive, ne veut pas se laisser voler sa vie, même au cinéma. Les créateurs sont des vampires dans ce sens'[17] ['Andréa, the film director, says in the film that all creators are thieves. Estelle, the mysterious and depressive woman, doesn't want to let her life be stolen away, even in the cinema. Creators are vampires in this sense'].

The conjunction of lesbian desire with both fusion and creativity also informs Joy Fleury's *Tristesse et beauté* (1985). When introducing Prudence as her talented pupil to her ex-lover Hugo, established artist Léa compromises the compliment with a pathologising note setting the tenor of the narrative to come: 'Sa sculpture est tellement passionnée qu'on dirait l'œuvre d'un cerveau *malade*' (my emphasis) ['Her sculpture is so passionate that you'd think it was the work of a *sick* mind']. That one comment on Prudence's art predetermines the (hetero)normative viewer's response to Prudence and to her feelings for Léa: passionate, but sick. When Prudence arrives at a party, Léa smiles radiantly, touching her and telling her that her eyes have the colour of their lake when it's been raining, to which Prudence asks the leading question 'La couleur de vos tableaux?' ['The colour of your paintings?'], thus hinting at a certain pictorial specularity as metaphor for the two women's psychic mirroring. Shortly afterwards, Prudence declares that, if she had a portrait or herself painted, she would contrive for Léa to be in it too – a statement invoking a far more obviously narcissistic model of lesbian desire, and pregnantly preceded by Prudence's seeming about to kiss the nape of Léa's neck. In this movie, the male node of the triangle contributes actively to the production of a fusional model. Hugo publishes a novel entitled *Une jeune fille de 16 ans* [*A Girl of 16*] – Léa was sixteen when they first met, but Hugo says that the chief protagonist is in fact Prudence, and Prudence for her part complies with this male forcing of the model by herself incorporating the character of Léa. She reads aloud the lines 'Devant la glace elle se poudrait attentivement' ['In front of the mirror she powdered herself carefully'], and acts out the lines exactly, powdering her body carefully in front of the mirror. She is thus both appropriating Léa's identity and performing her own as constructed by Hugo, again leading to a fusion of the two.

Equally baleful are the consequences of over-identification-in-desire rendered by Diane Kurys's *À la folie* (1993), which centres on the torturous relationship between sisters Elsa and Alice. As in *Les Biches*, one woman tries in some sense to become the woman she desires, and again, to this extent it may be more appropriate to think in terms of a replacement model of substitution rather than of fusion, be it narcissistic or not. Here, Elsa tries to take over Alice's life (her flat, her boyfriend Franck), then follows her and begins the whole pattern again when Alice escapes to New York. It is significant that, having purloined Franck from Alice, Elsa asks him what Alice does in bed, suggesting the sort of identification she claimed Alice to have evinced in childhood vis-à-vis herself. Proleptically, this forms an interesting parallel with *Les Blessures assassines* in the depiction of an atypically intimate relationship between sisters, but in the case of *À la folie* this results in intra-destructive actions, whereas in *Les Blessures assassines* the destructiveness is levelled outside the hermetically sororal matrix.

In contrast, ultimate destructiveness is implosive rather than explosive in André Téchiné's *Les Voleurs* (1996). Juliette's aspiration apropos her lover Marie (played by lesbian icon Catherine Deneuve)[18] to 'lui ressembler … C'est mon idéal' ['resemble her … She's my ideal'] is not in itself necessarily fusional – wishing to *be like* someone and wishing to *be* that person should be clearly distinguished. However, when Marie injures her ankle very shortly after rushing Juliette to hospital following the latter's suicide attempt, it is hard to avoid the inference of a Freudian 'slip' (in both senses) of identification. Further, in the 'scène de la baignoire' ['bath scene'] (a classic image in lesbian iconography), when Juliette asks Marie if she can see what Marie has written about *her*, Marie replies, 'Ce sont des impressions tu sais. En fait *ça me ressemble trop*, c'est pour ça que ça ne me plaît pas' (my emphasis) ['They're just impressions, you know. In fact they resemble me too much, that's why I don't like them'] – again hinting at the narcissistic model of lesbianism. And, as in *Thérèse Desqueyroux*, *Une Femme, un jour* and *L'Araignée de satin*, this model is visually reinforced by deployment of specular images: the two women's head and shoulders are seen in close-up through a mirror. If *Les Voleurs* mediates a model of identification which usually carries pathologising connotations, one might argue that Juliette emerges far healthier than before from the relationship with Marie, which has been the only relationship in her life free from the corrosives of money, power, domination and humiliation. As *Le Point* observes, Juliette 'est le personnage qui se sort le mieux de toute cette histoire. Elle est transfigurée par ce qu'elle à vécu avec Marie'[19] ['is the character who comes through best from the whole story. She is transformed by her experience with Marie']. On the other hand, it would appear that by investing herself entirely in Juliette, Marie literally lost herself in the sense of the successful professional woman she previously was. Ultimately, she effaces herself through suicide – and even this could be read as a form of morbid identification with Juliette's earlier such attempt.

Perhaps the most visually disturbing of all films in the corpus is François Ozon's *Regarde la mer* (1998). As noted in Chapter 2, an ill-defined but intensely charged dynamic grows between the middle-class Sasha and vagrant Tatiana; towards the end of the film, Sasha's hitherto absent husband Paul, arriving home to a deserted house, looks for his wife and baby daughter and finds a putrefying female corpse. Apart from the obvious horror of the inference that the editing incites us to make, that Sasha is the victim and Tatiana the culprit, it is also disturbing to note the virulent form of the fusional model of lesbian desire inscribed here: after brutally murdering her, Tatiana has purloined Sasha's identity by donning her dress and stealing her baby. In view of Tatiana's earlier, blackly offbeat reference to having aborted her foetus, it could be argued that the film is more about a woman traumatised by abortion than homicidally fusional in her lesbian desire, but given the fact that Tatiana undresses to get into bed with a sleeping Sasha just before the murder, the viewer cannot help wondering which sexual fantasies or acts may have preceded that murder, and why she dresses as Sasha after murdering her.

Similarly disturbing, if less visually shocking, is the consequence of female over-identification with a female desire-object in Anne-Sophie Birot's *Les Filles ne savent pas nager* (2000). As noted in Chapter 3, Lise becomes intensely jealous when her childhood friend Gwen starts experimenting sexually with boys. Tensions explode, and in a deranged attempt to win the sexual attention of Gwen's father – a metonym for the absent and rejecting Gwen? – Lise pushes him down the stairs. All Lise (shown out of focus at the back of the frame, the top of her head barely visible, with Gwen frantically huddling over her father in the foreground) can say to Gwen, distraught at her father's death, is 'Tu vois? Toi et moi, on est pareille' ['Do you see? You and me, we're the same']. These are the last words she utters, and they, along with her act, are pregnant with over-determined meaning. It is true that Lise had lacked a father-figure (her recently deceased father having left his family ten years before his death), and her kissing Gwen's father may seem like a crudely oedipal attempt to fill that void. This oedipal – or, more precisely, Electral – exegesis is imbricated in, and to my mind carries less weight than, the old psychoanalytical cliché of lesbian desire as based on a desire for identity and fusion: in eliminating Gwen's father, Lise has made Gwen just like herself, that is to say, fatherless. A crude, and axiomatically heterocentric, reading of Lise's poem to Gwen would equate 'Les petites filles ont peur de l'écume' ['Little girls are scared of spume'] with Lise's fear of sperm as a metonym for men, and her desire for Gwen as a desire for fusion and identity within a safe, pre-oedipal sphere. Such a reading can only shore up the notion that lesbian desire stems from immaturity – a not innocuous notion even when set aside the more heinous charge of murder.

Less obviously dramatic, but perhaps rather more complex, is the fusional/substitutional nexus constructed by Catherine Corsini's *La Répétition* (2000).[20] Many French reviews constructed Louise's obsession with Nathalie as jealousy, a wish to *be* the successful actress Nathalie has become, rather than to *have* Nathalie as a love-object.[21] This ascription to the woman of *being* rather than *having* reflects Lacan's gesturing towards ascription to the feminine role of *being* rather than *having* the phallus – a neat exemplar of how gendered binaries are policed even at the most obscure of connotational levels:

[l]es données analytiques indiquent également que la fille, voire d'une façon générale l'enfant, peut se concevoir soi-même comme l'équivalent du phallus, le manifester par son comportement, et vivre la relation sexuelle sur un mode qui comporte qu'elle-même apporte au partenaire masculin son phallus. (Lacan 1994: 168)

[Analytical data likewise indicate that the girl, indeed more generally the child, can conceive of herself as the equivalent of the phallus, manifest this in her behaviour and live her sexual relationship in a way which means that she herself brings her male partner his phallus.]

As such, these reviews imply the classical, pathologising model of lesbian desire as, ultimately, narcissism: attraction to the same/to indifferentiation and, in a semantic slide, to the self. I, however, contend that Louise seeks to become Nathalie *only in default of* having her. Put simply, I disagree with the French reviewers who see Louise's obsession with Nathalie as primarily a wish to be like her – a successful actress – and, increasingly, a desire to destroy Nathalie as the living proof of her own relative failure. Rather, I argue that Louise seeks to *be* like Nathalie, to appropriate Nathalie's identity, only when she has failed to *have* her as a desire-object.

An erotico-amorous current between the two women is, even though at first largely unilateral, indisputable. The camera zooms into a close-up of Louise's hand surreptitiously caressing Nathalie's underwear in a drawer; Louise refers to the scar on her wrist as being due to 'un chagrin d'amour', and we the spectator know that it stems from Louise's suicide attempt following possessive jealousy over Nathalie as a teenager; finally, when comforting Louise, Nathalie takes the physical initiative of kissing her, and what follows is an intense sex-scene between the two women. The image-track lingers on their breasts, head and shoulders, while the soundtrack conveys ecstatic moans plus unmistakable climax. We then cut to the two happily shopping, and here the director Catherine Corsini herself directs one to the narcissistic reading favoured by the critics, summing up this scene in the dress shop, rather than the sex-scene preceding it, as '*le* moment lesbien du film'[22] ['*the* lesbian moment of the film']. Tellingly, this scene centres largely on shots of the two women looking at their reflections in mirrors, thus iterating the old chestnut of lesbian as specularity/identification/narcissism. The final sequence of the film reiterates it: Louise is shown to have become the girlfriend of Nathalie's ex-boyfriend Sacha, thus appropriating Nathalie's past identity as Sacha's lover. It is not indifferent that the narcissistic insinuations are coupled with a near-homicidal stance on Louise's part in refusing a seriously ill Nathalie access to an ambulance crew. Here, the more sinister undertones immanent in the fusional model are brought into troubling focus: suffocation and death, murderous resistance to the attempt of one part of the dyad to break free.

The one film in the corpus which explicitly turns on its head the association of lesbianism with fusion is Chantal Akerman's *La Captive* (2000). Of salience is that Simon's ideal of love, says Akerman in interview, is of osmosis – a process of acquisition through absorption – whereas for Ariane, the girlfriend whom he rightly suspects of lesbian affinities, it is the opposite, and she actively wants something of the love-object to remain a mystery. In a neat reversal of psychoanalytic orthodoxy, the fusional model normatively ascribed to lesbianism is ascribed to a straight man (in Akerman's film there is no suggestion of the sexual ambiguity characterising Proust's Marcel), and its implied opposite to a lesbian-oriented woman. One can only lament the fact that such an inversion of the model is so rare in the corpus; yet the corpus is at least partly a reflection of cultural prejudices and anxieties at large, albeit also a potential modifier of them.

Connotationally, narcissism is proximate with incest, a form of attraction to the biologically *almost*-same/quasi-self; and in three films of the corpus – Nico Papatakis's *Les Abysses* (1963), Léa Pool's *La Femme de l'hôtel* (1984) and Jean-Pierre Denis's *Les Blessures assassines* (1999) – sibling incest too is configured as isomorphic with lesbian desire. *Les Abysses* and *Les Blessures assassines*, let us recall, are based on the real-life case of the Papin sisters, whose relationship was undoubtedly incestuous. I strongly refute the claim made by the intellectually respected journal *Les Temps modernes* that the 'oppression qu'elles subissent ensemble les lie plus sûrement qu'aucune expérience sexuelle'[23] ['oppression that they suffered together bound them together more securely than any sexual experience']. In *Les Abysses*, it is Michèle's fury at Elisabeth's erotic claims on Michèle's sister Marie-Louise that triggers the murders. *La France nouvelle* took a more dismissive stance, omitting mention of the sisters' social oppression, minimising the force of their threatened erotico-amorous bond and opting for the easy diagnosis of immaculately conceived madness, free from any social or interpersonal determinations: 'ces filles sont folles, ou au moins dans un état de paroxie . . . Leur attitude prend aussi des formes qui ne sont nullement obligatoires, par exemple l'homosexualité très nettement indiquée entre les deux principales protagonistes, incestueuses, du film'[24] ['these girls are mad, or at least in a state of paroxysm . . . Their attitude also takes on guises which were entirely unnecessary, for example the very clearly indicated homosexuality between the two main, incestuous protagonists of the film'].

In what first appears to be a similarly *ex nihilo* pathologising vein, but which may merit further probing, the director Jean-Pierre Denis refers to the relationship between the two sisters in his *Les Blessures assassines* as an 'affection anormale qui n'a rien à voir avec une relation homosexuelle d'aujourd'hui'[25] ['abnormal fondness which is nothing like a contemporary homosexual relationship']. I contend on the contrary that what mattered more than their biological connection was the simple fact that they loved and desired each other; and I am not alone in this. *Les Inrockuptibles* muses along similar lines:

> Les scènes de sexe entre les deux sœurs, l'apprivoisement progressif de leurs corps, sont parmi les plus réussies ... Mais on ne peut s'empêcher de se dire qu'il y avait là en germe une radicalité de représentation que le cinéaste n'ose pas tout à fait mener à son terme.[26]
> [Some of the best scenes are those of sex between the two sisters, the gradual taming of their bodies ... But one can't help thinking that there were seeds here of a radical form of representation that the director doesn't quite dare to see through to completion.]

I will return to this point in Chapter 5; for the moment, pushing to its logical conclusions the spirit of queer – which is, in essence, a resistance to all disciplinary (usually hetero)sexual norms – I will confront one of our last remaining sexual taboos and question the persisting condemnation and pathologisation of sibling incest. Temporarily bracketing the Pavlovian response of disgust, we should consider whether sibling incest really presents any material dangers beyond the risk that any progeny issuing from a brother and sister may have congenital birth defects. In the case of same-sex sibling love, there will axiomatically be no jointly conceived progeny, so where is the danger? In the case of the Papin sisters, it was not their love and desire for each other that drove them to murder, but the social forces that conspired to drive them apart, allied to a highly dysfunctional and unsupportive early (heterosexual) family life. To some extent at least, I argue for a 'normalisation' of the lesbian desire immanent in their relationship, and am reminded of an insight from Gide's eponymous character in his *Corydon* (1924): 'Je n'admets qu'une chose au monde pour ne pas être naturelle: c'est l'œuvre d'art. Tout le reste, bon gré mal gré, rentre dans la nature'[27] ['I only accept one thing in the world as being unnatural: the work of art. All the rest, willy-nilly, is part of nature'].

Rather more subtle, indeed tenuous, and conceptually complex is the collocation of lesbian desire with sibling incest in French-Canadian Léa Pool's *La Femme de l'hôtel* (1984). Conceptually complex because the following, not implausible interpretation juxtaposes lesbian desire between Andréa and Estelle with incestuous heterosexual desire between Andréa and her brother Simon:

> La relation d'amour tout à la fois réelle et impossible, c'est évidemment à un premier niveau celle qui lie Andréa avec Estelle. Comme un leitmotiv, un appel incessant ('Touche-moi') s'élève des yeux, de la bouche et du corps tout entier de la cinéaste et de sa comédienne. Un appel faussement nié, déplacé et finalement entendu par la femme de l'hôtel. Cet appel transmué en désir n'aura pourtant pas de réponse concrète, même une fois reconnu et déplacé par Estelle sur Simon ... Un amour impossible à vivre, mais pourquoi? Peut-être pour Estelle parce qu'homosexuelle? ... mais si l'on songe, d'une part au double Simon/Andréa, au lien Andréa/Estelle, et à la rencontre Estelle/Simon, au-delà des diverses impossibilités homosexuées, l'on peut entrevoir comme possible une attirance incestueuse entre le frère et la sœur, à l'origine alors de leurs respectives incapacités amoureuses. En effet, tout se passe comme si, pour parvenir à 'toucher/être touchée' par Estelle, Andréa ... ne pouvait vivre sa relation amoureuse que par personnes/personnages interposés: tentant de jeter par là, ses deux réels interdits, Simon et Estelle, dans les bras l'un de l'autre.[28]
>
> [On a primary level, the at once real and impossible love is obviously that linking Andréa and Estelle. Like a leitmotif, an incessant call ('Touch me') issues from the eyes, the mouth and the entire body of the director and of her actress. It's a call that is falsely denied, displaced, and finally heard by the woman of the hotel. This call transformed into desire will not however get a concrete response, even when it's been recognised and displaced by Estelle onto Simon. ... A love that is impossible to live out, but why? Perhaps for Estelle because it's a homosexual love? ... but if one thinks, on the one hand about the Simon/Andréa double, about the Andréa/Estelle link, about the Estelle/Simon meeting, beyond the various homosexually-slanted impossibilities, one can glimpse the possibility of an incestuous attraction between the brother and the sister, at the origin of their respective relationship failures. Indeed, the film's whole development suggests that, to succeed in

'touching/being touched' by Estelle, Andréa ... could only live her experience of love through the intermediary of other people/characters: trying,
thus, to throw her two forbidden love-realities, Simon and Estelle, into each
other's arms.]

Not only does it juxtapose these two forms of love, it posits Andrea as strad-
dling the two, and, more significantly, only allowing herself to realise them
vicariously; in symmetry, Estelle's heteronormative self-policing only
allows her to realise her desire for Andrea through the medium of a biologically related *ersatz*.

Sibling incest is not the only form of incest to be associated with lesbian
desire; far more commonly incest is implicitly immanent, if simultaneously
disavowed, in models of lesbianism as replicating a lost mother–daughter
relationship. In its most extreme forms, this model encodes lesbian desire
as regression to the realm of the Imaginary, entailing exclusion from the
Symbolic Order and, in the worst-case scenario (Kristevan), psychosis. In
this extreme form, the model intersects with the fusional model of lesbianism discussed above, for it recalls the infant's non-differentiation from its
mother. Engagement with all theoretical contributions to this paradigm is
impossible, such is their number; I will confine myself to summaries of the
most influential (again, drawing directly on my publications of 2002).

As we have seen, in *Histoires d'amour* Julia Kristeva posits 'les amours lesbiennes' as comprising 'la plage délicieuse d'une libido neutralisée, tamisée,
dépourvue du tranchant érotique de la sexualité masculine' ['the delightful
arena of a neutralised, filtered libido, devoid of the erotic cutting edge of
masculine sexuality']. This, she goes on to claim, evokes 'le dialogue
amoureux de la mère enceinte avec le fruit, à peine distinct d'elle, qu'elle
abrite dans son ventre' ['the loving dialogue of the mother pregnant with
the fruit, barely distinct from her, that she shelters in her belly']. Implicitly
repudiating the (in my view valid) charge of homophobia levelled at
Kristeva by Judith Butler (Butler 1989), Kelly Oliver avers that 'Kristeva is
more concerned with a preoedipal relation to the mother, which for women
requires a kind of homosexuality' (Oliver 1993: 81).[29] If Oliver is correct,
Kristeva should not wilfully confuse categories in their common accepta-
tions – or at least she should make it transparent that this is what she is
doing, for the stakes here are high. The sort of 'homosexuality' consisting
in a woman's putative, evanescent memories of a pre-oedipal relation to the
mother is ontologically and politically distinct from an erotic desire, and
possibly also love, between two differentiated, usually (but see above) non-
biologically-related women. Kristeva coopts the word 'lesbian' for her own

idiosyncratic permutation of the word, and in so doing stigmatises the material referent of its more common acceptation.

Although Irigaray's relationship to psychoanalysis, particularly to its Lacanian brand, is in many senses iconoclastic,[30] and is thankfully free of Kristeva's imputations of psychosis to lesbianism, she too conceives of the latter in terms of the pre-oedipal mother–daughter dynamic: 'étant donné que le premier corps auquel elles ont affaire est un corps de femme, le premier amour qu'elles partagent, est maternel, les femmes sont toujours dans un rapport archaïque et primaire à ce qui s'appelle homosexualité' (Irigaray 1987: 32)[31] ['given that the first body they have any dealings with is a woman's body, that the first love they share is mother love, it is important to remember that women always stand in an archaic and primal relationship with what is known as homosexuality']. Even when Irigaray tries to see beyond this 'primary' homosexuality of women, she cannot break free of familial paradigms:

> Essayons aussi de découvrir la singularité de notre amour pour les autres femmes. Ce qui pourrait s'appeler (mais je n'aime pas ces mots étiquettes), entre beaucoup de guillemets: ' "homo-sexualité secondaire" '. J'essaie de désigner ainsi une différence entre l'amour archaïque pour la mère et l'amour pour les femmes-sœurs. (Irigaray 1987, p. 32; my emphasis)
> [Let us also try to discover the singularity of our love for other women. What might be called (though I do not like these label-words) ' "secondary homosexuality" ', with lot of inverted commas. I am trying here to outline a difference between archaic love of the mother and love for women-sisters.]

De Lauretis sensibly eschews this maternal imaginary, which occludes the fact that lesbianism 'as a particular relation between women . . . is not only sexual but also sociosymbolic' (Lauretis 1994: 198). Patricia White is similarly mistrustful of the feminist preoccupation with the figure of the mother because of its 'writing out of lesbianism', where the 'homosexual' consists of same-sex relations without the 'otherness' of lesbian desire (White 1995: 89). Shameem Kabir, in her *Daughters of Desire: Lesbian Representations in Film* (1998), makes a valuable input to the debate: 'I would suggest that we accept that we are constituted in severance and lack. I can reject identifications with a maternal imaginary because I think we must not be duped into looking for origins and causes. It is a doomed project to recover what is lost' (Kabir 1998: 33).

If I have included discussion of the mother–daughter model of lesbianism in the present chapter, this is because in its extreme forms it certainly figures as a pathology: as a form of stymying anaclisis at best, of psychosis at worst. It rests upon either a disavowal of sexual desire, which de-eroticises the lesbian couple and infantilises one of the partners, or eroticises the mother–daugther relationship, without quite being able to face the logical conclusion of its argument: mother–daugther incest. None the less, quite a number of films in the corpus, albeit to varying degrees, and particularly to varying degrees of pathology, include traces of this model of lesbianism as regression to the mother–daughter relationship.

In Deval's *Club de femmes* (1936), Alice's attraction to Juliette is encrypted in, *inter alia*, the poem which Alice has chosen for Juliette's dictation exercise, containing the following lines: 'Mon enfant, ma sœur ... Songe à la douceur d'être là-bas ...' ['My child, my sister ... Think of the sweetness of being there ...']. The poem in question is, of course, 'L'Invitation au voyage' by the nineteenth-century poet Baudelaire, one of the most famous male writers to have depicted lesbian desire (in his collection of poems entitled *Les Fleurs du mal*).[32] The Baudelairian words chosen by the director for us to hear strongly connote, and arguably conflate, the hackneyed mother–daughter and the narcistically sororal models of lesbian desire, but more interestingly, they also evoke a utopic space in which Alice's erotic love could be openly lived. However, there are dangers in such a utopic exteriority, as Annamarie Jagose has convincingly argued:

> The tendency to figure 'lesbian' as utopic and outside dominant conceptual frameworks essentializes that category as transgressive or subversive. The inherent revolutionary character of 'lesbian' demonstrates the foundational flaw in its utopic figuration: that the exteriority of the utopic category is phantasmatic and conceals that category's proper position within the networks of power. (Jagose 1994: 5)

This alter-world comes dangerously close to the realm of the Imaginary and incompatibility with the 'networks of power' that forbid open expression of lesbian desire within a heterosexist Symbolic Order. Alice's protective, all-consuming love, unable to speak its name, will eventually drive her to murder, and thus to banishment from mainstream society into, literally, a lepers' colony.

The opening sections of Jacques Rivette's *Suzanne Simonin, La Religieuse de Diderot* (1965) stress Suzanne's brutal rejection by her mother before being forced into religious orders, and this deprivation of maternal love may well suggest for some spectators a facile aetiology of her initial passivity towards the lesbian-connoted advances of the religious 'mother' (Mother Superior) Mme de Chelles. Similarly, Guy Casaril's *Le Rempart des Béguines* (1972) opens with emphasis on the young (fifteen-year-old) Hélène's craving for physical affection from a female figure, Julia the cook/housekeeper, in lieu, the spectator is incited to surmise, of the affection her deceased mother might have provided. The focus of the film's narrative thereafter is the passion Hélène develops for Tamara, her father's thirty-eight-year-old mistress, who is literally to become her new mother through marriage to her father. This new mother, however, can only ever be a Kleinian 'bad breast' in that the inter-female bond depends upon a sado-masochistic dynamic, without which the younger, masochistic partner loses erotic interest (see above).

Equally open to a psychoanalytical reading, if along different lines, is the coming-out speech made in Belgian director Chantal Akerman's *Les Rendez-vous d'Anna* (1978) by the eponymous Anna to her mother. The unveiling of intimate secrets by a naked daughter to her mother occurs in a shared hotel bed plunged in womb-like semi-darkness, which constitutes a deeply over-determined context redolent of mother–daughter pre-Symbolic fusion – or even incest. The hotel receptionist's surprise at two women taking a room with a single bed foregrounds connotations of both lesbianism and possibly, for the more informed spectator (we, unlike the receptionist, now know they are mother and daughter), incest. When Anne starts to undress, revealing her naked back to the camera and to her mother, the latter gazes at her, saying she wants to watch her for a while: is this maternal or amorous scopophilia, or both? As she and her mother are framed lying next to each other in bed, in a medium shot with their faces towards the top of the frame and the very dim lighting evoking a uterine intimacy, the mother asks Anna to tell her about the evident love-interest behind the phone-call to Italy Anna had referred to. Anna accordingly recounts her initiation into lesbian desire and love-making, offering a psychoanalytic gem: 'Bizarrement, j'ai pensé à toi' ['Oddly, I thought about you'].

As Andrea Weiss astutely observes, the 'visual displacement of the lover by the mother' imposes 'onto the articulation of lesbianism a visual enactment of a pre-Oedipal, narcissistic identification between mother and daughter' (Weiss 1992: 117–18). Is Akerman complacently recycling an old stereotype in thus linking lesboerotic desire to mother–daughter intimacy? Or, more charitably, is this an attempt at psychological verisimilitude? Since mother–daughter intimacy may well be a common *initial* reference-point for many first experiences of intimacy between women, it is perhaps not surprising that her mother's image should have sprung to Anna's lesbo-virginal mind on first experiencing conscious desire for a woman. What would have been more interesting is some insight into Anna's feelings for the *non-mother* desire-object; but this the narrative forecloses. As a small compensation, we have Anna's effort to look beyond the mother–daughter framework in asking her mother, 'Tu n'as jamais aimé de femme?' ['Have you never loved a woman?'] The mother's response is an evasive, but not entirely dismissive 'J'ai pas. Je n'y ai jamais réfléchi' ['Don't know. I've never thought about it']. So, we have a hypothetical glimpse of a more adult, agentic desire between women, but this too is foreclosed. The scene winds down by substituting discourse on overt inter-female sexuality by diffuse inter-female sensuality: Anna tells her mother she smells nice, still wearing the same perfume, and they reminisce about the old pleasures of that fragrance; she turns over to take her mother in her arms in the bed, and her mother moves closer into her daughter's body. Olfactory and tactile pleasures serve as synecdoches for forbidden sexual ones (forbidden in the strongest of Symbolic terms: the mother refers to the Law of the Father in saying she would not dare tell her husband of Anna's confession, and Anne defers to this Law by agreeing that the confession not be divulged to her father).

Far more of a psychoanalytical conundrum is posed by one scene in Joy Fleury's *Tristesse et beauté* (1985). As noted above, Prudence is determined to wreak vengence upon Hugo for having years ago ruined her love-object Léa's life by abandoning her. A crucial epistemological enigma is posed by Hugo's wife's claim, which he does not deny, that Prudence is actually Hugo's daughter: 'C'est ta fille' ['She's your daughter']. If this is to be taken as literal truth – and there would appear to be no scope for a more metaphorical paternity, since Hugo and Prudence barely know each other – the whole narrative is skewed into an oedipal revenge fantasy in which Léa's role becomes that of Prudence's mother. No evidence is adduced, but this accusation certainly immobilises any fully confident articulation of lesbian desire independent of the mother–daughter incest taint.

In Geneviève Lefebvre's *Le Jupon rouge* (1986), Bacha is visibly jealous of the growing love between her closest, considerably younger friend Manuela (forty-four years old) and her even younger (twenty-seven years old), much less close friend Claude. As the fledgling lesbian lovers talk avidly, a shot with Bacha in the foreground looking disgruntledly at the two women in the background, shadowed, visually isolates her from their dyad and presages the drama of jealousy, which is about to explode. Of that moment, she says to Manuela she had been wishing the two younger women were her daughters, that she could have grandchildren and make jam ... a homely, sanitising spin that does not quite convince the viewer in retrospect, but more importantly for our purposes here, exposes the cultural repressions surrounding adult lesbian desire for a non-familial figure, and the mechanisms by which such desire can be camouflaged, de-eroticised and partially legitimised by invocation of maternal feelings towards a younger woman.

Mother–daughter affection is also the sanitised screen filtering and attenuating lesboeroticm between a younger and an older woman in Léa

Pool's *Anne Trister* (1986). Important for the erection of this screen are the film's opening sequences, in which Anne's mother fails to comfort her daughter crying on a bed, and subsequently declares to Anne's boyfriend Pierre, 'c'est sûre qu'elle n'a pas eu l'amour qu'elle attendait de moi' ['she certainly didn't get the sort of love that she expected from me']. So, 'inadequate' mothering is strategically emphasised by the narrative near the start of the film, so that it will influence the spectator's interpretation of twenty-five-year-old Anne's later love for forty-year-old Alix, a child psychologist treating emotionally dysfunctional children. That interpretation is over-determined from the outset: put crudely, the relationship between Alix and Anne has widely been construed in the mother–daughter mode, with a wounded Anne seeking from Alix the love unforthcoming from her real mother, and Alix responding with the sort of maternal, healing affection she also displays towards her seven-year-old patient Sarah. Typical of such a construction is the statement that '[c]et amour homosexuel, que la psychologue aura du mal à admettre, est pour Anne une quête de la mère qu'elle n'a jamais eue'[33] ['this homosexual love, that the psychologist will find it hard to acknowledge, is for Anne a quest for the mother she never had']. *Télérama* rightly regretted Pool's unnecessary heavy-handedness:

> parallèlement à l'évolution d'Anne, on suit les progrès d'une petite fille révoltée, Sarah, soignée par Alix. Quand Sarah barbouille de rouge son ours, Anne barbouille de rouge ses murs … Bref, un peu trop de psychanalyse et des symboles un peu trop évidents. C'est dommage, car Léa Pool est un auteur. Sa sensibilité est assez grande pour qu'elle n'ait pas besoin de nous fournir tant de clefs.[34]
> [in parallel with Anne's development, we follow the progress of a rebellious little girl, Sarah, being treated by Alix. When Sarah smears her teddy bear in red, Anne smears her walls in red … Basically, a bit too much psychoanalysis and rather too obvious symbols. This is a shame, because Léa Pool is an auteur. Her sensibility is sufficiently distinguished for her not to need to give us so many keys to interpretation.]

To reinforce the parallels between Anne and Sarah, there is not only their strong physical resemblance (both are dark, slight and brooding), but also the fact that Sarah at one point tries to touch Alix's breast; paradoxically, a less problematic mother–daughter dynamic is here invested with the eroticism that is often thought to be absent or minimal in adult lesbian relations reduced to the mother–daughter model. These parallels are only further reiterated by the film's editing: the juxtapositioning of frames first shows Anne caressing Alix's hand to comfort her, then Sarah touching

Alix's face during a therapy session. In the latter, the soundtrack conveys the sound of a strongly beating heart, evoking Sarah's (unconscious) wish for womblike fusion with Alix.

The dénouement is triggered by Anne's accident at her artist's studio. Alix is solicitous, by her side in the ambulance and at her hospital bed, and finally takes the physical initiative which she had earlier rebuffed coming from Anne. Alix first watches Anne crying on the bed, thus directly recalling the opening scene between Anne and her mother, then lays her head on Anne's hips, her hand on Anne's shoulder, and finally kisses and embraces her. The camera focuses in close-up on their gazing at each other, Alix looking grave, then shutting her eyes as Anne caresses her lips (as had the child Sarah earlier on), finally kissing them. And this time, Alix reciprocates. The film does not opt for a conventionally happy ending of unproblematic union, but it does imply some sort of future together for the two women. Alix is seen watching footage Anne has sent her of her father's tombstone in Israel, now with flowers growing by it. Significantly, Anne includes herself in the film, moving around, smiling, trying to find the best position in the frame for Alix to see her. As *La Croix* pertinently comments, '[l]a dernière scène, fort drôle, une bobine de superhuit qu'elle envoie d'Israël à Alix, la montre s'amusant avec cette notion de 'cadre' au sens cinématographique. Être dans la 'norme' ou pas, au fond, est moins important que d'avoir conscience de cette norme elle-même et de prendre ses distances en connaissance de cause'[35] ['the last, very funny scene, a super-8 reel that she sends from Israel to Alix, shows her playing with this notion of "frame" in the cinematographic sense. Being within the "norm" or not is basically less important than being aware of this norm and advisedly distancing oneself from it'].

Finally, I turn to a more recent film by Léa Pool, *Emporte-moi* (1998), in which representation of Hanna's lesboerotic feelings for a non-family member, schoolgirl Laura, is highly problematic because overlayed by representation of a passionate, quasi-incestuous love for her mother. In an early sequence, a close-up shot of thirteen-year-old Hanna lying next to, indeed practically on top of, her depressive mother in bed, trying to comfort her, visually suggests the mother–daughter model of lesbianism, whilst the soundtrack – Hanna declaring 'Je suis comme toi … je suis malade aussi' ['I'm like you … I'm sick too'] – evokes the fusional model, and to boot explicitly pathologises both. In classical oedipal triangulation mode, the father interrupts their intimacy and, albeit gently, orders Hanna to go to her own bedroom. Curiously, it is the father who tries to masculinise Hanna by insisting she get her hair cut short: in a moving close-up, we see a tear trickling down Hanna's stricken face as she gazes at her new, shorn image. Does this represent an unconsciously jealous paternal effacement of the mother–daughter intimacy via literal erasure of one standard 'feminine' marker (long hair)?

Significant too is that one of the few things Hanna's desire-object Laura is heard talking to her about is a sense of estrangement from her own mother, which is in symmetry with Hanna's own sense of melancholic loss of the mother (the hospital scene where she attempts to elicit some response from her drugged mother is almost unbearably painful). The narrative economy thus promotes a reading of the mutual lesboerotic attraction between Hanna and Laura as isomorphous with their mother-love and fear of losing that mother. The very last shot of the film emphasises the imbrication of mother–daughter love and eroticism: Hanna is reunited with her mother after the latter's long convalescence; the mother looks for all the world as if she is about to kiss her daughter on the lips, then opts for her neck instead, in an intensely moving close-up. Whilst I am wary of intentionalist modes of interpretation, it would be lying by omission not to cite the following:

> 'J'ai attendu d'avoir quarante-cinq ans et d'être mère d'une petite Giulia pour avoir le courage de réaliser mon premier film autobiographique', avoue Léa Pool. 'J'avais besoin de renouer avec mon passé et de comprendre les liens étroits unissant, irrémédiablement, une mère à sa fille.'[36]
> ['I waited until I was forty-five years old and the mother of little Giulia to be brave enough to direct my first autobiographical film', admits Léa Pool. 'I needed to go back to my past and to understand the tight bonds which irremediably link a mother to her daughter.']

It is the adverb 'irrémédiablement' which counts here, suggesting that those tight mother–daughter bonds ineluctably determine all that follow – *a fortiori*, determine any bonds between post-pubescent, (usually) non-biologically related females, which by virtue of this determination can always be minimised at best, pathologised at worst.

As a more affirmative coda to this investigation of 'sickness' models of lesbian desire mediated by certain French and francophone films, I wish briefly to mention Stéphane Giusti's *Pourquoi pas moi?* (1999), which provides a humorously deflatory parody of the pathologising approach to such desire. A French–Spanish co-production, *Pourquoi pas moi?* is a comedy of manners set in Spain, and has been likened to Almodovar's work. Its narrative centre is the efforts of a group of young gay people to come out to their parents. When the confessions are finally made, familial responses vary.

Ariane's father insults his daughter as an 'anomalie génétique' ['genetic abnormality'], and even talks about getting the homosexual gene medically removed (quite how is, of course, never specified). Eva's mother Manou, a well-meaning but deeply dim woman, also buys into this eugenicising discourse, frantically phoning round her family members to check that the abnormal gene did not come from them, so she can triumphantly pronounce her family normal. She assumes she will not be able to have grandchildren, a misconception which Josepha, Camille's mother, neatly undercuts by pointing out that Eva is 'lesbienne, pas stérile' ['lesbian, not sterile']. The fact that the pathologising model is articulated by one deeply antipathetic and himself neurotic character (whose wife threatens to leave him if he does not stop his rabid rantings) and an imbecilic child-woman for whom we have no respect considerably detracts from its perceived validity – at the very least within audience reception of this particular film.

In this chapter, nineteen (67.9 per cent) of the twenty-eight films figuring lesbian desire as in some way pathological were directed by men, and only nine (32.1 per cent) by women. Whilst bearing in mind the caveat that there tend to be more male than female directors anyway in France, as in other countries, the figure is worth noting, as is the fact that the gender gap is smaller than in Chapter 2 (seventy-six per cent male, twenty-four per cent female). A crude gloss on the difference might be that if women are going to stigmatise lesbian desire, they will be more inclined to see it as an illness than as a crime, whereas the opposite applies to men. Revealingly, most women feel relatively unlikely to turn criminal, whereas we all know that nobody is immune from illness. More interestingly still, criminality is ascribed a certain voluntarism, unlike illness.

As a coda to Chapter 3, I will identify one striking similarity that its corpus shares with the corpus of Chapter 2: the association of lesbianism with death. The reasons for this association in films mediating lesbians as criminal are, however, different from those underpinning the association in films figuring lesbians as sick. As we have noted, one of the two most predominant paradigms of lesbianism as pathology is the model of inter-female desire as leading to fusion and indifferentiation. As I have previously stated, for Western thought at least 'any excess of sameness appears threatening; the fear is that complete indifferentiation leads to lack of friction, supposedly the first principle of movement, activity, and life, and thus ends in inertia and death' (Cairns 2002b: 160). Whether criminal or sick, the lesbian is bad news in the majority of these films, all of which betray a 'hetero'-bias not just in the sense of 'heterosexist' but also in the sense of almost paranoically promoting difference *per se*.

Notes

1. I use the word 'lesbian' (as adjective and noun) and 'lesbianism' in address to a twenty-first-century readership, but am aware of its anachronism in reference to inter-female desire before the nineteenth century. Before that, words such as 'tribade'/'tribadism' or 'sapphism' would have been used.

2. It is not irrelevant to note the preponderance of American women writers, intellectuals and artists in the broadest of senses who made of Paris their literal as well as spiritual home in the 1920s. The most iconic of these was, of course, Natalie Clifford Barney, a lesbian writer and millionairess whose salon became the principal lesbian locus of the period. For an interesting filmic exploration of this phenomenon, see Greta Schiller's *Paris Was Á Woman* (US, 1995).

3. Dialogue is given in English without the French original, since I have only been able to obtain a dubbed version of the film.

4. As I have explained elsewhere, in *Memnon* (1868) Karl Heinrich Ulrichs defined the male homosexual character as the soul of a woman trapped in the body of a man and the female homosexual as the soul of a man trapped in a woman's body. The 'man-woman' theory, also known variously as the 'Zwischenstufen', the 'Third Sex' or the 'Intermediate Sex' theory, became the most widely accepted conceptualisation of homosexuality in the late nineteenth and early twentieth centuries. It was assimilated and disseminated by other influential sexologists such as Hirschfeld, Krafft-Ebing and Ellis, prevailing for many years among practically all European sexologists.

5. Interestingly, the movie being made in the diegesis is a re-make of Louis Feuillade's 1915 classic noir film *Les Vampires*, and the title of Assayas's film, *Irma Vep*, is an anagram of 'vampire'. For discussion of the vampire within lesbian iconography and filmography, see Chapter 2 above.

6. Jeander, ' "Les abysses": un drame sordide qui a aussi un sens caché', *Libération*, 27 April 1963.

7. Françoise Mallet-Joris, *Le Rempart des Béguines* (Paris: Julliard, 1951). In a recent interview with Mallet-Joris, Hélène de Monferrand, herself a renowned lesbian novelist (in both senses of the collocation: she is lesbian-identified and she thematises lesbianism in her novels), described *Le Rempart des Béguines* as 'un roman d'apprentissage', a definition endorsed by Mallet-Joris. (Hélène de Monferrand, 'Promenade dans l'œuvre de Françoise Mallet-Joris', *Lesbia Magazine*, June 2004, pp. 22–6 [24–5]).

8. Emmanuèle Frois, 'Diane Kurys ou l'amour vache', *Le Figaro*, 28 September 1994.

9. Maurice Fabre, 'Elisabeth Bourgine joue les incendiaires dans une boîte à bac', *France-Soir*, 31 May 1986.

10. The reasons for that restriction are complex. The most intelligible explanation may derive from observations articulated by Nancy Chodorow, helpfully summarised by Richard Dyer:

Chodorow stresses the fact that both boys and girls in this society form their first bond with a woman, the mother figure, and this is fundamental in establishing gender identity. Boys learn their anatomical difference from the mother and hence notions of autonomy, separation and uniqueness are central to male identity, whereas girls know their anatomical identity with the mother, and so notions of connection, relatedness, fusion and blurring characterise female identity. (Dyer 1990: 192–3)

Within the logic of Chodorow's argument, it follows that inter-female relations will be more inclined towards fusion than inter-male relations.

11. It is interesting to note how Franju has altered the words Mauriac ascribed to Thérèse through free indirect style:

> il fallait qu'[Anne] sût, comme Thérèse, que le bonheur n'existe pas. Si elles ne possèdent rien d'autre en commun, qu'elles aient au moins cela: l'ennui, l'absence de toute tâche haute, de tout devoir supérieur, l'impossibilité de rien attendre que les basses habitudes quotidiennes, – un isolement sans consolations. (François Mauriac, *Thérèse Desqueyroux* [Paris: Grasset, 1927]. I refer here to the Livre de Poche edition of 1989, p. 45)
> [it was necessary [for Anne], like Thérèse, to know that happiness does not exist. If they should possess nothing else in common, let them at least have that: boredom, the absence of any noble task, any higher duty, the impossibility of expecting anything but base daily habits – an isolation without consolation.]

Whereas in this original it is happiness in general which Thérèse does not want Anne to experience, in Franju's version it is love – arguably, a love that could usurp her place in Anne's affections. The opposite reading would be that Thérèse does not want Anne to experience love with another since Thérèse herself cannot have that experience with another – an other than Anne? And why not with Anne – because that would be a forbidden love? The two readings, apparently polarised, start to seem curiously proximate.

12. Henry Rabine, 'Les Biches', *La Croix*, 4 April 1968; my emphasis.
13. *Les Lettres françaises*, 28 March 1968.
14. Claude-Marie Trémois, 'Dominique Laourier', *Télérama*, 21 September 1974.
15. 'Céline et Julie vont en bateau', *Le Monde*, 24 September 1974.
16. 'Jacques Baratier, L'arraignée de satin', *Le Monde*, 1 April 1986.
17. Louis-Guy Lemieux, 'La femme de l'hôtel c'est . . . Léa Pool', *Québec, Le Soleil*, samedi, 10 novembre 1984.
18. Catherine Deneuve's status as a lesbian icon has antecedents in her role in *Belle de jour* (1967: see Chapter 2 above), but is most associated with her performance in the anglophone Tony Scott's 1983 hit, *The Hunger*. However, she maintains a publicly heterosexual lifestyle, and even initiated legal action against an American lesbian magazine which had taken the title *Deneuve*. In an out-of-court settlement in 1996, its name was changed to *Curve*. Defending herself against the charge of homophobia, Deneuve stated: 'it is a lesbian magazine, so lesbians will think I am suing them. It's not true. It does not

matter what the product is – whether it is perfume or a magazine. My name is a commodity, and you cannot put it on something without my permission. It is not fair. I hope people will understand the real issue here' ('Catherine Deneuve: The Ultimate Lesbian Icon Breaks Her Silence', *The Advocate*, 25 July 1995).

19. Michel Pascal, 'Entretien avec André Téchiné', *Le Point*, 17 August 1996.
20. I am grateful to Durham Modern Languages Series for permission to reproduce here certain comments on *La Répétition* from my chapter in Günther and Michallat (eds) 2006.
21. These reviews are too numerous to be cited in their entirety; the following two examples provide a flavour of their tone and focus: 'narcissisme exacerbé . . .' [exaggerated narcissism] (Frédéric Bonnaud, 'La Répétition', *Les Inrockuptibles*, 22 March 2001); 'Ce que cherchent les deux personnages de la *Répétition*, ce sont moins des garçons (ils ne font que passer) que le reflet de chacune d'elle dans le regard de l'autre' [What the two characters in La Répétition are seeking is not so much men (they only appear fleetingly) as the reflection of each in the other's gaze] (J.-M.L., 'Coups de théâtre', *Libération*, 15 May 2001).
22. Corsini in interview, in DVD extra (my emphasis).
23. *Les Temps modernes*, 6 April 1963.
24. Albert Cervoni, 'Les abysses', *La France nouvelle*, 1 May 1963.
25. Marie-Noëlle Tranchant, 'Une biographie des profondeurs', *Le Figaro*, 22 November 2000.
26. 'Sœurs Papin, films frères', *Les Inrockuptibles*, 21 November 2000.
27. Gide 1924: Folio edition 30.
28. Michèle Nevert, 'Touch Me', *Spirale*, October 1984.
29. Oliver is referring to the article 'Julia Kristeva in Conversation with Rosalind Coward', *Desire, ICA Documents*, 1984, pp. 22–7 (24).
30. See particularly her 'Misère de la psychanalyse', in Irigaray 1985; first published in *Critique*, 365, October 1977.
31. First delivered as a paper at the Fifth Quebec colloquium on mental health, 31 May 1980 in Montreal.
32. Charles Baudelaire, *Les Fleurs du mal* (Paris: Poulet-Malassis, 1857), first edition.
33. J.-L.M., ' "Anne Trister" peint', *La Croix*, 24 July 1986.
34. Claude-Marie Trémois, 'Anne Trister ... et Louise Marleau', *Télérama*, 30 July 1986.
35. J.-L.M., ibid.
36. B.B., 'Emporte-moi. L'adolescence revisitée de Léa Pool', *Le Figaro*, 3 August 1999.

CHAPTER FOUR

Girls on the Edge: Liminality

This chapter forms a hermeneutic of films in which lesbian desire is a borderline case, situated on the edges of intelligibility. It scrutinises two discrete categories of filmic moments: those that mediate desire between women as implicit or latent; and, to a lesser extent (lesser only because there is less germane material available), those in which desire between women forms a queer rather than an unproblematically lesbian current. Whilst wary of unrestrained voluntarism, and certainly not intent on imagining lesbian desire as a truly constant if censored presence in French and Francophone cinema, I consider the points made by Lynda Hart below to be seminal:

> 'Until recently,' D. A. Miller writes, 'homosexuality offered not just the most prominent – it offered the only subject matter whose representation . . . appertained exclusively to the shadow kingdom of connotation, where insinuations could be at once developed and denied.' Consigned to the realm of connotation, homosexuality is constitutively dubious. . . . Those who believe in the text's one true meaning (Barthes's 'philologists') insist on the primacy of denotation. Those whom Barthes names the semiologists challenge the elevation of the denotative over the connotative, pointing out that the former is merely a system like any other. Barthes wants to rescue connotation from both sets of criticism, retaining it as a 'computable trace of a certain plural of the text (that limited plural of the classic text)'. . . . Once in motion, connotation is promiscuous, insatiable, and aggressive. . . . Homosexuality is thus most prominently represented when it is virtually under erasure. . . . But is it not precisely in the undecidability . . . of women's relationships that much of the pleasure lies *between* women? The continuum of desire, the absence of discernment, is what makes lesbianism a 'writerly' text. (Hart 1994: 66)[1]

By 'writerly', Hart refers to a well-established concept in literary criticism. In *S/Z* (1970), Roland Barthes distinguished between (usually realist) texts that are merely *lisible* (readable), involving no genuine participation from the reader other than the consumption of a fixed meaning, and texts that are *scriptible* (writerly): more fragmentary or dislocated writings, which challenge the reader to participate in creating textual meanings rather than just consuming them. Whilst the specificity of the filmic as opposed to the literary medium should be respected, Barthes's distinction may reasonably be applied to the former as well as to the latter, for the base-line is that certain films, just like certain written texts, encourage compliant consumption and others a more dynamic role from the spectator in the forging of meanings. This base-line certainly informed theoretical discourse on film from the late 1960s and 1970s: *Cahiers du cinéma* and then *Screen* did an immense amount of work on subject-positioning and its implications for the politics of spectatorship.[2] For our purposes, what is of interest is the creation of 'lesbian' meanings from filmic material which is connotational as opposed to denotational, covert as opposed to overt, *scriptible* as opposed to *lisible*. My one dissent from Hart relates to her rhetorical question '[b]ut is it not precisely in the undecidability . . . of women's relationships that much of the pleasure lies *between* women?' As in my reaction to Clare Whatling below, I resist what might bluntly be termed the 'pis-aller' school of lesbian spectatorship, for it seems to me that the valorisation of the 'undecidability . . . of women's relationships' may turn out to be nothing more than making a virtue of necessity. Yes, it is true that the lesbian spectator in French/francophone, as in anglophone cinema, has few unambiguously lesbian scenarios in which to revel, and the politically motivated trend of appropriation is understandable; but let us not subordinate intellectual lucidity to an automatic privileging of the undecidable, the un(remark)able *per se*. To do so might well be to foreclose or at least to limit the creation of less compromised envisionings.

Chapter 1 stressed that theories of appropriative lesbian spectatorship and its resisting readings are not such a new phenomenon as we might think: as Julia Erhart observes, the value of subtexting or reading against the grain was signalled by the editors of the 'Lesbian and Film' section of *Jump Cut* which appeared as early as 1981 (Erhart 1997: 86). More recently, Tamsin Wilton has argued that

> [w]atching a film is clearly hard work for the lesbian spectator. To read much lesbian film theory is to understand lesbian spectatorship as a constant struggle to insist on and locate 'lesbian' as a reading/viewing position. This is in itself a mighty battle, in the teeth of Freudian/Lacanian film theory which sets up a rigidly (one might say, anxiously) gendered polarity whereby the unstable, multiple inflections of genders, sexualities and desires are mercilessly beaten into the square hole of heterosexuality. . . . The lesbian spectator is forced to defend herself against a plethora of fantastic phallocentric

assumptions that psychoanalysis has bred, and that have become influential even within feminism. . . . In arguing for a more complex model of cinema spectatorship, I am suggesting that we need to separate gender identity from sexuality, too often conflated in the name of sexual difference. Unless the separation that Stacey advocates occurs, the unfortunate lesbian viewer is doomed in film theory to ricochet back and forth between 'castrated male' and 'fetishized phallic female', existing only as an antidote to male anxiety . . . (Wilton 1995: 157–8)

I contend that what constrains the lesbian viewer into such ricocheting is no more than the presumption that the cinematic gaze can only be male. As argued in Chapter 1, this presumption is historically contingent rather than ahistorically necessary, as is its forcing of the lesbian subject-position into that of 'castrated male' and 'fetishised phallic female'. To put it bluntly, lesbian viewers do not need to be theorised in relation to men and their phallic-castratory anxieties. If lesbians are not women in the heteronormative acceptation of the word 'woman', they most certainly are not men, and they can certainly desire a woman on screen without doing so from a so-called masculine subject position, whatever that might mean (the unicity of the masculine subject being no less a fallacy that that of the feminine).

Two years after Wilton, Whatling brought a refreshingly non-anguished perspective to the debate which went beyond the adolescence of lesbian film criticism and its infatuation with the paternal authority of psychoanalysis, arguing for the liberatory effect of the covert lesbian inscription over the overt:

And let us not underestimate the spectatorial pleasure that results from the piecing together of the lingering looks, the long smiles and the moments of finger-tips barely touching that form the covert lesbian subtext of such films. . . . In addition, it is precisely because such films work at the level of the covert, depending on the individual viewer's subcultural knowledge to piece together the lesbian coding within the text . . . that these films vindicate the lesbian viewer of any responsibility for the veracity (or otherwise) of the representation. As distinct from the overt 'lesbian' text whose burden of representation we carry with us (Does it represent us fairly, if not will all lesbians be equated with its assumptions? Am I embarrassed by the images unveiled? Am I at least so anxious at the thought of being misrepresented that I cannot even enjoy the images when attractive to me? All questions which apply to lesbian-produced or lesbian-featured images), the covert representation of lesbianism as, for instance, platonic friendship, at least allows us to make of it what we want. Since we owe the dominant cinema nothing, in one sense its images are up for grabs, there for us to make of them what we will. What the covert text also offers us of course is the thrill of the

forbidden, the nostalgic sense of lesbianism as taboo, its images, rendered
covertly, for our eyes only. (Whatling 1997: 89)

Before turning to Whatling's 'thrill of the forbidden' (and questioning its
political implications), this chapter will consider certain less exhilarating
permutations on the liminally lesbian model. It will analyse these permutations in the following order: location of lesbian desire in an outsider
figure; disavowal of lesbian identification despite obvious lesbian desire;
the frequent influence of men or of the masculine, including the role of
men when visibly present – typically, in triangular structures; women's
defection from a lesbian relationship into the arms of a man through bad
faith/internalised lesbophobia; machismo in butch lesbian characters; the
lesbian figure and/or couple as eroticised object of the voyeuristic male
gaze within the diegesis; and, finally, the role of men through their *absence*,
giving rise to the possibility of an all-female space. Thereafter, it will focus
on filmic moments which play on that thrill of the forbidden. It should be
understood that the epithet 'liminal' is sometimes more text-based and
sometimes more to do with the potential perceptions and creations of the
hypothetical resisting 'reader'/spectator. Most notably, in the case of triangulations the liminality is merely a function of that set structure, and
does not by any means always lend itself to particularly lesbo-appropriative readings.

First, then, location of lesbian desire in an outsider figure is effected by
François Ozon's *Huit femmes* (2002). Among Ozon's eponymous eight
women, all played by either established or rising female stars, two stand out
in a lesbian spectatorial context: Catherine Deneuve for her lesbian icon-
icity (see Chapter 3, note 18), and Fanny Ardant for the punning potential
of her name. Ozon situates lesbian desire mainly in socially marginalised
characters such as the exoticised black housekeeper Chanel (Firmine
Richard), the lower-class maid Louise (Emmanuelle Béart), and Chanel's
great love Pierrette (Fanny Ardant) who, although of bourgeois origin, has
a murky past as a louche nude dancer and, it is insinuated, prostitute.
Chanel's passive devotion to Pierrette and her victimhood smack dubiously
of the black slave/white owner archetype: she abjectly begs Pierrette to
forgive her for being jealous, is pushed roughly to the ground for her pains,
and declines to defend herself. Louise the maid's admission that she loved
her female ex-employer, whose photo she keeps on her person, comes as
something of a shock since her function within the narrative economy
hitherto has been mainly that of mistress to master of the house Marcel.
Despite her ravishing beauty according to conventional feminine canons,
she is also, in class terms, an outsider. Further, her participation as mistress

5. Star gazing: in *Huit femmes* (2001), four out of eight celebrity actresses play women with lesboerotic leanings (see Chapter 4). Canal +/Fidelite Productions/The Kobal Collection/Moireau, Jean-Claude

to the adulterous Marcel in the deconstruction of bourgeois veneers is ver-
tiginously fortified by the revelation of her non-complicity in hetero-
norms. In contrast to the lower-class women's relative moral integrity, the
originally middle-class Pierrette shows classic bourgeois bad faith. In
attempting to seduce middle-class, married Gaby (Catherine Deneuve),
Pierrette presents her own lesbian past as a *pis-aller*, a compensation for
and refuge from dissatisfaction with men. In recommending a lesbian
adventure to Gaby, she again presents it in relation to men rather than an
independent choice: 'L'amour entre deux femmes n'a rien de choquant.
C'est même un plaisir que vous devriez essayer pour vous laver des
hommes' ['There's nothing shocking about love between two women. I'd
even say it's a pleasure that you should try in order to get men out of your
system']. The camera then focuses on her suggestive trailing of finger up
Gaby's fur-clad arm and shoulder as she archly alludes to 'complicité féminine' ['female complicity']. Ironically, yet coherent with the heteronormative discursive economy reflected by the film, what triggers sexual activity
as opposed to mere innuendo is rivalry over a man. Gaby moves to shoot
Pierrette, they struggle bodily for the gun (classic symbol of the penis, and,
in the chain of signifiers, of phallic mastery), and then their hostility suddenly transmutes into carnal desire. As they hold the clinch, the camera
highlights their breasts rubbing together, Pierrette mounting Gaby,
holding down her wrists and kissing her passionately. Cue kitschly sugary,
non-diegetic music to convey a sense of utopic magical pleasure. That pleasure is utopic in the sense of a no-place within the Symbolic Order – an
Order to which they both cling, for as soon as the other characters enter
the room, the lesboerotic dalliance is liquidated and disavowed.

The second permutation mentioned in the typology above was disavowal
of lesbian identification in spite of obvious lesbian desire. Marie in André
Téchiné's *Les Voleurs* (1996) and Ariane in Stéphane Giusti's *Pourquoi pas
moi?* (1999) show less bad faith than Téchiné's Gaby, but both refute
explicit identification as lesbian despite their obvious sexual attraction to
women. When asked 'Vous n'aimez que les femmes?' ['Are you only
attracted to women?'], Marie ripostes in a depoliticised register fairly
typical of the French context (see Chapter 1), 'Les femmes, je sais pas, mais
Juliette, sûrement' ['I don't know about women in general, but Juliette, certainly']. And in *Pourquoi pas moi* Ariane's political myopia under the guise
of liberal individualism is marked. She declares to her girlfriend Camille,
'Je n'aime pas *les* filles, Camille, je t'aime toi' ['I'm not attracted to girls in
general, Camille, I'm attracted to *you*']. Camille's retort implies the need
to prioritise the political: 'Je suis une fille, Ariane, donc, politiquement,

tu aimes les filles, forcément' ['I'm a girl, Ariane, so, in political terms, of course you're attracted to girls']. Later on, Ariane insists that she never consciously chose between her former straight life and Camille. Of course, a queer advocate would vindicate both Marie and Ariane's refusal of fixed sexual identifications. The plea of Camille's mother Josepha (herself heterosexual) to Ariane to show a bit more 'solidarité communautaire' ['solidarity with the community'] counters the queer optic by implying the strategic necessity of identity politics for vulnerable minority communities, but the force of her argument is, unfortunately, neutralised by her function as caricatural vehicle for sending up politically correct straight sympathisers with the gay cause. Josepha loses credibility by her dilettantish approach to gay history, referring to 'Strangewall' instead of Stonewall and insisting there must have been martyrs killed there. (In an anglophone context, the chiming of 'strange' with queer is a delectable detail.)

Is such depoliticisation and its attendant potential for rendering lesbianism invisible[3] more typical of male representations of lesbian desire in film? My answer, in good Derridean spirit, always already provisional, is: on the whole, yes, for rather obvious reasons: particular sexual acts that temporarily derogate from the masculine monopoly are less threatening than assumption of a (supposedly) permanent identity which axiomatically excludes the masculine. The French Republican tradition of hostility to sexual identity politics also plays a part here, but it should be noted that this tradition co-exists with French culture's inveterate if unacknowledged privileging of the masculine.[4] One could further complicate the question by noting that Téchiné is gay, and that Giusti used to be – his reconversion to straightdom apparently having occurred during the filming of *Pourquoi pas moi?*,[5] but to avoid tightening the conceptual knot I will leave this additional point in abeyance. Téchiné's lead actress Catherine Deneuve reinforced Giusti's depoliticised position in an interview given to *L'Express*: when asked if acting a 'femme homosexuelle' ['homosexual woman'] had seemed so risky she had hesitated about accepting the role, she replied that for her, Marie was not homosexual, but merely in love with someone who happened to be a woman.

Lesbia Magazine, the main mouthpiece for lesbian reception since 1982, provided two contrasting viewpoints on *Les Voleurs*. Jacqueline Pasquier implied a silencing of the feminine:

> Rien de ce qui a pu se passer entre elles n'est dévoilé, et donc leurs motivations restent très floues. C'est donc parce que ces femmes n'ont pas le droit de s'exprimer, de parler de leur amour, que nous sommes déçues. Encore.[6]

[Nothing of what may have happened between them is revealed, so their motivation remains very unclear. It's thus because these women are denied the right to express themselves, to talk about their love, that we are disappointed. Yet again.]

However, she elevated this French filmic mediation of lesbianism over anglophone counterparts: 'Ceci dit, au moins ça change de "lesbienne-comme-meurtrière-un-peu-cinglée" du cinema du Commonwealth'[7] ['That said, at least it's a change from the "lesbian-as-slightly-crazy-murderer" that you get in the cinema of the Commonwealth'] – and it is interesting that the two stigmatising models she vilifies in anglophone films are hardly absent from French and francophone films, as Chapters 2 and 3 of the present study testify. Catherine Gonnard was more adamantly unimpressed:

l'amour au féminin se termine toujours mal et Téchiné ne déroge pas à la règle vieille comme le cinéma: une bonne lesbienne est une lesbienne morte. Téchiné aime les femmes et ça se voit! Deneuve ne croit pas à son personnage, nous non plus d'ailleurs.[8]

[love between women always ends badly and Téchiné doesn't depart from this rule, which is as old as the cinema: a good lesbian is a dead lesbian. Téchiné likes women and it's obvious! Deneuve doesn't believe in the character she plays, and nor do we.]

My third permutation was the frequent influence of men or of the masculine, which is arguably the most common seme in liminally lesbian configurations. The following analysis will centre first on the role of men when visibly present, in triangulations involving two women and one man. Terry Castle's assertion in her study of literature may have some relevance to our filmic corpus here:

by plotting against what Eve Sedgwick has called the 'plot of male homosociality', the archetypal lesbian fiction decanonizes, so to speak, the canonical structure of desire itself. Insofar as it documents a world in which men are 'between women' rather than vice versa, it is an insult to the conventional geometries of fictional eros. (Castle 1993: 90–1)

Before the (so-called) sexual revolution following 1968, French films[9] featuring lesbian desire certainly corresponded to Castle's literary archetype. Before 1968, for obvious socio-economic reasons, a lesbian relation entirely independent of men was virtually unimaginable for the directors in question, virtually all of whom were male. To the extent that these films do show men ' "between women" rather than vice versa', they may indeed be construed as 'an insult to the conventional geometries of fictional eros'. This is not, however, to argue for their overwhelmingly subversive impact, because narrative resolution nearly always returned the insult and reinstated heteronormative order. More resonant for our corpus, perhaps, is what Valerie Traub says of the triangular structure in the anglophone movie *Black Widow* (1986):

> Spectator desires for narrative congruity and coherence thus battle with the heterosexist framework that disallows 'lesbian' desire as a possible reality. From a 'lesbian' perspective, Reni's offer of Paul to Alex is not merely a coercive gesture; in inverting the male homosocial system by which women are exchanged between men, Paul's body becomes a courier, communicating indirectly those desires that Reni and Alex cannot express. (Traub 1991: 315)

From a total corpus of thirteen films, I will discuss textual clusters grouped together according to the ways in which the triangle is finally 'resolved' (or not). The resisting lesbian reader will find this section relatively fallow ground, for the simple reason that the liminal here is more to do with that triangular structure than with the potential for spectatorial appropriation.

First, let us examine the three trios which ultimately excise the male figure. In the Belgian Harry Kümel's *Les Lèvres rouges* (1971), the desiring circuit runs between newly married couple Valérie and Stefan and Hungarian countess/vampire Elisabeth, who cynically charms both, the better to wrest wife from husband. Yet this is not such a simple victory over heteronormativity as it may seem. Superficially, Stefan appears at least intermittently to represent the worst of patriarchal excesses, for he gradually becomes viciously misogynous: for example, attacking Valérie with a belt. But what is intriguing is that this attack occurs just after his 'mother' has remonstrated with him for having married Valérie: the so-called mother, as we see through the cross-cutting of shots of them on the phone, is in fact a man in drag, which proliferates the queer potentialities of the film. Is Stefan a repressed gay man? If so, his marriage represents the paradigm of the closet produced by heteronormativity, and viscerally demonstrates its noxious potential: an excessive *mimétisme* of masculine supremacy over, and abuse of, women. Perhaps more disturbingly still, his character alludes to a virulent misogyny popularly, if erroneously, identified with certain gay men for whom women are not only dispensable but despicable. Finally, it is of crucial importance that the remaining lesbian dyad is – symptomatically – destroyed by the narrative, through the spectacularly gruesome death of Elisabeth.

Extra-textually, the hegemony of the heteronormative is also presaged by Joy Fleury's *Tristesse et beauté* (1985), for the promotional copy on the video jacket-cover foregrounds Hugo's wish to re-establish contact with his ex-lover Léa. This copy is highly misleading, since the film's affective centre of gravity is the love borne by Prudence, a talented young sculptress, for the now established artist Léa, and, more importantly in narrative terms, Prudence's resolve to avenge Léa of the long-term damage caused her by Hugo's rejection. Prudence's revenge stratagem includes engineering a situation in which she has sex with Hugo but sets him up for humiliation, appearing to find intercourse painful, stopping him touching her breasts, then crying out 'Léa!' – at which he, along with his member, slumps. And her declared intent to destroy Hugo's family is tragically fulfilled by her luring out his infatuated son Martin onto the sea, where he drowns. The death also appears to confer closure for Léa on her painful relationship with Hugo: she bestows a compassionate, non-desirous kiss upon him, then turns to Prudence whose face she strokes gently, causing the younger woman to regain consciousness. Léa has finally made her choice, and the solemnity of that decision is emphasised by the blue filter of the closing scene, in which Prudence is literally brought back to life.

Third in the group of films ultimately excluding the male coordinate from the trio is Christine Lipinska's *Le Cahier volé* (1993),[10] in which the triangle has a genuinely structuring function. Set in summer 1945, the film explores schoolgirl Virginie's love for two young men and a young woman, Anne. Anne's sexual possessiveness is signalled early on by her baleful interruption of a playfully erotic interchange between Virginie and the two young men; but Virginie wants to have hetero-sex for heuristic reasons, 'pour voir' ['just to see']. More macho than Maurice, Jacques exercises his right to hetero-patriarchal supremacy by publicly humiliating Virginie through reading out to the small-minded villagers diary extracts in which she has recorded details of her sexual relationship with Anne. Sex with him is an anti-climax for Virginie, who merely wants rid of her (hetero)virginity, and the narrative ultimately establishes beyond doubt that her love for Anne, both amorous and erotic, far surpasses her mere attraction to the two young men.

Yet working against this narrative grain is the incongruous voice-over at the end of the film. A male voice refers to a trio which is similar to the diegetically inscribed one but bears different names (Violette instead of Anne, Louis instead of Jacques . . .), and suggests that the woman and the two men had, for her (Virginie), been one person only, an ideal first love, sometimes a man, sometimes a woman. Thus the lesbo-affirmative logic of the narrative economy is traduced by a masculine-authored bracketing of the central lesbian love with, at best, an edulcorated androgyny. And, even more lamentably, that lesbian love is stereotypically condemned to the ultimate fate of death: as *Lesbia Magazine* remarked, 'pour les auteures comme pour les cinéastes, les amours lesbiennes sont rarement heureuses . . . *Le Cahier volé* ne déroge pas à la règle'[11] ['for women authors as for directors, lesbian loves are rarely happy . . . *Le Cahier volé* is no exception to this rule']. Anne's suicide, driven by parental interdiction on her love for Virginie, is narratively and ideologically double-edged, for it may be read either as an indictment of societal strictures on same-sex love, or as yet one more contribution to a noxious cultural cliché.

Within the corpus of films featuring triangulations, the first of the three scripting a centrifugal implosion whereby all three (the two women and the one man) go their separate ways is Jean Rollin's *Fascination* (1979), a vampire movie set in 1905. Seeking refuge from his aggressors in an apparently deserted château, professional thief Marc chances upon the mysterious couple formed by Elisabeth and Eva, who take pleasure in each other's bodies and are visually encoded as hyper-feminine (wearing frilly, flouncy white dresses, giggling and simpering in front of Marc). Both women also appear to experience a fleeting attraction to Marc, with Eva taking the physical lead, but purportedly only the better to entrap him for the all-female vampiric feast on which the film culminates. It is unclear whether Elisabeth is jealous of Marc for getting Eva's sexual attention or vice versa, for she appears to be falling for him, and later declares she loves him. This heterosexual love is, however, negated at the very end of the film by her statement that she never really loved him. Lesbo-eroticism is seen to be generalised in the secret company of women who assemble for the midnight cannibalistic orgy: two other women are framed kissing sensually on the lips, and a further (Hélène) comes on to Elisabeth. However, the fact that several of the women also evince attraction to Marc suggests again that the presence of a man at best compromises, at worst enucleates lesboeroticism.

The second centrifugal implosion of the triangle occurs in French Canadian Léa Pool's *La Femme de l'hôtel* (1984), where to begin with the triangulation is highly atypical. Instead of a straight man infiltrating a lesboerotic dyad, we have a gay man (Simon) used as a courier (cf. Valerie Traub on Bob Rafelson's *Black Widow* above) for the expression of unavowable desire between his sister, director Andréa, and the eponymous 'femme de l'hôtel', Estelle. As we have seen in Chapter 3, Michèle Nevert's review adeptly captures the ontological complexity of this inter-female desire, along with its possible imbrication in incestuous sibling desire. Howard Feinstein for his part draws attention to the autofictional basis of this atypical trio, citing Pool's observation 'The triangle is always present in my films', a point to which I will return in discussion of one of Pool's later films, *Emporte-moi* (1999).

The third instance of centrifugal implosion is found in Philippe Faucon's *Muriel fait le désespoir de ses parents*, which premiered on the French cultural TV channel Arte in 1995 and was only released in cinemas in December 1997. Tracing the eponymous teenager Muriel's assumption of a lesbian identity, the film focuses mainly on her attraction to straight-identified Nora. Nora's boyfriend Fred is about the most lesbo-friendly one could hope for in a young man obviously desirous not just of his girlfriend but also, more obliquely, of Muriel. Significantly, this tolerance is located in a black youth, countering common perceptions of black men as more macho and (hetero)sexist than the majority of their white counterparts. He chooses the single bed in a hotel room, leaving the double to the two girls. But he also buys Muriel a short dress, saying he's fed up seeing her in trousers, which could be interpreted as an effort to feminise and annex her to his Symbolic territory. Further, he seeks confirmation of his privileged place in Nora's desiring hierarchy by asking if she prefers his or Muriel's caresses. He then asks, 'Tu as envie d'essayer avec elle? T'oses pas?' ['Do you want to try it with her? Afraid to?'] His motives are opaque; is he genuinely trying to get her to embrace her authentic desires regardless of their social risks, or merely playing some kind of game? Nora replies with (her now familiar) prevarication and potential bad faith: 'Mais non, c'est pas ça mais . . . des fois j'ai un peu peur de ce qui risque d'arriver entre nous trois' ['No, no, it's not that, but . . . sometimes I'm a bit scared of what might happen between the three of us']. So, she acknowledges the dangers of their triadic attraction, but omits to confirm her sexual desire for Muriel; moreover, she ostensibly weights the balance in Fred's favour by adding that she doesn't like it when he hugs Muriel too closely. Yet to the audience (and even conceivably to the eavesdropping Muriel), the equation could be inverted here and the jealousy attributed to Muriel's wanting Fred rather than her, Nora.

Inexorably, the narrative works towards implosion of the triad. When first Fred then Muriel kiss the sleeping Nora, wondering if she will notice the difference, Nora wakens and fails signally to appreciate the joke. After Muriel has tactfully retreated, Nora asks Fred sarcastically if he'd like a *ménage à trois* and warns him that he will have to choose. Through ellipsis and the subsequent turn of the narrative, we conclude that Fred and Nora have split up and that Nora and Muriel have become estranged. Yet the rupture with Nora proves salutary, for it opens the path to a less closeted relationship with Caroline, a girl with whom she had exchanged smiles at a party before the row with Nora. This time, in creating a lesboerotic dyad rather than acquiescing in a dubiously 'queer' triad of others' making, Muriel has assumed agency rather than let others shape her sexual subjectivity.

The first of the two films which ultimately maintain the delicate balance of the trio with the male figure as its anchoring-point is Guy Casaril's *Emilienne et Nicole* (1970). Here, Castle's 'conventional geometries of fictional eros' are structurally destabilised, but ideologically, masculinity is accorded ultimate victory. Claude is just as sexually attracted as his wife Emilienne to the interloper in their marriage, the comically named (for an anglophone viewer at least, 'nooky' being a slang term for sexual activity) Nouky – indeed, their heterosexual relations ante-date the two women's lesbian relations. The camera iterates and reiterates triangular structures, or rather, invasions of a dyad by a third party. Early on in the narrative, Emilienne is framed outside the door (privileged sign of liminality) behind which Nicole and Claude are having sex; shortly afterwards, when Nouky turns up at Emilienne's home and performs cunnilingus (teasingly suggested though not actually shown by the camera), a point-of-view shot from the perspective of the peeping [-Tom] Claude subsequently shows the two women kissing, their outstretched bodies in close-up as they mutually caress. Typical of the soft porn 'lesbian' movie designed to titillate straight men, the conversation reverts to men even at a lesbian nightclub where the two women have just kissed. When at Emilienne's behest Nouky moves into the marital home, the male viewer identifying with Claude is treated to kitsch wish-fulfilment. Claude has two attractive women, and his sexual gratification is humorously symbolised in being kissed by both after he has fallen flat on his face into an oozing cream cake; when the two women rush upstairs, he pursues them and is welcomed with a plethora of kisses. And when Nouky has a baby by Claude, his situation again gratifies the 'ideal'[12] (read, traditionally masculine) viewer: he has two women, and his baby son two mothers (cf. *Gazon maudit*, particularly with respect to the scene of straight-slanted family bliss in cooing over the baby). Whilst the threesome experiences various unilateral ruptures, the narrative ends with a visual mediation of reunion, via a medium close-up shot of the three naked: the two women face each other, nipples aligned, but the man is in the literal and symbolic centre, gripping both and sporting a fatuously proud grin. Fundamentally, the bond between the two women, whilst durable, is always subordinate to Claude's dominion. Of crucial importance is the fact that Claude's voice-over shapes the spectator's interpretation of otherwise ambiguous situations; the fact also that he, unlike the two women, is never on the outside: he remains central, the pivotal point. The whole film seems to cater for (some) straight men's abiding fascination with lesbian sex as, essentially, an arousing precursor or supplement to hetero-sex in which he reigns supreme.

6. *Gazon maudit* (1995): rare are such moments of unadulterated pleasure in French versions of sapphism on screen. The Kobal Collection

7. In *Gazon maudit* (1995), cheating husband Laurent sulks as bisexual wife Loli savours her own lover Marijo (see Chapter 4). The Kobal Collection

I have linked *Emilienne et Nicole* with *Gazon maudit* (1995), but Josiane Balasko's later film differentiates itself from Casaril's in two important ways: it is a *comédie de mœurs* rather than a soft core pornographic film, and it had far greater commercial success than Casaril's offering. Indeed, it is one of the few films in our corpus to have achieved international fame (some would say notoriety). *Femme* Loli, married to philandering Laurent by whom she has two small children, falls for dyke Marijo; a farcical three-some is formed as Laurent and Marijo vie for victory and Loli, in a fit of jealousy over Marijo's female ex, finally dumps Marijo, who then gets Laurent to impregnate her; Loli eventually welcomes Marijo and child back into the bosom of the family. I have commented before on the nor-malising effects of this supposedly comic *ménage à trois*: '[B]y the end of the film . . . the temporarily dislocated heterosexual family has been restored to its natural order, with its ability to accommodate extension and appendage simply serving to reiterate its perennial strength' (Cairns 1998: 232–3). This view has not changed; what I would like to add here is some reference to French lesbian reception of Balasko's box-office hit. Shortly after the film was released on 8 February 1995, three reviews appeared in *Lesbia Magazine*: one by Jacqueline Pasquier and two by Catherine Gonnard. Pasquier's is the only laudatory one of the three:

> Avec *Gazon maudit* on assiste à une évolution significative du ménage à trois . . . En 1995, le nouveau trio c'est le mari, la femme et la maîtresse de la femme. Pour porter à l'écran cette histoire audacieuse et la démarginaliser, Balasko a fui le ton dramatique, s'épargnant ainsi les nombreux pièges du sujet; son film 'grand public', et ce n'est pas péjoratif sous ma plume, est une comédie insolente, poussée volontairement jusqu'à la farce, ce qui permet à l'auteur d'aller en déça de son propos: une histoire d'amour homosexuelle peut arriver à toute femme mais aussi à tout homme. . . . Balasko raconte cette histoire d'amour simplement, avec tolérance, générosité, insolence, gaieté, invraisemblance, innocence, et même si le film comporte quelques longueurs on en sort gentiment 'décoiffé'.[13]
> [With *Gazon maudit* we witness an important evolution of the ménage à trois . . . In 1995, the new threesome is the husband, the wife and the wife's mistress. In order to make a film out of this daring story and to demargin-alise it, Balasko avoided a dramatic tone and thus avoided the numerous traps that the subject sets up; her film 'for the general public', and I don't mean that negatively, is a cheeky comedy, deliberately taken to the extremes of farce, which allows the author to go beyond her original aim: a homosexual love-affair can happen to any woman but also to any man. . . . Balasko tells this love story with simplicity, tolerance, generosity, insolence, gaiety, implausibility, innocence, and even if some parts of the film drag a bit, you emerge from the cinema totally inspired.]

It is interesting that one of Pasquier's points for praise – Balasko's suggestion that any woman, indeed any man, may experience homosexual love –
is, contrarily, a stance mocked by Gonnard in its erasure of lesbian
difference.[14] Gonnard's reviews lambaste the film on various fronts, often
to mordantly humorous effect. *Inter alia*, the first review ironises on the
cynical marketing of the film and its mendacious packaging of lesbianism
as a new vogue.[15] Her second review sends up the stereotypical yet domes-
ticating representation of the only 'true' dyke in the movie, Marijo (Loli
being seen as bisexual at best):

> Dès les premières images, on est rassuré: si la Marijo de Balasko est une
> 'camionneuse', elle l'est gentiment à l'instar de celles qui portent des polos
> colorés, un méga trousseau de clefs, fument des cigarillos, sont toujours
> prêtes à vous bricoler un truc qui ne fonctionne plus depuis des lustres, et
> ont un cœur d'or . . . C'est une goudou standard . . .[16]
> [From the very first images, we're reassured: if Balasko's Marijo is a 'bull-
> dyke', she's a nice one, like those who wear coloured polo shorts, carry a huge
> bunch of keys, smoke cigarillos, are always ready to fix something that hasn't
> worked for years, and have a heart of gold . . . She's your standard type
> of dyke . . .]

Gonnard's second review also denounces the improbability of Marijo's
sudden maternification (to be discussed in Chapter 5 below). For the
moment, it behoves us to ponder Gonnard's final point:

> j'ai bien peur que l'avancée que représente le film sur le personnage de la les-
> bienne, bien plus acceptable que dans la plupart des films où les pauvrettes
> finissent régulièrement très mal, ne soit bien minime même si enfin on
> découvre que l'on existe, que l'on n'est pas des erreurs de la nature et qu'une
> femme tout à fait 'normale' peut tomber sous le charme d'une 'camionneuse'
> même en ayant dans son lit un Don Juan de banlieue, car la Marijo ne change
> rien à l'ordre des choses, elle essaie seulement de s'y trouver une petite place.
> Les lesbiennes dans les harems, ou comme initiatrices des maîtresses de ces
> messieurs ont toujours été bien acceptées, ne l'oublions pas.[17]
> [I fear that the progress this films represents as far as the lesbian character
> goes, who here is far more acceptable than in most films, where the poor
> things often come to a very bad end, is in fact very minimal, even if we at last
> discover that we exist, that we're not an error of nature and that an entirely
> 'normal' woman can fall under the spell of a 'bull-dyke' even when she
> already has a small-time Don Juan in her bed. For Marijo doesn't change
> anything about the established order, she merely tries to mark out a little
> place for herself within it. Let us not forget that lesbians in harems, or as ini-
> tiators of the mistresses of these gentlemen, have always been accepted.]

The essence of Gonnard's charge here – that rather than threatening the established sexual regime, Marijo merely seeks accommodation within it – is convincing, particularly given her recuperation at the end of the film. A year later, *Lesbia Magazine* published a fourth review, this time by Véronique Lorin, who regrets the stereotypically butch representation of the 'real' lesbian, Marijo, and classes Loli as bisexual rather than lesbian. She dismisses the triangulation as tired old hat within popular French filmic formulae.[18] And her verdict, with which I concur, somewhat damns with faint praise, resigned as she is to the limitations of the hetero-norms of the mainstream film industry: 'Ceci dit, le film reste réussi, il est à la hauteur de ses ambitions: il nous divertit et nous fait rire, il ne faut pas en attendre plus' ['That said, the film remains a good one, it fulfils its ambitions: it entertains us and makes us laugh, and we shouldn't expect any more from it'].

Finally, I turn to the five films which ultimately excise one of the two women from the triad, allowing a heterosexual dyad to triumph. The sapphic semaphore in Henri-Georges Clouzot's *Les Diaboliques* (1954) was intercepted by two 1950s reviewers, if in symptomatically skittish parentheses: 'Nicole, bientôt, paraîtra prendre son amant en grippe et la femme en pitié (peut-être même un peu plus, laisserait entendre Clouzot, qui se souvient du rôle de Simone Renant dans *Quai des Orfèvres*)'[19] ['Nicole will soon take a sudden dislike to her lover and pity on the wife (perhaps even something more, implies Clouzot, remembering Simone Renant's role in *Quai des Orfèvres*)']; 'Un complot est ourdi par la femme et la maîtresse, unies dans leur rébellion contre leur tyran et par une complicité plus équivoque (on ne fait qu'effleurer cette trouble affection, heureusement)'[20] ['A plot is hatched by the wife and the mistress, who are united in their revolt against their tyrant and by a complicity that is more equivocal (fortunately, this dubious affection is only briefly hinted at)']. What evidence is there beyond that already adduced in Chapter 2 to support a reading against the heteronormative grain? First, when the poisoned Michel is put to bed by Christina and asks if the bed is hers or Nicole's, she replies 'Le nôtre' ['Ours']. Second, Nicole is mistaken for the headmaster when they return to the school with Michel's (supposedly) dead body, which generates the notion of Nicole assuming Michel's position as Christina's husband. Third, when even the hitherto indomitable Nicole is unnerved by apparent ghostly visitations and wants to leave the school, she resists the urge because she doesn't want to leave Christina on her own; turning from bellicose butch into feminised woman, she tearfully attempts to touch Christina, but Christina withdraws her hand, enjoining Nicole to leave and forget what's happened, just as the spectator is implicitly enjoined to forget the lesboerotic seeds sown by the film only to be erased by its implausible narrative resolution. The resisting lesbian spectator will feel fully vindicated by the knowledge that, contrary to Clouzot's heterosexualised ending (which unites Nicole with Michel as conspirators in Christine's death so that their own couple can prevail), in the novel on which Clouzot's film is based, *Celle qui n'était plus*,[21] 'it is the two women who are lovers seeking to eliminate the husband so they can run away together' (Hayward 2003: 9–10). To read against the grain may take some pluck given the film's voluntarily corrupt ending vis-à-vis the literary original, but that dénouement is so improbable and so imbued by sensationalist virtuoso that, quite simply, it fails to convince at least this spectator.

The lesbian coloration to the trio in Claude Chabrol's *Les Biches* was also acknowledged by a number of contemporary French reviewers upon the film's first release in 1968. The first of these reviewers was Jean-Louis Bory, whose own gay identification was perhaps not immaterial to such sensitivity. However, his relative lucidity was limited by its own episteme: 'Deux biches vivaient en paix, un cerf survint: tel est le thème, il relève de la fable populaire . . . Délicate balance de cet homme entre deux femmes dont l'une au moins est plus masculine que lui'[22] ['Two does lived peacefully, a stag appeared: such is the theme of the film, it's part of popular legend . . . This man is delicately balanced between two women of whom at least one is more masculine than he']. Given his historical positioning (March 1968, thus before *les événements* of May 1968), it is unsurprising that Bory insinuates Frédérique's status as lesbian by reference to her masculinity: prior to the cultural watershed at least heralded by if not embodied in the events of May 1968, and for some time afterwards, the notion of a non-lesbian masculinised woman was rare. Another gay male critic, Henry Chapier of the left-wing *Combat*, followed suit:

Premier chapitre pudique, romantique, et tendre sur ces moments lyriques et fragiles qui font le charme insolite des amitiés particulières: un monde remis, chaque soir et matin, en question, menacé par les regards d'autrui, et aussi par la tension de ces rapports privilégiés . . . Deuxième chapitre: un homme surgit . . . peu à peu, Frédérique découvre 'avec l'animal' le bonheur de toutes les femmes.[23]

[The first chapter is discreet, romantic, and tender in its treatment of those lyrical, fragile moments that form the unusual charm of 'special friendships': a world that day and night is called into question, threatened by the gaze of others, and also by the tension of these privileged relations . . . Second chapter: a man appears . . . little by little, Frédérique discovers 'with the animal' woman's true happiness.]

It should be noted that the collocation 'amitiés particulières' was a euphemism for a homosexual relationship at least as early as 1943, the publication date of Roger Peyrefitte's now famous *Les Amitiés particulières* which daringly portrayed sexual love between two schoolboys.[24] The temptation to read Chapier's comments as ironic is unsupported by the tone of his review in its entirety, which is earnestly laudatory. And *Les Nouvelles littéraires*, an establishment literary journal, was unashamedly heteronormative in its analysis, diagnosing lesbian desire as lack: 'En tout cas, [Chabrol] nous propose aujourd'hui une analyse psychologique qui n'est pas dépourvue de finesse, celle de deux filles que leurs jeux incomplets laissent insatisfaits et qui décident de s'offrir un beau mâle'[25] ['At any rate, [Chabrol] now offers us a psychological analysis which is not without subtlety, that of two girls whose incomplete games leave them unsatisfied and who decide to treat themselves to a handsome male'].

So, how exactly *is* power distributed between the three coordinates of the triangle in *Les Biches*? Largely unarticulated but visually obvious desire between Frédérique and the younger woman nicknamed Why turns sour when Why falls for Paul and Frédérique then steals him away from her. Why voluntarily adopts a servile role; Frédérique is still tactile with her, brushing her hand past Why's when she passes, caressing her forehead and her hair, but treats her, as does Paul, as subaltern. The tensions inherent in the triad become acute in a scene where the three get progressively more drunk, Why strokes Paul's hair, then Frédérique takes Why's hand. As the two women hold on to each other, their hands – that recurrent lesbian motif – significantly occupy the centre of the frame, thereby excluding Paul, who expresses his castratory anxieties in the ambivalent utterance, 'Je devrais vous trouver charmantes . . . Vous *êtes* charmantes, mes biches' ['I should find you charming . . . You *are* charming, my does']. Why leaves Paul's side to go to Frédérique's and says she loves them both, at which point the threesome is framed in an inebriated group hug-cum-grope. When the couple retire to bed, Why is seen fingering their bedroom door (as observed above, symbol *par excellence* of liminality), and the camera cross-cuts between images of her in apparently primal oedipal-scene longing whilst Frédérique and Paul fornicate behind the door. The viewer is interpellated by the question: Exactly who, or what, is Why desiring? The possibilities proliferate: desire *for* Frédérique would be lesbian, desire *for* Paul would be straight, desire *to be* Frédérique would be fusionally lesbian or substitutionally straight, desire *to be* Paul would be phallically lesbian (or even transsexual) – a truly queer nexus of desiring eventualities. Valerie Traub's comments cited above apropos the anglophone *Black Widow* may have a particular validity for *Les Biches*, if for 'Reni and Alex' we substitute

'Frédérique and Why' (by peculiar coincidence, the male courier bears the same name, Paul, in both films): 'in inverting the male homosocial system by which women are exchanged between men, Paul's body becomes a courier, communicating indirectly those desires that Reni and Alex cannot express' (Traub 1991: 315).

More mundanely, the trio in Louis Malle's *Milou en mai* (1989) issues in unproblematised conquest by the interloping male figure: Claire initially attempts to hold the younger Marie-Laure in thrall to her stylised dominatrix powers, but Marie-Laure soon succumbs to the more socially sanctioned charms of Pierre-Alain. When the latter two sit flirtatiously on the lawn together, Claire's attempts to mark out Marie-Laure as her own territory are conveyed by the spatial relations within the frame: she sits down very obviously between the two, temporarily rupturing their embryonic dyad. The soundtrack complements this by relaying Claire's verbal attempts to ridicule what is in effect the essence of Pierre-Alain's structural identity within this film, as May '68 student cipher. She implicitly denigrates his naïve revolutionary discourse by opining that barricades do not need to be erected in order to improve the status quo and to encourage exchange, dialogue, reflection: for that, there is painting, sculpture – art – as opposed to petty sectarian discourse. This is an interesting disinvestment in the overtly political on the part of a gay women who potentially has more to gain from political activism than from aesthetic contemplation.

Yet Claire makes her own political point, in the wider sense of the word 'political', by her performative satire of heteronormativity. Deciding to exploit lorry driver Grimaldi's obvious attraction to her by puncturing his machismo, and in so doing achieving at least a displaced symbolic revenge on Pierre-Alain by metonymically targeting a proximate male figure, she provocatively suggests that the whole (bourgeois) family put into practice the utopic social theories preached by Pierre-Alain by each member having sex in front of everyone else. The gullible Grimaldi says he is up for it, but Claire remains complete mistress of the situation, undressing seductively and asking, deflatingly, if he is getting a hard-on. *Pace* the naïve conviction of *Le Figaro*'s reviewer that Claire is prepared to succumb to Grimaldi,[26] this is a cynical performance of straight sex on Claire's part, but with the power structures reversed: he is hesitant, submissive, while she regally calls the shots. In the Deleuzian lexicon, Claire the sadist certainly has institutional power in her greater cultural capital and higher class status than Grimaldi. As to whether Grimaldi is even alert to the possibilities of a subversive contract between them predicated on his own submission is highly questionable: more plausibly, he would appear to be quite simply her victim.

Frustratingly, the response of Pierre-Alain, the real if indirect target of this satire, is passed over by Malle.

Sylvia Calle's *Ô trouble* (1998) follows suit, albeit in more jocosely ironic vein. Calle's short evokes androgynous Inès's passion for canonically feminine flatmate Laura, her jealousy of Laura's straight attractions, and her build-up to an abortive love declaration. Triangulation is adumbrated in a flashback sequence in which a pre-pubescent girl longingly gazes at another pre-pubescent girl dancing with a man. The sequence is assumed by the viewer to be a childhood memory of herself and Laura, but it also reflects the diegetic present – she, the subject, is framed alone, gazing at the feminine object of desire in the arms of a man. The love declaration is finally prompted by Inès's furious jealousy of her brother, who has monopolised Laura's attention for a whole evening. Laura asks Inès why she is so upset; Inès vilifies her brother, flinging every imaginable insult at him in his absence, then finally spits out that she loves Laura. Laura replies ruefully and rapidly 'Oui je sais' ['Yes I know'], gives her a brave smile, then departs – upon which Inès comically faints. The termination of the film at this point forecloses knowledge of whether Inès's brother triumphs, but what is clear in this wry short is that lesbian desire certainly does not.

The triangulation in French-Canadian Léa Pool's *Emporte-moi* (1999) is considerably more complex. Early on, a haunting, slow-motion underwater sequence suggests a potentially incestuous relationship between thirteen-year-old Hanna and her older brother Paul by, for example, showing the two kissing slowly on the lips. However, when Paul is introduced to Hanna's exogamous desire-object Laura, the lesbian current between the two girls is challenged, prompting Hanna's jealousy about the growing attraction between Paul and Laura. When Hanna and Paul seek shelter for the night at Laura's home, the triangle is visually literalised as the three lie in bed together. Laura and Paul end up kissing and falling asleep in each other's embrace; distraught at her exclusion, with the melancholy soundtrack supplementing the visual mediation of her distress, Hanna steals away. Ironically, just as she shuts the bedroom door behind her, Laura turns over from Paul to cuddle up to Hanna – too late. The American gay magazine *The Advocate* throws an interesting light on the autofictional nature of Pool's sexual triangulation, and on its pervasiveness in her wider filmic *œuvre*:

Like Hanna, Pool has an older brother. Hanna's first (and unconsummated) sexual experience is with him under water; it's a lovely, innocent scene. Her second, much more passionate encounter is with a girl her own age who then begins to play around with her brother. 'The triangle is always present in my films,' says Pool, who notes similar plot elements in *La Femme de l'hôtel* (1984), *Anne Trister* (1986), *Corps perdu* (1988), and *Rispondetemi* . . . 'This is part of my life,' she adds simply. And the triangle always involves both sexes. 'At one point I thought I had to choose,' Pool says. 'I was with guys all through my 20s and at the beginning of my 30s. At 28 I fell in love with a woman teacher. After this I thought I had to make a choice. Am I gay? Even gay society asks you to make a choice. I've had a lot of reproach even for *Set Me Free* that the film is not gay enough.'[27]

Pool's words here underscore the discreetly queer nature of her take on sexual relations and her refusal of the homo/hetero binary. Some lesbian spectators may lament her resistance to communitarian co-option, but in that resistance resides much of her subtlety and aesthetic integrity.

Which conclusions might be drawn from this exposition of desiring triangulations involving two women and a man? A statistical summary, however alien to the dominant methodologies of film studies, is telling. Of the thirteen films in question, only three (roughly twenty-three per cent) – *Les Lèvres rouges*, *Tristesse et beauté* and *Le Cahier volé* – ultimately exclude the male figure; and, significantly, only one (a little over seven per cent) of these three (*Tristesse et beauté*) even hints at a future for the remaining lesbian dyad. A further three (again, roughly twenty-three per cent) – *Fascination*, *La Femme de l'hôtel* and *Muriel fait le désespoir de ses parents* – script a centrifugal implosion whereby all three go their separate ways, whilst two (just over fifteen per cent) – *Emilienne et Nicole* and *Gazon maudit* – maintain the delicate balance of the trio, with the male figure as its anchoring-point. The remaining five (just over thirty-eight per cent) – *Les Diaboliques*, *Les Biches*, *Milou en mai*, *Ô trouble* and *Emporte-moi* – destroy the lesbian dynamic by excluding one of the two women, leaving the other to the man. The resisting lesbian reader may well derive pleasure from these filmic triangulations, but for the *principled* resisting lesbian reader (see Chapter 1), in all but seven per cent of cases this will be an ephemeral pleasure, leading to the blunt political conclusion that such triangulations are, on the whole, sterile territory.

The fourth permutation in my typology, namely, women's defection from a lesbian or proto-lesbian relationship into the arms of a man through bad faith and/or internalised lesbophobia, is represented by Henri Calef's *Féminin-Féminin* (1973), Léonard Keigel's *Une Femme, un jour* (1974) and Tonie Marshall's *Pas très catholique* (1994). This fourth permutation could, of course, be viewed as a sub-set of the third category, namely the influence of the male/masculine principle; but in the interests of a nuanced reading,

I will treat it as a discrete variant. In an anglophone context, Whatling argued in 1997 for the perverse pleasures of a filmic 'lesbian abject':

> Of course it is not saying anything new to note that much of the 'lesbian' desire articulated on the screen treads a very fine line between lesboeroticism and lesbophobia, the first often recuperated to the last. Still, I would argue that such scenes are not without their own abject pleasures. Indeed, it is in reading these films, not despite, but because of their heterosexual recuperation, that we really begin to get to the foundations of the lesbian abject. (Whatling 1997: 103–4)

Whilst revelling in abjection may strike some as masochistically retrograde, Whatling's advocacy is somewhat more sophisticated:

> In their iteration of the attempted lesbian seduction of the non-lesbian such films, even though they rest upon an immediate or eventual diegetic failure or recuperation, nevertheless visualise a powerful lesbian desire. For the viewer, seeing it all and appropriating regardless, it does not ultimately matter whether the lesbian on screen gets the girl or not, what matters is that we, the audience, think we might if we just look long enough. In appropriating these moments, regardless of their diegetic recuperation to heterosexuality, they operate as stolen moments, all the more tantalising for their unlicensed nature. (Whatling 1997: 110)

I will return to Whatling's claims to assess their possible purchase on Calef's, Keigel's and Marshall's French-language films.

As noted in Chapter 3, in Calef's *Féminin-Féminin* (1973) Marie-Hélène leaves Françoise after the latter has voiced reservations about the very excess of their happiness together. Marie-Hélène's sudden volte-face and return to her ex, Jacques, is a narrative blindspot; no explanation for it is supplied other than Françoise's cautioning against their mutual elation. When Marie-Hélène is seen with Jacques at the airport after leaving home, the image-track emphasises anguish through her distressed facial expression and her nervous sucking on cigarettes – hardly the picture of a woman swept off her feet by true straight love. Yet the male revenge narrative is kicking in, for next we see Françoise begging her own ex, Georges, for help, even implying the possibility of their getting back together. That is truncated by Georges's retort that he's engaged to another woman. The cut to Marie-Hélène provides even more egregious wish-fulfilment of male revenge fantasies, showing her thanking Jacques for being so understanding as to allow her to give Françoise an explanation, and saying she feels relieved, thanks to him. A slight blip is registered in the form of her devastated look when they get back to the flat to find Françoise gone, but it is quickly annulled by the classic solution of his undressing her.

Keigel's *Une Femme, un jour* (1974) similarly condemns the lesbian couple to sabotage by the male principle, which from the start of their relationship sedulously haunts Caroline if not Nicky. When the two women start kissing at night in their car, the heavy hand of the Paternal Law clamps down, for they are intercepted by policemen quipping, 'Ça se bécote dans la voiture . . . Si c'est pas malheureux. Et nous, alors, à quoi on sert?' ['They're smooching in the car . . . How pathetic. And what about us, then, what're we good for?'], illustrating a certain crisis of masculinity faced with the possibility of lesbian self-sufficiency. Eventually, Caroline capitulates to hetero-norms and leaves Nicky for a comfortably-off male dentist; as *Le Quotidien de Paris* says of the lesbian rapport, 'il ne s'agira que d'une brève rencontre, l'héroïne cédant à la pression du *sur-moi*, aux conventions sociales, et à la facilité du rôle d'objet que l'ordre établi lui réserve – depuis des siècles – dans l'ombre de l'homme'[28] ['it will only be a brief affair, the heroine giving in to the pressure of the super-ego, to social conventions, and to the temptation of an easy life in the role of object that the established order has historically reserved for her']. The camera frames Caroline in bed with her new man, but sexually unfulfilled; and the last word she utters in the film strikes an ironic note: on holiday with the dentist and son, she mutters melancholically 'Nicky' upon seeing a market stall (Nicky is a market stallholder), whereupon the camera cuts to an equally depressed-looking, but solitary, Nicky.

Marshall's *Pas très catholique* (1994) features a far more independent heroine than Caroline in Maxime, who at the age of twenty-two had left her rich husband and infant son in order to become a private investigator. She is encoded as a denatured woman in her lack of maternal feelings, and the suggestion of a lesbian potential will be isomorphic with this – although ironically she never embraces that potential, despite sleeping with Florence, for she insists she prefers men. One particular sequence encapsulates this irony. The camera sets up the two women in bed together, with Florence licking Maxime's ear sensuously and the camera then reproducing her desirous gaze at Maxime's naked back from the waist upwards. The accompanying dialogue denotes the disparity of desire between them, but also connotes at least a degree of bad faith on Maxime's part, for the editing places her denial directly after her having slept with Florence:

> *Florence*: T'as un très joli sexe, très fin, juste un petit peu rose sur les
>   pointes . . .
> *Maxime*: Eh ben on n'est pas toutes pareilles?
> *Florence*: Non, le mien est plus touffu, plus caché.

Maxime: J'aurais pas remarqué.
Florence: Pourquoi tu ne veux pas vivre avec moi?
Maxime: . . . J'aime les hommes Florence tu sais bien . . .
Florence: Alors pourquoi tu veux faire l'amour?
Maxime: Parce que tu fais très joliment ta cause t'es agréable . . .
[*Florence*: You've got a very pretty cunt,[29] very delicate, just a teeny bit
pink at the edges . . .
Maxime: Aren't we women all the same?
Florence: No, mine is more hairy, more hidden.
Maxime: Can't say I'd noticed.
Florence: Why don't you want to live with me?
Maxime: . . . I like men, Florence, you know that . . .
Florence: So why do you want sex?
Maxime: Because you put your case beautifully, you're very attractive . . .]

Later on Maxime begins a straight relationship, but her lesbian 'interlude'
cannot be consigned to the dustbin, for the dialogue cited above reveals
marked inconsistencies between Maxime's words and her behaviour.

To what extent, then, may Whatling's theory be applied to Calef's,
Keigel's and Marshall's French-language films? I disagree with Whatling's
insistence that 'it does not ultimately matter whether the lesbian on screen
gets the girl or not, what matters is that we, the audience, think we might
if we just look long enough' (Whatling 1997: 110), for this insistence subordinates the objective integrity of the text to the vagaries of the individual viewer's fantasy rewrites. Only the most doggedly optimistic – or the
most naïvely delusional – of lesbian viewers could emerge triumphant from
a screening of Calef's film, whose ending sticks in a lesbophobic boot by
contriving Françoise's suicide, or from Keigel's, with its relentless accent
on the insuperable social barriers to lesbian love. True, there are moments
of lesboerotic arousal to be savoured in both films, as there are, and in
greater abundance, from Marshall's less lugubrious movie, but must we
resign ourselves to scrabbling for the crumbs of 'stolen moments', or, to
vary the metaphor, prizing the fruit simply because it is forbidden? In
holding out for more dignified and empowering forms of viewing pleasure,
I would presumably be open to Whatling's charge of clinging to a 'lesbian
utopian project', for she carries on thus:

> Whilst detailing what I have elected to term a nostalgia for abjection in this
> chapter, however, I remain convinced that no less nostalgic in its intentions is
> the lesbian desire for positive images, a desire which, burdened by expecta-
> tion, will never be realised. In structuring disappointment into its narrative
> pleasures, at the very least I believe that a nostalgia for abjection works against
> the inevitable failure of the lesbian utopian project. (Whatling 1997: 111)

Whilst contending that 'nostalgia for abjection' sounds suspiciously like glorifying grief in the most regressive of Romantic traditions, I concede that 'structuring disappointment into its narrative pleasures' may be a realistic and productive spectatorial strategy for lesbians. Yet to call for more balanced scripts in which lesbian relations sometimes succeed rather than inevitably failing is hardly to adopt either a utopian or a puritanical positive images agenda; it is merely to request from script-writers and directors the same sort of diversity of treatment as straight relations have traditionally been accorded on celluloid.

Moving away from triangular structures, I now turn to the fifth discrete permutation identified above (which is also, arguably, a sub-set of the category focussing on the influence of the male/masculine principle): machismo in butch lesbian characters. In Nelly Kaplan's *La Fiancée du pirate* (1969), masculine-identified Irène objectifies women just as brutally as does the traditional (hetero)sexist male. This film depicts the gradual autonomisation of Marie, a hitherto downtrodden young woman. After her mother's death she begins to use her sexual power against those authority figures who have previously exploited her: largely the men of the village, who all become her sexual clients, but also her female boss Irène, a wealthy, land-owning farmer. Unfortunately, Irène's masculine attire, gait and general appearance (short hair, leather jacket, trousers), in themselves morally neutral, find a disturbing parallel in her wholesale integration of macho behaviour patterns. In the opening scenes we witness her physical brutality towards Marie, who at that point is wholly economically dependent on her. The camerawork traces the transmutation of a potentially sensitive response to Marie's maternal loss, as she touches the young woman in an apparently consolatory gesture, into self-centred exploitation as she breathes 'J'ai envie' ['I want it'] and lowers the just bereaved young woman onto the bed, undoes her front buttons, caresses her breasts and kisses her neck. Not unsurprisingly for someone who has just that morning lost her mother and undergone social trauma, Marie remains impassive, indeed inert. Irène in fact treats Marie no better than any of the men in the village do. She tries to dominate Marie after the latter begins to earn money of her own through prostitution, treating her as a possession, hypocritically insulting her as a 'traînée' ['hussy'] after discovering her amongst a crowd of men she had invited home and got drunk in order to enlist their services in burying her mother.

Only one of Irène's gestures elevates her ethically over the parochial, small-minded men of the village who also buy Marie's sexual services: the fact that she alone invites Marie to a community film-show, whilst the others ostentatiously shun her. In a later sequence, when Marie has begun to titivate herself from the proceeds of her new earnings, Irène says she's become beautiful, and that she'll give Marie anything she wants if she stays the night. The two have sex, and this time, Marie assumes an agentic role. But symptomatically, their intercourse is voyeuristically framed by the camera's presentation of it through the field of vision of a watching male client.

This introduces the sixth permutation (which like the fourth and fifth can be considered a sub-set of the influence of the male/masculine principle): the lesbian figure and/or couple as eroticised object of the voyeuristic male gaze within the diegesis. Guy Casaril's *Emilienne et Nicole* (1970) seems to cater overwhelmingly for the (stereotypical) straight man's abiding fascination for lesbian sex as essentially a titillating precursor or supplement to straight sex in which he reigns supreme. In the point-of-view shot from the perspective of Claude gazing at his wife Emilienne and mistress Nouky kissing then mutually caressing, there is a literalisation of the trope of male voyeurism. Nouky then invites him into this tenuous lesbian space via her complicitous smile, and his initial pique is remedied within minutes: when all three are engaging in social chit-chat, she profits from Emilienne's momentary absence to kiss him.

In the Belgian director Chantal Akerman's *La Captive* (2000), the Proustian-inspired Marcel character Simon most obviously incarnates the voyeurism characterising classic masculine purviews on lesboeroticism in two sequences.[30] First, in a specular opening forming a filmic *mise en abyme*, the viewer watches Simon watching a home-video projection of a group of young women having fun frolicking on a beach. The haptic concurs with the visual in suggesting a diffuse sensual pleasure between the women: the camera records their frequent tactility with each other, as well as homing in on the enigmatic, aroused smile of (Albertine-based) Ariane, Simon's girlfriend. Towards the end of the projection we see Simon's silhouetted head in the bottom left-hand corner of the diegetic screen, emblematising his wish to intrude on, set against his spatial marginalisation within, this space of inter-female pleasures. Second, Simon later secretly follows Ariane into the Musée Rodin, gazing at her gazing at a statue of a female bust (note the mirroring topos), then at her being kissed on the cheek by her female 'friend' Andrée.[31] His scopic fascination for these lesboerotic images amounts to a very particular brand of fetishism, in which his inability to penetrate the charmed circle is disavowed through his vicarious, ocular participation within it.

Finally, we come to the seventh permutation. Thus far, I have considered the frequent influence of men (or of the masculine principle) when they are visibly present. Equally preponderant, and considerably more fertile ground for the lesbian spectator, is the role of men through their *absence*. This absence engenders the possibility of all-female spaces, the most obvious paradigm being the gynaeceum: usually a girls' boarding school (as popular legend has it, matrix of lesboerotic pulsions), but by extension any female-only living environment, such as the women's hostel or prison. In 1990 Richard Dyer helpfully identified the literary, sexological and socio-logical roots of what began in the early twentieth century and was to become a cinematic (sub-)genre in its own right:

> The gynaecum [*sic!*] tale provided a literary model and at the same time there was an interest in the phenomenon of the Schwärmerei, the schoolgirl crush, among contemporary commentators, including sexologists such as Havelock Ellis who published his 'The school-friendships of girls' in 1897. The growth of large boarding schools signalled a shift in the education of middle-class girls, making such intensities possible and even common . . . (Dyer 1990: 39)

Two years later, Andrea Weiss's seminal study *Vampires and Violets: Lesbians in the Cinema* (1992) traced the implantation of this (sub-)genre within European and North American cinema, providing an admirably wide-ranging contextualisation:

> Ellis's preoccupation with all-female environments was taken up, popular-ized, and significantly refocused in several European and American films of the late 1920s and early 30s. Where Ellis saw danger, these films – especially two by female directors – imagined pleasure. *Mädchen in Uniform* (Leontine Sagan, Germany, 1931), *Club de Femmes* (Jacques Deval, France, 1936), and *The Wild Party* (Dorothy Arzner, United States, 1929) all focus on the joys rather than the perils of all-girl living; any potential danger is posed by an outside threat rather than by the women's attachments *per se*. These films, set in women's schools, established a veritable genre that appears through-out movie history, continuing with the several remakes of *Mädchen in Uniform*, including a 1957 technicolor version with Romy Schneider and Lily Palmer, and the Mexican version *Muchachas en Uniforme* (1950). Two films in this genre which retain *Mädchen in Uniform*'s female eroticism but abandon its radical feminist politics are *Olivia* (Jacqueline Audry, France, 1951), based on the autobiographical novel of English girls' boarding-school life by Dorothy Strachey Bussy, and *Theresa and Isabel* (Radley Metzger, France, 1968), the soft-core porn depiction of Catholic schoolgirl affection, featuring a memorable sex scene in the church pews. (Weiss 1992: 8)

Within our French-language corpus (and it should be noted that Radley Metzger's *Thérèse and Isabelle* is, *pace* Weiss, *not* a French film,[32] so will not be treated here), one of the first three instantiations of the genre is a film mentioned by Weiss above, namely Jacques Deval's *Club de femmes* (1936). (The first, and also the first film of my entire corpus, was Armand du Plessy's *La Garçonne* [France, 1923], which despite my best efforts has proved unobtainable.) Again *pace* Weiss, the film is set not in a 'women's school', but rather in a female hostel run by a brisk but kindly proto-feminist, Matilde, aided by the dykish-looking house doctor, Gabrielle. While Gabrielle's lesbian orientation is only tacitly suggested, that of nine-teen-year-old Alice is clearly established despite the film's taboo on use of the words 'lesbienne', 'homosexualité' or any of their cognates. Her doomed love for the more naïve Juliette is one of the two main plot-lines, the other being a stabilising heteronormative antedote: Claire's antics to smuggle her boyfriend into the women-only institution, her pregnancy and eventual guarantor of a conventional happy ending via the birth of a baby girl adored by all. Whilst the general ethos and atmosphere of this all-female commu-nity is certainly warm, supportive and pro-women if not feminist in our con-temporary sense of the word, Weiss's inclusion of this film amongst those that 'focus on the joys rather than the perils of all-girl living' requires quali-fication, for Alice's experience of love and desire for Juliette is one of clan-destinity, frustration and finally, tragedy. Gabrielle mitigates the potentially disastrous consequences of Alice's *crime de passion*, but whether this is a gesture of covert lesbian solidarity or a simple cover-up to preserve the good name of her institution (or indeed a mixture of the two) remains opaque.

Appearing in the same year (1936), but curiously ignored by Weiss's foundational study, was Jean de Limur's *La Garçonne*. Based, like du Plessy's film of the same name, on the novel *La Garçonne* by Victor Margueritte (1922),[33] de Limur's film is only of peripheral lesbian interest in its entirety, but that periphery is very often our vantage point in the present chapter, and the film deserves at least brief attention. Set in the early twentieth century, it traces the fortunes of Monique: her betrayal by her fiancé, her assumption of a career and economic independence, her obliquely erotic dalliances with a *bona fide* lesbian, Niquette (played by the famous Arletty),[34] and with a female singer, her mistreatment at the hands of a sexist boor, and her final happiness with a man of moral integrity. For its time, the film is liberal in the positive value placed on a woman's quest for independence, but ultimately it ties into the conventional heterosexual-romance formula. However slight the space for a lesbian reading of this text, that space is no mirage. In terms of the cinematic lesbian continuum, we have the topos of the gynaeceum – literally here: a girls' (boarding) school, run by Monique's beloved aunt. It is a truly 'joyous' (see Weiss above), all-girl environment, animated by energy and noise, where Monique prefers to live as opposed to in her parental home, even though she is no longer a schoolgirl. The prevailing atmosphere in the school is one of exhilaration: the soundtrack foregrounds laughter and excited voices, the image-track the girls' robust movement as they run around. The aunt's boarding school retains its iconic status as a prelapsarian, all-female idyll; Monique's 'fall' comes first in the form of painful betrayal by her fiancé, yet true to the Freudian formula, if narratively incoherent, her primary attachments to her own sex are succeeded by the supposedly more mature encounter with difference, that is, with the male.

Also set in the literal gynaeceum, but this for its entire narrative run as opposed to a prelapsarian incipit, is Jacqueline Audry's *Olivia* (1951). As Weiss states, Audry based her film on the 'autobiographical novel of English girls' boarding-school life by Dorothy Strachey Bussy' (Weiss 1992: 8).[35] Weiss avers that Audry's film retains '*Mädchen in Uniform*'s female eroticism but abandon[s] its radical feminist politics' (Weiss 1992: 8). I opine that, for its time, its French context of adaptation and production, and despite its sombre ending, *Olivia* was in fact an exceptionally daring film.[36] This context-bound temerity inheres in its overt inscription of a desire that not only excludes the male principle but is also age-asymmetrical. It is thus all the more surprising to learn that 'the film, though it was panned by many of the (male) critics and provoked snide remarks from the right-wing press, did not create a scandal, was not banned and apparently enjoyed a moderate international success' (Tarr 1993: 35). That success was a box-office rather than a critical one, however, for very obvious reasons articulated by *Les Cahiers du cinéma* soon after the film's release: 'Quant à l'homosexualité féminine, on sait quelle indulgence amusée et supérieure lui portent les mâles. Sans juger la valeur même des films, ni "Jeunes Filles en uniforme", ni "Olivia" n'apportent de quoi distraire cette suffisance' (Kast 1953: 51) ['As for female homosexuality, we know how males treat it with an amused and superior indulgence. Without judging the merit of the films in itself, neither *Girls in Uniform* nor *Olivia* offer anything that diverts them from this self-importance'].

An English schoolgirl trapped in a sensual young woman's body, Olivia soon falls passionately in love with one of the two headmistresses at her new French boarding school, Mlle Julie, whose elegant and seductive demeanour prompts her to remark wondrously 'Elle n'a pas l'air d'un professeur' ['She doesn't look like a teacher']. No more primarily a teacher than a mother-figure to Olivia, contrary to Tarr's designation of her as 'adored teacher-cum-mother figure' (Tarr 1993: 38), Julie is above all Olivia's desire-object. The schoolgirls' claim that this is a school divided into two camps – the 'Julistes' and the 'Caristes' – implies that each schoolgirl necessarily becomes an exclusive acolyte of one of the women. Ironically, the two women share an amorous history. It is a measure of how far heteronormativity persisted in the late twentieth century that the summary of the film provided by the Bibliothèque du Film presents Julie and Cara as sisters,[37] whereas there is no supporting evidence for this. And even if they were sisters, their attachment would in all honesty have to be called incestuous.

Olivia's rapt facial expression, her body language and the soundtrack confirm her nascent passion for Julie as the latter reads from Racine's *Andromaque* (an obvious intertext for doomed passion) and the camera lingers on her ample bosom. Christiane Jouve's assertion that there were '[p]as de sous-entendus dans "Olivia", tout est dit, tout est clair' ['no innuendo in *Olivia*, everything is said, everything is clear'] is at once understandable and yet not quite accurate. Olivia's love for Julie is certainly spoken and certainly clear to the audience; but the sexual expression of that love was not. What is implied but could not have been shown was, obviously, homosexual sex, for that between a minor and an adult was, in effect, criminalised by French law from 1942 to 1982 by being penalised more heavily than straight sex between minors (at the time, those under 21) – a legacy of the fascist Vichy régime during the Second World War, which had first introduced the disparity on 6 August 1942. Ironically, the law had been endorsed on 8 February 1945 – thus, during the 'Liberation' period in France – by the hallowed freedom-fighter, General de Gaulle.

In the Christmas ball sequence, the schoolgirls' bodies are blatantly eroticised: from girls they are transformed, via their dress and the camerawork, into alluring young women. Julie's roving eye spots Cécile, an American schoolgirl whose sexually precocious body, endowed with ample breasts and feminine curves, incites the most explicitly lesboerotic frame of the entire film: Julie kissing Cécile's neck voluptuously, voraciously (and in so doing forming a no doubt unintended intertextual allusion to the figure of the lesbian vampire).

Cara accuses Julie of making the schoolgirls depraved, and even of actually penetrating the girls' bedrooms: the verb chosen is polysemic, casting Julie alternatively as a predatory (and paedophile) male in drag or a phallic lesbian, but what is clear is the imputation that Julie abuses her power over her under-age charges. The dramatic trigger to the dénouement is Cara's death (understood to be suicide). Genuinely distraught, Julie declares to Olivia and her other acolytes that Cara was the only being in the world she had really loved, and that now she wants above all to avoid doing harm. Later on, she allusively refers to her hitherto successful management of a socially reproved sexual orientation, and to her new sense of guilt: 'Toute ma vie cela a été la même lutte, mais j'ai toujours été victorieuse et fière de l'être. Et maintenant je me demande bien souvent si la défaite n'aurait pas mieux valu pour tout le monde' ['All my life it's been the same battle, but I've always won and been proud of winning. And now I often wonder if defeat might not have been better for everyone']. So, consonant with cliché, lesbianism is connoted as dangerously destructive at the very end of the film. But two points are significant. First, while one of its two chief incarnations (Cara) is punished by death, the other (Julie) is left to thrive in other climes: she decides to leave the school for Canada, accompanied by her devoted young (female) Italian teacher. Second, when *Lesbia Magazine* reviewed the film after its showing at the Sceaux women's film festival of 1984, both the title of the review ('6ième festival de films de femmes à Sceaux: le triomphe d'"Olivia"' ['Sixth Women's Film Festival at Sceaux: *Olivia* triumphs']) and its content clearly suggested that 'modern' lesbian reception privileged the fulgency of the lesbian loves depicted in the film over its mediation of lesbophobia: 'Olivia, le plus beau film d'amour entre femmes qu'il me fût jamais permis d'admirer'[38] ['Olivia, the most wonderful film about love between women that I've ever had the privilege to admire'].

Far more reproving of the girls' school as matrix of lesboerotic pulsions is the much later *L'Araignée de satin* (1984), directed by Jacques Baratier and set in a girls' boarding school named Les Fauvettes in which lesbianism is presented as isomorphic with 'drogue, folie, meurtre'.[39] The verdict of the left-wing newspaper *Libération* was scathing, imputing a hypocritically unavowed pornographic quality to the film:

> *L'Araignée de satin* est pathétique. On ose à peine penser que la seule raison de Baratier pour se lancer dans l'entreprise est d'y aligner un maximum de collégiennes sexy typées et photographiées David Hamilton. . . . A chacun ses fantasmes, mais il y a moins de gâtisme macho et de puritanisme cochon dans n'importe lequel des pornos de série . . .[40]
> [Baratier's *L'Araignée de satin* is pathetic. One hardly dares to think that Baratier's only reason for throwing himself into the venture is to line up as many sexy schoolgirls as possible of the stereotype photographed by David Hamilton. . . . Each to his own fantasy, but there's less macho idiocy and smutty Puritanism in any standard porn film . . .

Libération had a point, but, as I have previously argued, the lesbian spectator can herself exploit the material products of exploitative intentions or commercial infrastructures, enjoying the visual and aural stimuli whilst discarding the dubious politics. Such stimuli are evident in an early sequence featuring two young women kissing, one touching the breasts of the other at whom she is gazing intently and passionately. This seems to constitute a memory: the moving image freezes into a static photographic image being gazed at by the headmistress, who then kisses the older school-girl, with the camera tracking down their bodies as she caresses the girl's hair, head, waist and other bodily parts.

Later on, a long sequence featuring a school ball (and invoking as inter-text a similar scene discussed above in *Olivia*) provides a superficially more institutionalised conduit for lesboerotic currents, but it fails to subdue certain subversive eddies. Solange appears in highly androgynous guise, almost in male drag, and is later joined by two similarly transvestite-styled girls. Two hitherto unknown schoolgirls kiss each other sensuously on the lips in public. All goes on under the benevolent gaze of the headmistress and even the school chaplain, a slightly sinister character who clearly rel-ishes these secular pleasures and performs for the younger girls 'magic' tricks which echo the earlier mention of black magic. There is even a per-formance of lesbian sex in silhouette, which turns out to be one step too far. When one of the participants bites the breast of the other, Lucienne screams and leaves the stage, prompting the school doctor to admonish the headmistress in scandalised terms. By close of play the chief lesbian 'culprit' has been arrested and extirpated from the school community, which in itself survives, consonant with the defiance emblematised by the unrepentant headmistress's words 'Je suis pour ceux que j'aime une provo-cation' ['For those I love I am a provocation'].

The second most prominent variant on the topos of the all-female space, the women's prison, first appears in Francis Girod's *La Banquière* (1980), which retraces the tumultuous life of real-life personage Marthe Hannau. Renaming Marthe as Emma, the film opens in retro style, pastiching early silent films in its use of black-and-white images and accelerated motion. This period-style opening includes the first avatar of Emma's lesbian prac-tice (if not identification) in her suggestive eye-contact with a woman who follows her into a lift, then in the cut to the two women being discovered in bed by the stranger's incensed husband. Later on, unjustly arrested on sus-picion of embezzlement, Emma is placed in a cell where the other women prisoners taunt her about her previous cross-dressing and lesbian relations. When one woman simulates soliciting, saying, 'Vous voulez danser mon-sieur? Oh . . . tu sais que t'es plutôt beau mec, pour une gonzesse' ['Would you like to dance sir? Oh . . . you know you're rather a good-looking guy, for a chick'], her words on one level attain their goal of humiliating Emma, but on another level underscore the conflation of gender identification and sexual orientation, and may even betray a latent lesboerotic response on the part of the woman ostensibly mocking lesbianism. The discursive node here is indeed knotty. Another woman in the cell asks jeeringly, 'Je te plais?' ['Do you like me?'], at which point Emma slaps the woman and a fight breaks out. As she is led away by a prison warder, the women shout after her 'sale mec' ['dirty geezer'] and 'goudou' ['dyke']. So much for female solidarity in adversity. Finally, another lesbian sub-plot evolves when the female prison warder, who has grown rather partial to Emma, leans over her after she has collapsed, with the camera setting her up in a pose resembling that of a lover about to kiss her love-object; and, indeed, one of the women prisoners calls out 'les gouines' ['dykes']. Thus Girod mediates an ambiguous picture of the women's prison as simultaneously lesbophobic in its collective spirit but with secret lesboerotic crevices: in some senses, a mirror-image of 1930s French society outside prison.

The one film in our corpus to focus exclusively on a community of female prisoners is Charlotte Silvera's *Prisonnières* (1988). The only lesbian relationship forged is between Sabine and Lucie, the latter considerably older than the former. Whilst their relationship forms only one narrative element, as *Les Cahiers du cinéma* comments, it is the love-story between Sabine and Lucie which will become the film's real focus.[41] When Sabine (who, it is later revealed, has a boyfriend) first sees Lucie, the older woman is shielding her face from the sun, and Sabine's gaze lingers on that face in a low-angle shot. The camera again draws attention to Sabine's gaze on Lucie when the latter is serendipitously moved to the same work detail. The two are soon joking complicitously, with Sabine flirtatiously teasing the usually earnest Lucie. Lucie's solicitousness when Sabine gets irate about other prisoners' heterocentric prurience prompts the younger woman to tears and thence to a confession of love at first sight for Lucie. The scene is shot in low, warm lighting, promoting a sense of intimacy in its contrast with the frequently cold, grey colours that predominate elsewhere in the film. For the first time in the film, music accompanies the image-track, conveying a heightened emotional experience on the part of both women. Soon after, the camera focuses in close-up on their linked hands (a central trope in the semiology of lesbianism, be it written or screenic). Lucie's love for Sabine is conveyed visually, through her exaltation (conveyed in a point-of-view shot) whilst watching Sabine's joyful energy playing a ball game. Later, emotionally charged music is again used, here to amplify the import of Lucie taking the sexual initiative in opening Sabine's shirt and kissing her passionately on the neck, whilst the revolving camera follows their lyrical embrace in an exhilaratingly vertiginous movement. Despite the obvious dissonances between the genres in question, the passionate kissing on the neck in this women's prison film was related by one of my interlocutors to the figure of the lesbian vampire (just as I myself have above related a particular frame in boarding-school film

Olivia to vampiric iconography), leading to the inference that a certain blurring of generic margins may well obtain in treatment of an axiomatically marginal subject.

The strength of Lucie's love for Sabine is confirmed by the fact that, whereas she had previously been a model of good behaviour, she almost attacks the woman (Marthe) responsible for Sabine's solitary confinement. In a tragic penultimate sequence, Lucie, bereft of Sabine, and possibly tormented by censorious religious discourse, attempts suicide. The film is not, however, unmitigatedly pessimistic about their love, for the epilogue shows Lucie alive three years on, in the outside world after serving her term, and still in some sort of relationship with Sabine (we see a younger friend saying to her that Sabine's mother has sent Lucie a 'mandat' ['money order']). *Les Cahiers du cinéma* treats this lesbian love in universalising mode:

> L'enjeu de *Prisonnières* n'est pas d'ailleurs de l'utopie mais dans la possibilité d'intégrer, comme y parvient Lucie, la loi de l'amour après celle de la prison, de regagner son identité à la force de la fiction qu'on se donne (cet amour, dont il est bon d'avoir montré qu'il n'était pas une passion vicariante et résistait à la libération de Lucie).[42]
> [The issue in *Prisonnières* is moreover not utopia but the possibility of assimilating, as Lucie manages to do, the law of love after the law of prison, of recapturing one's identity by dint of the stories one tells oneself (this love, which it was good to have shown not to be a substitute passion, and which survived Lucie's liberation.)]

In my view, the fact that the film ends here, whereas the Sabine – Lucie relationship has been only one of several narrative foci, implies the director's particular privileging of the one positive legacy of the penitentiary experience, that is, inter-female love, rather than love in the more general sense espoused by *Les Cahiers du cinéma*.

Finally, from the Senegalese director Joseph Gaï Ramaka, we have *Karmen Geï* (2001). This is the fifty-second film version of Bizet's famous opera *Carmen* of 1875, but to my knowledge the first to depict the eponymous heroine as a black bisexual. The film begins in a women's prison, with a shot of Karmen's legs wide apart and her body gyrating to music – a highly provocative opening given Senegal's status as a predominantly Muslim country. Her thighs are shown in a close-up shot which becomes a point-of-view shot as we realise that the sexualised visual focus derives from prison governor Angélique. The camera reveals the arousal of the latter – severely tailored and attempting to maintain an equally severe demeanour – through close attention to her eyes and to her tensed jaw muscle. Karmen gets up and dances sensuously, accompanied by a drumbeat and the heady clapping of the all-female audience. The camerawork again emphasises Angélique's arousal by reprising the close-up shot of her. Sedulously, Karmen approaches Angélique, starts rubbing first her legs then her groin against Angélique's knees, then beckons Angélique up onto the dance floor with a tilted finger on the governor's chin. Angélique the prison governor reacts to the seductive manœuvres of Karmen the prisoner with visibly uncontainable passion, thus reversing the established power structure as she reveals herself to be the helpless prey of the theoretically disempowered prisoner.

Soon afterwards, Angélique is shown gazing through prison bars at Karmen as the latter passes by flirtatiously; again, what is curious is the reversal of norms, for the shot is constructed so as to give the illusion that it is the prison governor who is 'behind bars', and Karmen the prisoner who is governing the situation. Sexually, this is of course precisely the situation. When Karmen gives Angélique the eye, there is a reprise of the earlier visual detail as Angélique's jaw muscle tenses. In due course, Karmen is taken by another warder to the governor's boudoir. Angélique strips down to her knickers and lies next to Karmen, caressing her, while a close-up shot details her hand on Karmen's shoulder. The soundtrack conveys heavy panting, the image-track Karmen's buttocks on top of her in close-up, plus the not insignificant and never elucidated detail of Angélique's wedding ring. A slow tracking shot sensuously reveals the length of their horizontally outstretched bodies.

The foregoing are the only visibly lesbian elements of conduct on Karmen's part. After escaping from prison, she goes on to seduce men, and in fact during the very first scene following her escape is aggressive towards a female competitor for a man, finally attacking her. Here there is no sense of the solidarity with women immanent in the prison scenes and which is recalled by her much later on waving a flag in the direction of the prison, to 'mes femmes, et ma geôlière' ['my women, and my woman jailor'] (in synchrony with a shot of the governor looking out for Karmen from a boat).

Finally, a word on the diffuse lesboeroticism marking the communal prison scenes. As noted above, the other women prisoners are highly appreciative spectators of Karmen's lewd dancing and seduction of the governor, chanting along with her and eventually joining in the dance. But there is also a later scene when, as the women start to discuss Karmen's dalliance with their governor, their conversation is invested with ribald lesboeroticism ('All slits look alike . . .' 'Want to know what I'd do with the warden? [body gyrating] I'd put her here, and then here!' Let her taste mine!' [spoken in the indigenous Senegalese language Wolof, with subtitles]), their bawdiness accompanied by loud clapping, and the camera focusing on the lascivious wiggling of female rumps.

Ramaka figures the legendary Carmen figure as bisexual at best rather than lesbian, and her relationship with the female prison governor Angélique could be viewed by cynics as a mere means of gaining favour and, eventually, freedom: it is after she has sexually intoxicated Angélique that she stages her escape, and in the world outside the women's prison her libidinal attractions appear to be firmly heterosexual. On the other hand, she weeps at the news of Angélique's suicide; and when speaking to her old male friend Samba, she says ambiguously 'Je l'aime', which due to the neutrality of the direct object-pronoun here could refer to loving either a man or a woman. When Samba asks directly about the prison governor, however, she replies 'J'aurais pu l'aimer. Mais elle a [*sic*] l'amour triste' ['I could have loved her. But her love is sad']. Angélique's love for Karmen may be stereotypically doomed, but *Libération* locates Karmen's most profound love in women and music:

> Jeïna Diop Gaï, gazelle dreadlocké et fière, entre dans le film en exécutant une danse longue, lente, envoûtée, ostentatoire jusqu'à la provocation, se transformant en une Salomé saphique, dansant jusqu'aux transes pour sa géôlière. . . . Karmen, profondément, ne fait l'amour qu'avec des femmes et des sons.[43]
> [Jeïna Diop Gaï, a proud gazelle wearing dreadlocks, enters the film by performing a long, slow, bewitching dance that is so ostentatious it becomes provocative, transforming herself into a Sapphic Salome, dancing to the point of trance for her [female] jailor. . . . Essentially, Karmen makes love only with woman and with sounds.]

At the very least, it is reasonable to say that the women's prison is depicted as a lesbo-friendly environment in Ramaka's film, and that this depiction is non-judgemental – all the more remarkable given the greater prevalence of institutionalised homophobia in Senegal than in France.[44] (Of course, a more reactionary counter-claim would be that these lesbo-friendly women *qua* criminals by definition represent a corrupt ethics.)

What general conclusions may be drawn about filmic mediations of all-female spaces, be they schools, hostels or prisons? It could be argued that, whilst these spaces appear empowering because they allow inter-female desire and love to develop unfettered by male opprobrium, their ontological integrity as lesbian paradigms is dubious because they are constitutively dependent on, precisely, the absence of men. Put in more vernacular terms, the argument is that the so-called lesbian love and desire found in such spaces is a mere *pis-aller*, in default of amorous/sexual opportunities with men. This argument is impossible to verify: axiomatically, an all-female community cannot be compared with a mixed community within the heteronormative societies by which we are all interpellated; in such societies, any kind of control group is unconstitutable. That said, it is not negligible that in the three cases where the lesbo–susceptible female subject is shown operating outside the all-female community (*La Banquière*, *Prisonnières* and *Karmen Gei*), she hardly loses all interest in women. None the less, and paradoxically, it is the prison that becomes the space of liberation for that subject.

The tension between confinement and liberation of lesbian desire is not alien to the last part of this chapter, which zooms in on what Whatling terms 'the *thrill* of the forbidden, the nostalgic sense of lesbianism as taboo, its images, rendered covertly, for our eyes only' (Whatling 1997: 89; my emphasis). The foregoing has analysed *mises en scènes* of lesbian desire compromised by the male principle; what follows celebrates the spectatorial project of reclamation, but insists upon a principled resistant reading, that is, one that does not traduce the integrity of the text. Retaining a chronological approach, it will in some cases revisit films already discussed, but in a more self-consciously appropriative, if unapologetically fragmentary, mode. One of its objectives will be to identify currents of queer as well as of inter-female desire in liminally lesbian films.

Queer currents *avant la lettre* permeate Jean de Limur's *La Garçonne* (1936). Designer Monique is coveted by Niquette, a wealthy and beautiful *femme*-figure who none the less plays with gender as performance, on one occasion donning a top hat with a short skirt. At first she acts as patron to Monique by commissioning work from her. But from their very first meeting the resisting viewer will note the sultry look she bestows upon Monique, along with the sexualised undercurrents of her remark that Monique will have to do things other than 'installations' if she is to succeed. Via shot-reverse-shot, the camera hints at Niquette's masculinised intention of buying Monique's bodily services as well as her artistic labour, along with Monique's inchoate awareness of this and her consequent unease.

Niquette is not the only woman openly to display her desire for other women in this film. At a bohemian salon, various forms of libertinage flourish, including lesboeroticism. Niquette gazes lustfully at a black woman dancer's body, but other lesbian moves are also being made, including butch – femme seduction. In a reversal of normative expectations according to which the butch emulates the active male and the *femme* the passive female, it is the *femme* who solicits the woman in male drag, pulling her arm and dragging her off to pursue her desire. Further, a very feminine-looking blonde woman flirts more circumspectly with another *femme*, adjusting her dress as a pretext for bodily contact; the image of their reflection in the mirror shows the blonde practically licking her lips.

In contrast, Henri-Georges Clouzot's *Quai des orfèvres* (1947) mediates lesbian desire as a verbally and socially censored yet pure and ethically elevated force. The lesbian desire inheres in one character alone, Dora, an extremely attractive, conventionally feminine-looking female photographer (but see Mayne 2004) and old friend of Maurice. Jenny, Maurice's wife and Dora's desire-object, appears entirely oblivious of Dora's sexual attraction to her, and certainly does not reciprocate it. When Dora sensuously arranges her legs for a photo-shot, Jenny says she doesn't like people to 'tripoter' ['grope']. The representation works almost exclusively non-verbally, and only one utterance towards the end of the film, placed in the mouth of inspector Antoine, confirms to at least the cognoscenti the lesbian nature of Dora's attachment to Jenny:

> *Antoine*: Vous l'aimez bien, hein, votre amie [Jenny].
> *Dora*: . . . *je l'aime.*
> *Antoine*: Je sais . . . vous êtes un type dans mon genre . . . avec les femmes, vous n'aurez jamais de chance.
> [*Antoine*: You really like her, don't you, your friend.
> *Dora*: . . . *I love her.*
> *Antoine*: I know . . . you're a guy like me . . . with women, you'll never be lucky.]

Antoine's final, self-deprecating words align Dora's desire for women with a masculine identity despite her very feminine appearance, and thus reflect (albeit *inter alia*) the tyranny of gender norms in the policing of sexual orientation. The closest Dora comes to articulation of her non-normative sexuality is, typically for the time, coded: when Maurice says he should have had a wife like her, she looks enigmatically into the distance and says wryly 'Je suis une drôle de fille' ['I'm a funny kind of girl'] – the 'drôle', meaning 'funny' as in 'strange', here offering an apt, if anachronistic, equivalent of 'queer'. *Lesbia*'s verdict was blunt but enthusiastic:

> il y a Simone Renant qu'on soupçonne dès les premières scènes d'avoir un fort penchant pour Suzy Delair. Je n'en croyais pas mes yeux, il [Clouzot] a osé! C'est décrit avec justesse, Jouvet et les spectateurs ont compris l'amour qu'elle porte à cette grosse vache . . . [45]
> [there's Simone Renant whom you suspect from the very first scenes of having a strong penchant for Suzy Delair. I couldn't believe my eyes, he [Clouzot] had dared to do it! It's aptly evoked, Jouvet and the viewer understood the love she has for that fat cow . . .]

The lesbian space created in Georges Franju's *Thérèse Desqueyroux* (1962) is more discreet territory, tightly encrypted in potentiality. One of the most important indices to Thérèse's desire rather than simple affection for Anne, who becomes her sister-in-law, is the flashback to memories of happy, quasi-idyllic times with Anne before Thérèse's marriage: their cycling together across lush meadows, the frames infused with an edenic luminosity consisting in far more than their symbolically white dresses – signifying, particularly within the Catholic framework of Mauriac's work, a prelapsarian (here, pre-marriage) paradise. Thus does Franju visually convey Mauriac's written insistence on the purity of the two young women's bond; but rather than 'purity' in the conventional Christian sense, it is a purity consisting in freedom from men and from the petty, strictured society dominated by men which ends after she marries.[46] In a direct quotation from the Mauriac original, Franju's Thérèse says of Anne that she (Thérèse) is 'insatiable de sa présence' ['insatiable for her presence'],[47] and gazes forlornly after Anne when the latter has to leave, the camera mournfully tracking her slow departure. It is significant that Thérèse explains her wish to marry Bernard as being perhaps first and foremost because this would give her the joy of becoming Anne's sister-in-law. Again, this echoes the Mauriac original, but with the empowering omission of Mauriac's patronising epithet 'puérile', for what Mauriac said was 'Il y avait cette joie puerile de devenir, par ce marriage, la belle-sœur d'Anne'[48] ['There was that childish joy of becoming, through this marriage, Anne's sister-in-law']. Out in the family garden one night, Anne places her head on Thérèse's shoulder, reprising an earlier gesture, but this time goes one step further by asking Thérèse to kiss her. She then kneels in front of Thérèse and rests her head and arms on Thérèse's lap and legs, claiming 'Tu m'aimes, toi' ['*You* love me']. They go back to the house hand-in-hand. Things turn sour, however, when Anne becomes desperate to track down her straight love-interest Jean, and thinks Thérèse is lying when she says he is in Paris. What is interesting is the line of attack her skein of confused feelings assumes, for she accuses Thérèse of having lost her uniqueness through integration into the institution of marriage. Predictably, Anne too is recuperated, for she too goes on to marry.

For the most part critics fastidiously ignored the lesbian potentialities of the Thérèse – Anne relationship, but two exceptions are worth citing. *Europe* pointed to sublimation: 'A vrai dire était-elle faite pour le mariage? Un trouble instinct ne la portait-elle pas vers une amitié très particulière pour sa future belle-sœur, sous le prétexte très ambigu d'une recherche de pureté "absolue"? C'est ce que laisse entendre le début du film, sans insister toutefois'[49] ['Was she really made for marriage? Was she not drawn by some dubious instinct towards a very particular friendship with her future sister-in-law, under the very ambiguous pretext of a quest for "absolute" purity? This is what the start of the film implies, without for all that being heavy-handed']. And the establishment literary journal *Les Lettres françaises* alluded with heartwarming alacrity to the lesbian nature of the relationship: 'L'atmosphère du roman, Franju l'a spontanément retrouvée, le film devient un document sur la séquestration d'une femme; mais il y a pourtant un éclair de clarté joyeuse chez cette femme: les moments passés avec Anne, sa belle-sœur' ['Franju has spontaneously rediscovered the novel's atmosphere, and the film becomes a document on the sequestration of a woman; but there is none the less a spark of joyous light in this woman: the moments she spends with Anne, her sister-in-law'].

Eighteen years on, Claude Mulot's *L'Immorale* (1980) reverts to the superficially more libertine mode of *La Garçonne* (1936). Applying Judith Roof's schema, Mulot's movie could aptly be grouped along with such films as *Emmanuelle* and *Melody in Love*[50] by virtue of its soft porn quality and its episodic narrative structure:

> *Emmanuelle*, a prototypical soft-core porn film, and *Melody in Love* both contain lesbian scenes. Narratively, these are not central or climactic moments in the films, whose plots generally consist of a series of episodic sexual encounters. Both films appear to be aimed at a mixed audience and contain the formula typical to soft-core porn films: a series of sexual encounters in an episodic narrative about the sexual initiation of a woman or a young man. (Roof 1991: 17–18)

After a car accident, Carole suffers amnesia; in an attempt to reconstruct her memory from audiotapes she had previously recorded for a contracted book, she discovers that she had been a high-class prostitute. The audio narrative of the tapes introduces a visual narrative structured on flashback to (parts of) that past, filmed in a rather preciously retro sepia-coloured lens. Among the somewhat tedious procession of largely straight-sex cameos recalled by the retrospective narrative, one is of interest to our corpus. Carole is sent on a special assignment to meet her first butch, as brothel-boss Norma puts it, adding that this is not a common type of client. Our first shot of the presumed hunk is of a mysterious figure who is clad in male attire but soon strips to reveal a very female body. The sensationalising soundtrack at this point evokes her strong erotic impact on Carole, and the shot-reverse-shot foregrounds not just the woman's body but also Carole's appreciative response. Next the two women are framed in bed, with Carole having her stomach caressed by the feminine-encoded white gloves now donned by the previously butch woman. Carole's voice-over comment, whilst far from conveying any emotional investment, rates this 'lesbian' sexual experience fairly favourably, through ludic litotes: her

bourgeois morality forces her to admit that what followed wasn't that disagreeable, and a whole lot less disagreeable than sex with certain male
clients who could have been her grandfather.

Similarly free-floating and apparently inconsequential is the lesbian
desire suggested in Marie-Claude Treilhou's *Simone Barbès ou la vertu*
(1980). The three discrete sections of Treilhou's film are linked only by the
fact that they record one woman's experiences over a single night. Simone
is first seen at work (a porn cinema) with a female colleague, whom she
kisses slowly and touches playfully on the nose at the end of her shift
(leaving the colleague, it has to be said, entirely impassive). The second
section shows her at a nightclub, where she goes to find her 'amie'
['[girl]friend'] but eventually gets fed up with waiting. The nightclub is
frequented largely though not exclusively by lesbians, and was based on the
real-life lesbian clubs Le Monocle and Moune.[51] This sequence is filmed
in saturated red, suggesting seduction and loucheness. Its main interest lies
in its *mise en scène* of gender-bending *avant la lettre*. The female staff are
mainly dressed as men, whereas the clients include *femmes* as well as butch
types; the 'Amazones' act features two women dressed scantily as gladia-
tors, simulating a sword fight (practically the only thing in her evening to
elicit a smile from Simone); another act features a long-haired but otherwise pretty macho, black-leather-jacketed female rock-artist who sings
aggressively about being a 'nana-mec' ['chick-guy']. The third and final
section of the film forms an awkward hiatus with the first two, and is of
limited interest to the lesbian spectator: Simone drives a male stranger
home, briefly contemplates having sex with him, then decides against it.

To recall Hart's postulate, is Simone's lesbian status 'constitutively
dubious'? The respected and mainstream *Cahiers du cinéma* assumes
without question her lesbianism and also its centrality to the film, referring
to her as 'une amoureuse bafouée par sa petite amie qui se prostitue dans
les coulisses de la boîte'[52] ['a lover scorned by her girlfriend who prostitutes
herself in the wings of a bar']. Treilhou's interviewer in the lesbian and gay
journal *Masques* addressed the dubiety directly, implying a certain cyni-
cism on the director's part:

> Tu disais tout à l'heure, en parlant de Simone, qu'elle avait un rapport homo-
> sexuel, mais qu'elle n'était pas 'définie' comme homosexuelle, comme lesbi-
> enne. Dans la dernière partie du film on la voit avec un homme. Cette
> ambiguïté ne t'a-t-elle pas servi?
> [You said earlier on when you were talking about Simone that she had a homo-
> sexual relationship, but that she wasn't 'defined' as homosexual, as lesbian. In
> the last part of the film we see her with a man. Did you not exploit this
> ambiguity?]

Treilhou's evasive response minimised the specificity of Simone's relations with her 'amie' and along with them the ontological integrity of Simone's lesbianism as staged in the second section: 'Je ne sais pas. Ce que j'ai voulu faire, en tout cas, c'est naturaliser le milieu. On y rentre comme on rentre n'importe où ailleurs'[53] ['I don't know. What I wanted to do, at any rate, was to present the [lesbian and gay] scene as natural. You get into it as you get into anything else'].

A similarly fudged directorial spin was also put on the far more commercially successful *Coup de foudre* (1982), which has become a cult movie for lesbians beyond France despite the constitutive dubiety of its lesbianism. The only verbal reference to lesbianism in the film comes from Léna's husband Michel when he angrily accuses her of being a 'gouine' ['dyke']; and director Diane Kurys has hedgingly qualified the relationship between the two women as a little more than friendship, a little less than passion.[54] What, then, is the case for a lesbian sub-texting of this film?

In the early 1950s, housewives Léna and Madeleine meet by chance at their children's school play. Via medium – close-up two-shots, a long lingering look between them is given prominence. The haptic and the olfactory function as oblique signifiers of their as yet unconscious desire: Léna smells Madeleine's hand (ostensibly her skin cream) and emits a strong impression of sensuous, if not yet sensual pleasure. Similar responses, graduating from the sensuous to the sensual and finally to the sexual, are conveyed on several other occasions: when Léna, who has been fitting a dress for Madeleine, starts dancing with her and elicits a response of feigned protest poorly concealing actual pleasure; in the hedonistically charged scene in which the two women lie next to each other as Léna reads to Madeleine; in the scene at the public swimming baths where Madeleine says that Léna's breasts are 'adorables', looks moved, then asks suddenly why she feels so at ease with Léna.

The borderline between sensuous–cum–sensual and sexual desire is crossed when, after Madeleine's loaded and rhetorical question as to whether one can't start again at thirty, Léna responds by saying she wants to kiss her, and places her head on the other woman's neck (recalling the same intimate pose in *Thérèse Desqueyroux*). And when Madeleine leaves her husband, she asks Léna to live with her. The camera directs our attention to the skirting of Léna's finger around Madeleine's breast as they lie in a hotel bed, but the gesture is suspended, signalling the kicking-in of unconscious censorship. Other techniques deployed to relay the increasingly desirous love between the two women include voice-over to transmit the contents of the numerous letters which pass between them once Madeleine has left, including her fairly unambiguous supplication to Léna to write to her if she

loves her even a little, and poignant non-diegetic music signalling
Madeleine's sense that Léna has betrayed their dreams, coupled with her
pleading that Léna leave her own husband. Finally, the camera's construction of the neglected Madeleine as broken invalid in a point-of-view shot
from Léna's perspective when she first glimpses her after she (Madeleine)
has suffered a breakdown underscores the profundity of Madeleine's love,
along with the correlative gravity of her depression at Léna's failure to
honour it.

Thereafter the narrative resorts to ellipsis, giving us to understand that
in the diegetic interstices the two women have set up business together and,
it would appear, a shared life. When Michel appears and jealously van-
dalises their clothes shop, Madeleine holds Léna in a supportive and
excluding embrace; and by the end of the film, when Michel has again
appeared unannounced, this time at the women's family home shared by
their children, Léna orders Michel to leave the next morning. So, an 'alternative family' has been formed, but the label 'lesbian' family would certainly be refused by director Kurys, and it is significant that the film ends
by spotlighting Kurys's own, younger and wistful persona, alias Sophie,
the daughter through whose eyes we only now realise the whole film has
been framed and indeed directed.

Fabienne Worth's claim that the film's '[h]omosexual undertones . . .
have not been commented on by the French critics' (Worth 1993: 63) is not
entirely accurate. Many of the French reviews did address these undertones, with roughly sixty per cent (at least of those I have been able to track
down) denying the lesbian nature of the women's bond and opting for an
interpretation of platonic friendship. Some of these verdicts are unsurprising, given the overt ideological positioning of the publication. Thus,
the Catholic La Croix concedes that there is a 'coup de foudre' ['love at first
sight'] between the two women (it could hardly deny it, give the film's title),
but predictably and patronizingly avers that this is in no way sexual.[55] The
satirical Le Canard enchaîné appeared blind to its own need for sending
up in the following piece of schoolboy smut: 'Mais son parti pris antimas-
culin finit par faire rire. Est-ce là la rançon de l'homosexualité féminine?
Moins sectaire que l'auteur, on admet que toutes les gousses sont dans la
nature. Et on félicite les deux cons joints'[56] ['But you end up laughing at
its anti-male prejudice. Is this the price of female homosexuality? Less
sectarian than the author, we acknowledge that all dykes have their place in
nature. And we congratulate the two cons joints'].[57] The lesbian dimension, however, is also erased by other reviewers from less ideologically
transparent publications, such as L'Express (8 April 1983). Interestingly,
Le Provençal's dogged interviewer uncovered Kurys's concession of

ambiguity and, more importantly, the agency of one of her lead actresses in bringing the lesbian sub-text into the foreground. When the interviewer asks about Léna's gesture towards Madeleine's breast when they share a hotel bed, Kurys replied (getting her actresses names mixed up – a revealing lapsus in itself) 'Je n'avais rien indiqué à Miou-Miou: c'est elle qui a fait ce geste. Finalement j'ai gardé la scène et laissé cette ambiguïté. Les sentiments, vous savez, ça n'est jamais très carré!'[58] ['I hadn't recommended anything to Miou-Miou; she's the one who made this gesture. In the end I kept the scene and left in this ambiguity. Feelings are never very straightforward, you know!']. Indeed.

Only one reviewer unequivocally conceded the epithet 'lesbian', affirming the amazing credibility of the lesbian couple, which was adjudged charming by virtue of its rarity in French cinema;[59] it is perhaps not immaterial that he was writing for the left-wing *Libération* only one year after the decriminalisation of homosexuality in France by the new, left-wing administration headed by president François Mitterrand. The right-wing *Le Quotidien de Paris* pushed the question with Kurys but ultimately deferred to the credo of directorial intention:

> Et voilà que Madeleine et Lena se rencontrent, et qu'une irrésistible attirance, à leurs propres yeux longtemps inexplicable, les pousse l'une vers l'autre. . . . Alors, une histoire de femmes, je précise une histoire de lesbiennes, j'insiste grossièrement, une histoire de 'gouines'. . . . 'Non, c'était autre chose, c'était plus et mieux que cela, plus qu'une amitié, moins qu'une passion, et je sais de quoi je parle, nous dit Diane Kurys, Lena, c'était ma mère'.[60]
>
> [And so Madeleine and Lena meet, and are driven together by an irresistible attraction which long remains a mystery for them . . .. So, a story about women; let me be more precise, a story about lesbians; I insist crudely, a story about 'dykes'. . . . 'No, it was something else, it was something more and something better than that, more than a friendship, less than a passion, and I know what I'm talking about', says Diane Kurys: 'Léna was my mother'.]

As the centre-left *L'Express* opined, 'On comprend alors que le lien charnel, s'il existe, qui unit Madeleine à sa mère ne soit jamais évoque: si Sophie peut le percevoir, elle ne saurait en aucun cas le concevoir'[61] ['We realise that the carnal link, if there is one, binding Madeleine to her mother is never evoked: if Sophie can perceive it, in no way could she conceive it']. The fact that Kurys refutes the word lesbian does not, of course, prevent us from privileging the integrity of the text and its independent semiotic processes over the director's own intentions, particularly in the light of her clearly problematic relationship to emotive autobiographical material.

Although the francophone-Swiss paper *Le Matin*'s statement that the women's attachment remains platonic begs the question and its final statement is politically quietist, its review does provide an important ideological contextualisation for that attachment:

> On ne nous dit pas que Madeleine et Léna éprouvent l'une pour l'autre une attirance homosexuelle, mais il se peut que leur attachement ne demeure platonique qu'en raison des tabous de l'époque et de l'innocence du milieu petit-bourgeois où elles évoluent. Ce qui les lie serait alors un amour qui a la chance de ne pas savoir son nom et qui, par force, ne le dit pas.[62]
> [We're not told that Madeleine and Léna experience a homosexual attraction to each other, but it may be that their attachment only remains platonic because of the taboos of the time and the innocence of the petit-bourgeois background in which they develop. What binds them together would, then, be a love which is lucky enough not to know its name and which, inevitably, doesn't say it.]

As Fabienne Worth goes on to say, *Coup de foudre* is a French archetype, foregrounding homosociality rather than homosexuality; for Worth, '[c]'est un film qui fait plaisir à tout le monde sans faire de mal à personne, il a d'ailleurs beaucoup plu aux États-Unis mais il évite la polémique en évitant l'aspect sexuel'[63] ['It's a film that pleases everyone without hurting anyone; it was, moreover, a great success in the United States but it avoids polemic through avoiding the sexual dimension'].

So far, I have analysed French/francophone press reception of Kurys's film. What of wider, international academic critique? I would contest Judith Roof's assertion that '[w]hatever sexual desire exists between the women is put off in favor of affairs with art teachers, plans for dress shops, and groping with young men on trains . . . We are finally left with a dislocated desire represented by the absence of any consummation' (Roof 1991: 81). This assertion neglects several factors: Léna's verbalised desire to kiss Madeleine – hardly a platonic statement; the fact that consummation may not receive visual representation but is none the less hinted at through various strategic combinations of suggestion and telling ellipsis; and the political importance of the film's ending – the fact that Léna leaves her husband to live with Madeleine in 1950s France is a fairly potent subversion of heterocracy. More apposite is the verdict of Andréa Weiss, who acknowledges that 'the film's formal qualities – so dependent are they on the codes of art cinema – restrain the women's relationship as the narrative seeks to extend it', but states that as a consequence, 'the shroud of ambiguity surrounding the exact nature of the women's relationship leaves space for the lesbian imagination' (Weiss 1992: 125).

The space for the lesbian imagination left by French Canadian Léa Pool's *La Femme de l'hôtel* (1984) is far more exiguous. Film director Andréa's fascination for Estelle, the woman she meets at a hotel, is at least initially an aesthetic one, bound up with the filmic work she is creating: her character's trajectory begins more and more to resemble Estelle's (namely, that of a lost, *angst*-ridden woman suspected of mental illness, but who might more aptly be described as being metaphysically and existentially nauseous). The first direct contact she initiates is to approach Estelle, a complete stranger, and to announce that she'd been looking for her. As remarked in Chapter 3, the two women gradually build up an intimacy based on a shared elaboration of the diegetic character's story. Hitherto entirely detached from her physical environment, Estelle links arms with Andréa as they discuss this story. Estelle's anguish moves Andréa, whose equivocal desire is mediated in the voice-over conveying her thoughts vis-à-vis Estelle: 'J'ai besoin d'elle . . . Je voudrais qu'elle ait besoin de moi' ['I need her . . . I want her to need me']. In the letter she leaves for Andréa, Estelle thanks her 'd'avoir su entendre ce qui n'a pas été dit' ['for having known how to hear what was not said'], evincing the potential eroticism, albeit diffuse and unarticulated, of their rapport. For Pool, showing love is reductive; she avers that she preferred to express it differently, in desire – in the inaccessible, in flight.[64] The reader is left with the question: why should showing love through desire – in a Lacanian ideolect, this could not be other than in the inaccessible, in flight – be easier or preferable to showing love period?

If lesbian desire in *La Femme de l'hôtel* seems to be 'there' but occulted, in René Féret's *Mystère Alexina* (1985) it is, paradoxically, both obviously 'there' and yet constitutively dubious in a very particular sense. Loosely based on the diary of a certain Alexina as presented in Foucault's *Herculine Barbin dite Alexina B.: Mes souvenirs* (Foucault 1978), Féret's film is prefaced by an opening title asserting the historical veracity of the narrative. In our corpus, the story of a nineteenth-century officially classified hermaphrodite who had fallen in love with a woman (Sara) presents an epistemological conundrum: given the uncertain nature of Alexina's sex and gender, it raises questions of queer *avant la lettre*. The very title, by its punning evocation of the masculine within Alexina ('mystère' being identical to a gallicised pronunciation of the English word 'mister'), connotes the figure of transsexuality. If Alexina is not a woman, her/his (or his/her?) amorous desire for a woman cannot qualify as lesbian. Despite intuiting the complexity of the matter ('si Alexina ressentait de l'amour pour Sara, c'était tout simplement parce qu'elle était un homme. Ça coule de source. Donc, elle n'est pas lesbienne. CQFD') ['if Alexina felt love for Sara, it was quite simply because she was a man. That's obvious. So, she's not a lesbian.

QED'], *Lesbia Magazine's* review ultimately, and, from a queer optic, oppressively, dismissed Féret's film: 'Étonnant de voir qu'en 1985 on fait des films sur ce genre de méprise, au lieu de choquer encore plus le grand public en lui montrant deux vraies femmes en train de s'aimer'[65] ['It's astonishing to see that in 1985 films are being made about this kind of mistake, instead of shocking the general public even more by showing it two real women loving each other']. What remains of relevance to this study is the social repression of a sexual love between two subjects whose performance of gender is at least initially wholly feminine (Alexina's sex is not reassigned as masculine until a good two-thirds of the way into the narrative).

In a point-of-view shot the camera draws attention to Alexina's acute awareness of Sara's breasts silhouetted against the screen (an obvious visual metaphor for the concealment which is to dominate their love) behind which she is undressing in their shared, partitioned bedroom. The effect of the lamp is to shadow and enlarge the breasts, standard symbol of feminine sexuality. Passion eventually triumphs over Sara's religious scruples, and the camera soon reprises this frame, but advances the narrative in showing Alexina now acting upon her desire by moving through to Sara's bed, embracing her and telling her she loves her, lowering her onto the bed, kissing her, and rubbing her breasts. Sara offers no resistance – on the contrary, the soundtrack conveys rapid climaxing on both parts. Afterwards, when Alexina sobs, Sara takes the initiative and declares that Alexina is not made like other girls, that's she's a boy – Sara's boy. She decides to call Alexina Camille, a fittingly androgynous name, but has legitimated to herself their sexual love by deciding that since Alexina is in fact a boy, their union is entirely proper. Having sanitised the issue discursively and morally, she lets rip physically, and the scene turns into a series of erotic kisses, bodily entwinings and torrid tussles. However, their idyll is no sooner begun than rapidly beleaguered from all sides. Alexina naïvely tells her confessor at church the truth as she sees it, in fairytale mode: that her friendship for Sara had gradually changed into love, and that, for the love of Sara, she had changed herself from a woman into a man. Her innocent intuition of gender's non-essential properties (far before Judith Butler's promulgation of gender as performative) is poignantly doomed within the harshly inflexible binarisms of nineteenth-century sexual mores.

And poignancy proliferates in this film. Disqualified by church pressure from her teaching post, Alexina determines to come back to Sara after sex reassignment. After several medical examinations, a doctor pronounces her male; significantly, the main criterion in his decision is that she is attracted to a woman. What more flagrant example of heteronormative blind-spotting? Yet Féret's film also illustrates how religious and medical discourses of the time could be in conflict: for the Church, Alexina is 'ni un homme, ni une femme' ['neither a man, nor a woman'] – denied any sexual/gendered identity or legitimacy at all, from one perspective; from another, this is in fact a more liberal stance than that of the medical institution in the sense that it recognises (though not with enlightened motives or effects) sexual/gender indeterminacy. So, as a compromise, s/he is classified as a hermaphrodite, in a medical report conveyed by voice-over; in civil terms, however, s/he is legally pronounced a man, partly because of the size and functioning of her/his genitals, and partly again because s/he is attracted to a woman. Her/his sex is officially registered as male, and her/his name officially changed to Camille. Tragedy now becomes the dominant tenor in Féret's movie, with voice-over conveying Alexina's despair about ever being with Sara again. The film closes on an intensely melancholic image of Alexina/Camille draped lifelessly on a bed, engulfed by curiously faded colours which, from the intertitle ending the film, we infer to have been smoke, for we learn that in 1860, Camille/Alexina committed suicide by asphyxiation.

Press reaction to the film was slight, and the one review making any allusion to homosexuality goes on to deny its relevance to the film: 'Homosexualité? On y croit au début, conditionné par le thème qui hante la sélection 1985 via *Colonel Redl*, *Adieu Bonaparte*, *Birdy*, *Mishima*, *le Baiser de la femme araignée*. Fausse piste'[66] ['Homosexuality? That's what one thinks at first, conditioned by the theme that has haunted the 1985 line-up via *Colonel Redl*, *Adieu Bonaparte*, *Birdy*, *Mishima*, *le Baiser de la femme araignée*. It's a false track']. Yet the dismissal of the 'piste' ignores the rich potential of this film for a lesbian tracking always already problematised by a queer dis-identification of desire.

In contrast, Geneviève Lefebvre's *Le Jupon rouge* (1986) leaves no doubt as to the lesbian nature of the relationship between forty-four-year-old Manuela and twenty-seven-year-old Claude, both previously straight-identified. More liminal is the nature of the deep and abiding bond between Manuela and the much older Bacha. Ironically, it is Bacha who introduces to Manuela the woman who is to divide Manuela's attentions and of whom Bacha will become violently jealous. When Manuela rushes up to Bacha saying she has just heard about the death of Wanda, with whom Bacha had spent four years in the same block at Ravensbrück, Bacha spits out, 'Je veux même pas que tu prononces son nom' ['I don't want you even to utter her name']. Does this indicate a sense of betrayal by Manuela in comparison with a 'friend' who never let her down? Or the sullying of a sacred memory of true love from Wanda because of Manuela's defalcation from that amorous ideal? Or else an unbearable association between two

women she has loved and one of whom has let her down? Whatever, Bacha
declares that she never wants to see Claude again; and the film ends on a
weakening, if not a dissolution, of the Manuela – Claude dyad, to the
advantage of the re-established 'friendship' between Manuela and Bacha.

Philippe Faucon's *Muriel fait le désespoir de ses parents* (1995) also
explores the ambiguities of female 'friendship', for while teenaged
Muriel's sexual identification is clearly lesbian, her best friend Nora's is
decidedly more labile. Nora kisses Muriel in the toilets, laughs, then when
asked by Muriel why she had kissed her like that, equivocates with a throw-
away, 'C'était pour déconner parce que j'avais envie' ['It was just for a laugh
'cos I felt like it']. Her riposte implies that she had felt like kissing Muriel
rather than messing around, but that insinuation is hastily retracted when
Muriel asks 'De quoi?' ['Felt like what?'] and she insists 'De déconner'
'[Having a laugh']. However, while ultimately she refuses to actualise it,
Nora does display lesbian potential both in her deeds (such as the kiss) and
in her coded words. For instance, she asks Muriel, 'T'as déjà été attirée par
une autre fille?' ['Have you ever been attracted by another girl?'] Muriel
prevaricates by asking why she asks, then returning the question, to which
Nora replies in the negative. This exchange takes place as they walk along-
side a river (iconic metaphor for woman: aqueous, boundary-less and thus
boundary-resistant in politico-sexual terms) in medium shot, with the
camera revealing their tentatively desirous eye-contact. It is at the riverside
that Nora will later take Muriel's arm and kiss her slowly and sensuously.

Nora also flirts verbally with Muriel while in the car with her boyfriend
Fred and with friend Antoine, who clearly find it irritating, and remarks
suggestively on Muriel's lack of a bra and thus her (Nora) having 'quartier
libre' ['leave from barracks'], stroking Muriel's neck, asking 'Tu veux des
câlins? . . . Je t'en ferai plein' ['Do you want cuddles? . . . I'll give you
loads']. Again Nora exploits the verbal ambiguity between the literal and
the figurative: when Muriel says she doesn't know where they are going,
meaning which direction in the car, Nora, who knows perfectly well they
are going back to her place in literal terms, replies, 'Moi non plus je ne sais
pas où on va' ['Me neither, I don't know where we're going']. Alas, Nora
lacks the courage of her intuition and, as we have seen above, finally opts
for the safe shores of heteronormativity over the boundless unmapped of
inter-female desire.

In André Téchiné's *Les Voleurs* (1996), the sexual ambiguity of Juliette
(referred to by *L'Express* as 'une jeune fille androgyne')[67] is flagged up on
her first appearance via a framing comment from Alex, the policeman who
interviews her for petty theft: he says he hadn't realised that she was a girl
when he first saw her, due to her boyish clothes. (She also has short hair.)

Thus one of the identificatory axes crucial to binaristic determination of sexual orientation – gender – is foregrounded from the outset, and is deployed in complicity with the old cliché of the lesbian as tomboy/garçon manqué. However, Juliette soon turns out to be less of a monochrome stereotype, not least in her sexual practice and sexual identification (the latter is never articulated and remains unfixed). She comes on to the same Alex, and they enter into an erotically robust relationship in which rough, ruthless sex certainly appears to induce physiological climax in her (notably in the sodomy scene). However, her desirous *love* for a woman is literally written on the body: she has a tattoo of the name Marie on her stomach.

Such transparency of love between women is absent from Virginie Despentes's *Baise-moi* (2000). Commentary on this polemical film tends to be over-determined by the plethora of heated debates it provoked by virtue of its non-simulated (hetero)sex-scenes and extreme violence. However, very little of that discussion has centred on its potential for lesbian sub-texting. What textual evidence would support a lesbo-appropriative interpretation of the bond between central protagonists Manu and Nadine?

At a relatively early point in the narrative, having successfully evaded retribution for their murders, they nonchalantly take a hotel room and dance together in unambiguously erotic mode. Nadine gazes at Manu desirously, though whether the desire is for Manu herself or rather for what Manu might do with men is obviously a moot point in the context of mainstream reception. What is undeniable is that the two women simulate sex poses with each other, and that the camera deliberately focuses in close-up shots on their vibrating bodies in very close proximity. In a different scene, they gaze at each other whilst having sex with two different men on adjacent beds, and this specular siting of the other and self-in-other seems to enhance the erethism of their own activity at that precise moment. When one of the men suggests the two women do a sixty-nine together, Manu stares at him coldly, superciliously, and spits out the imperative 'Dégage' ['Clear off']. What Manu's mordant response forecloses is not the possibility of lesbian sex, but the risk of male voyeurism framing and delimiting that lesbian sex.

As well as the accretion of indices to a subtextual erotic current, there is an intense affective charge to the relationship between the two women. It is telling that the only emotion ever shown by Nadine is in reaction to Manu being shot dead: here, Nadine weeps, kisses Manu on the lips, and remembers Manu saying to her, 'Je propose qu'on reste ensemble' ['I suggest we stick together'] (a memory conveyed through voice-over). Finally, it should be noted that the images Nadine recalls before shooting herself are of that first – primal? – scene noted above, that is, of the two women dancing

8. Hailed by some as France's answer to *Thelma and Louise*, *Baise-moi* (2000) takes the
female road-cum-revenge movie to controversial extremes (see Chapters 2 and 4).
Le Studio Canal/Take One/The Kobal Collection

erotically together, the first of which features a very scantily clad Manu
thrusting her breasts forward not for a man, but for Nadine.

Opening the film's semiotic field out onto a wider international purview,
several reviews in the French press cast *Baise-moi* as a French version of
the American Ridley Scott's cult movie *Thelma and Louise* (1991). Both
represent cases of lesbian liminality as well as being proximate in other,
more obvious ways (both, for instance, fit into the two discrete genres of
the women's revenge saga and the female road movie). It should be noted
that Alan Rudolph's *Mortal Thoughts* (US, 1991) also features the triad of
two women-together/murder/lesboerotic subtext. Barbara Creed's commentary on anglophone films illuminatingly extends the comparativist
optic:

> Babuscio has argued that the death of one or both friends has become a nar-
> rative convention of the buddy film; it works to suppress questions of homo-
> sexual desire at a point where the narrative has run its course and the audience
> is wondering what the men will do next . . . The buddies have rejected both
> society and heterosexual domesticity – will they declare their love for each
> other? We see a similar convention at work in other female friendship films
> with lesbian undertones such as *Single White Female*, *Fried Green Tomatoes*,
> *Beaches*, *Outrageous Fortune* and *Poison Ivy*. (Creed 1995: 98)

Finally, while the excesses of biographical-intentionalist readings should be eschewed, it is not immaterial that one of the two main actresses in *Baise-moi* manifests definite lesbian, or at the very least lesbo-friendly, sensibilities: when asked by *Le Nouvel observateur* about her plans, Raffaëla Anderson (Manu) replied:

> Dans l'immédiat, participer le 24 juin, sur un char, à la Gay Pride. Et puis mon rêve serait de tourner une comédie musicale avec Catherine Deneuve. Je l'ai toujours admirée. Dans 'les Voleurs', de Téchiné, quand elle prend un bain avec Laurence Côte dans une baignoire, elle est proprement bouleversante.[68]
> [In the immediate future, to participate on 24 June in Gay Pride, on a carnival float. And then my dream would be to film a musical comedy with Catherine Deneuve. I've always admired her. In Téchiné's *Les Voleurs*, when she takes a bath with Laurence Côte, she's literally overwhelming.]

Even the mainstream, albeit left-wing, newspaper *Libération* conceded the possibility of a dynamic between the two women transcending platonic friendship: 'c'est quand même une grosse affection d'ordre amoureux qui unit les deux buteuses'[69] ['you have to admit that what unites the two hit-girls is an enormous affection of amorous nature'].

The lesboerotic content of Keren Yedaya's short *Les Dessous* (2001) also depends wholly on the subject-position of the viewer, and it could be argued that its pointed and sustained display of the female body might be appreciated by a male voyeur just as much as a lesbian spectator. Yet the fact that it featured in a lesbian film festival suggests a distinctiveness, a particular appeal to lesbian modes of spectatorship. It figures Marie endlessly trying on underwear ('les dessous' of the title) in a department store, gazing at and touching her body, assuming conventionally seductive poses to gauge the level of attractiveness of each garment (and her bodily parts within them). The camera shots are mainly medium close-ups (not quite showing the full body, since the ankles and feet – not conventionally erogenous zones – are left out). However, there are also point-of-view shots from Marie's perspective when she is out on the shop floor, conveying her nascent interest in other female bodies. She becomes intrigued – or aroused, depending on one's spectatorial biases – by the sounds of two young women in the changing room adjacent to hers, just as the lesbian viewer may be stimulated by the snapping sound of knicker elastic on Marie's buttocks. In a process of cinematic erethism, the camera fetishises her hips, crotch and thighs. A hand-held camera sequence emphasises the jerkiness and urgency of her movements as she works herself up into something of a frenzy. As she tries on lacy knickers, the soundtrack relays her sighing deeply as if approaching orgasm. Is this purely autoerotic, or informed by the close proximity of other female bodies? The latter interpretation would seem to be supported by her clear visual dissatisfaction with her own body. There is also considerable investment in what is going on outside her own changing room. She hears another customer being denounced for trying knickers on over naked genitals, and the ostensibly trivial, indeed comic event is dramatised by the shop assistant's aggressive demand that the elderly client take off the knickers immediately, to which the client ripostes she didn't know it was forbidden (which may function as a metonymy for lesbian arousal). As if to consolidate her solidarity with the criminalised victim, Marie ends up stealing a piece of underwear. And she, in contrast with the older woman, triumphs from a new-found self-confidence in her roving desire: she smiles at the girl she had spotted earlier, asks if she's bought the bra after all, and when the girl replies ruefully in the negative, declares it a pity. Her gaze follows the girl as she departs with her censorious mother, but ultimately Yedaya establishes Marie's secret victory. Having left the underwear department with her stolen garment, she is last featured at the store's café, tucking sensuously into food, smiling triumphantly. This brief film is ambiguously situated between celebration of female auto-eroticism and of lesboeroticism: and perhaps its main message is that the former may be a precursor of the latter, if one is prepared to transgress petty societal taboos.

Chronologically the last text in this chapter's corpus, François Ozon's *Swimming Pool* (2002), whilst ostensibly a very heterocentric film, is in fact eminently susceptible to a lesbian-resistant reading. As *Le Monde* remarked apropos the trailer, 'On s'attend à un suspense policier avec dérapages sexuels possibles, tentations lesbiennes à la clé. Il y a de ça, mais en filigrane'[70] ['We expect a detective suspense film with possible sexual deviations, and lesbian temptations thrown in. There is that, but only implicitly']. The lesbian sub-coding relies on two factors. First, and most persuasively, the frequent point-of-view shots conveying the vision of chief protagonist Sarah linger repeatedly and portentously on the (conventionally) sumptuous body of Julie, the twenty-year-old daughter of Sarah's philandering male editor and ex-lover, erotically detailing the iconically seductive bodily parts: breasts, thighs, and – less conventionally – stomach. Second, the relationship between the older and younger woman evolves into an intimate sharing of taboo secrets, a complicitous onslaught on masculine power which eventuates in the rehabilitation and vindication of a third woman: Julie's dead mother, whose unpublished novel, once rejected by Julie's editor father, is reborn in Sarah's own, which also incorporates Julie's diary. The film conveys a temporary psychic uniting of these three

9. A point-of-view shot from *Swimming Pool* (2002): Sarah wrests the desiring gaze from its male stronghold (see Chapters 1 and 5). Headforce Ltd/Canal+/The Kobal Collection

female subjectivities, but with strong differentiation and distanciation of the three women involved.

Finally, as a fitting coda to this study of liminally lesbian encodings in French/francophone film, I cite an anecdote from Ozon which emblematises the palimpsestically allusive, layered and distancing nature of the liminally lesbian film:

Comme Charlotte Rampling a été très amie avec Dirk Bogarde, je lui disais pour m'amuser: joue comme lui. Parce que je la voyais parfois sur son transat, regardant avec envie la jeune fille, comme lorsqu'il incarnait le vieux musicien dans *Mort à Venise* de Visconti. Il jouait ce créateur, inspiré de Mahler, qui a cherché toute sa vie la beauté et qui, soudain, se trouve tétanisé parce qu'il la voit, là, incarnée, devant lui, sous les traits d'un jeune garçon. . . . Je regarde Charlotte qui regarde Ludivine et cela me renvoie plus ou moins à *Mort à Venise*.[71]

[As Charlotte Rampling was very good friends with Dirk Bogarde, I said to her for fun: act like him. Because sometimes I saw her on her sunbed staring desirously at the young girl, like when he was the old musician in Visconti's *Death in Venice*. He played this creator, inspired by Mahler, who'd been looking for beauty all his life and who, suddenly, is paralysed because he sees it, there, incarnate, in front of him, in the features of a boy. . . . I look at Charlotte who is looking at Ludivine and I'm vaguely taken back to *Death in Venice*.]

The 'vieux musicien' in *Death In Venice*, Gustav Aschenbach, experiences latent homosexual desire, and Dirk Bogarde was a gay male icon; Ozon's musings operate a transvestism of desire, implying lesbian desire via contiguity with male homosexuality.

Significantly, like many of the movies treated in this chapter, *Swimming Pool* was a commercially successful film appealing to a mainstream audience. It is thus fitting to conclude on the shrewd judgement of Fabienne Worth, an unusually positioned critic in that she is here writing from a lesbian viewpoint on French film but within a wider, American-based context: 'The ability to play with the homoerotic, while keeping the heterosexual frame in place, seems to characterise the success formula of the French film dealing with homosexuality' (Worth 1993: 63). Worth's words prompt a formula which in this context is far from glib: having one's cake and eating it.

Notes

1. Hart's quotation is from D. A. Miller, 'Anal Rope', in Fuss 1991: 124–5.
2. Key figures in this scholarship were, inter alia, Steven Heath and Colin McCabe. A useful starting point is *Screen Reader 1: Cinema/Ideology/Politics* (London: SEFT, 1977).
3. The noun 'invisibilisation' along with the adjective 'invisible' in reference to mainstream cultural and political practices are, symptomatically, widespread in self-reflexive French lesbian discourse.
4. For an overview of this masculine privileging, see part one of Cairns 2000.
5. 'Stéphane Giusti est sûrement un garçon plein de bonnes intentions, et de ressources (homo devenu hétéro en cours de tournage nous annonce le dossier de presse)' ['Stéphane Giusti is obviously a nice lad full of good intentions and resources (he's a gay man who turned straight during the filming, so the press cuttings inform us)'] (Didier Péron, 'Sur les homos ça pionce', *Libération*, 6 January 1999).
6. Jacqueline Pasquier, 'Aux voleurs!', *Lesbia Magazine*, October 1996, p. 32.
7. Pasquier, ibid.
8. Catherine Gonnard, 'L'arnaque des voleurs', *Lesbia Magazine*, October 1996, p. 33.
9. It should be noted that, despite my best efforts, I have been unable to unearth any lesbian-connoted francophone as opposed to French films that pre-date 1968.
10. Lipinska's film is an extremely loose adaptation of *Le Cahier volé: petite chronique des années 50* (Paris: Fayard, 1978) by feminist writer and publisher Régine Deforges.

11. Catherine Gonnard, 'Le cahier vole, pas la peine d'en arracher les pages', *Lesbia Magazine*, April 1993, p. 35.

12. Just as it can be argued that any written text posits an 'ideal' reader possessing the requisite disposition (ethical, cultural, and so on) for that particular text to achieve its full effect, so the same can be said of filmic texts and their viewers, for there is no generic or material difference between the two media that would prohibit the transference of the concept.

13. Jacqueline Pasquier, 'Gazon maudit de Josiane Balasko', *Lesbia Magazine*, March 1995, p. 32.

14. Catherine Gonnard, 'Cinéma', *Lesbia Magazine*, March 1995, p. 31.

15. Gonnard, ibid.

16. Catherine Gonnard, 'Au ras du gazon', *Lesbia Magazine*, March 1995, pp. 33–4 (p. 33).

17. Gonnard, ibid., pp. 33–4.

18. Véronique Lorin, 'Quand les lesbiennes crèvent l'écran', *Lesbia Magazine*, April 1996, pp. 26–8 (26).

19. 'Les Diaboliques', *Radio Cinéma Télévision*, 3 February 1955.

20. Lucie Derain, 'Des monstres dans un bocal: Les Diaboliques', *La Vigie marocaine*, 8 February 1955.

21. Pierre Boileau and Thomas Narcejac, *Celle qui n'était plus* (Paris: Denoël, 1955).

22. Jean-Louis Bory, 'Chasse à courre en bleu', *Le Nouvel observateur*, 20 March 1968.

23. Henry Chapier, 'Les Biches', *Combat*, 21 March 1968.

24. Roger Peyrefitte, *Les Amitiés particulières* (Marseille: J. Vigneau, 1943).

25. G. CH., 'Les biches', *Nouvelles littéraires*, 21 March 1968.

26. Dominique Borde, 'La petite révolution en campagne', *Le Figaro*, 17 May 1994.

27. Howard Feinstein, 'Pool of desires', *The Advocate*, 23 May 2000.

28. Henry Chapier, 'Une femme, un jour de Léonard Keigel. Un cri passionné et tendre', *Le Quotidien de Paris*, 4 February 1977.

29. Translator's note: 'cunt' is far lower in linguistic register than 'sexe', but no other English word fits here: 'sex' is not used in English to designate the genitals, 'the genitals' is too medicalised, and 'fanny' introduces a humorous note that is not in the original.

30. I am grateful to Durham Modern Languages Series for permission to reproduce here certain comments on *La Captive* from my chapter in Günther and Michallat (eds) 2006.

31. The work of art as mediator of desire is a key Proustian topos.

32. The confusion probably arose from the fact that the novel on which Metzger's film is based was a *bona fide* French text: Violette Leduc's semi-autobiographical *Thérèse et Isabelle* (Paris: Gallimard, 1966).

33. Victor Margueritte, *La Garçonne* (Paris: Flammarion, 1922). It was deemed such an affront to traditional values that its author was stripped of his *Légion d'Honneur*.

34. Susan Hayward, as noted above, stated that Simone Signoret appealed to both sexes because of her playing with the fixity of gender. In the same article, Hayward links Signoret very strongly with Arletty: 'some critics in the 1950s said that Arletty lived on in Signoret. Arletty, though not a star in the sense of Signoret, was a precursor to this duality/equilibrium of genders and it made her very attractive to both men and women' (Hayward 1995: 73). Keith Reader also refers to Arletty as 'an at least sexually ambiguous figure (with an attested bisexual history)' in his chapter ' "Mon cul est intersexuel?": Arletty's Performance of Gender', in Hughes and Williams (eds) 2001.

35. Dorothy Strachey Bussy, *Olivia* (London: The Hogarth Press, 1948).

36. It is interesting to discover that when in 1954 *Olivia* was released in the United States as *The Pit of Loneliness* (an obvious allusion to Radclyffe Hall's iconic but deeply depressing lesbian novel *The Well of Loneliness* [London: Falcon Press, 1949]), it was censored for American audiences; for further details, see Russo 1981.

37. See the 'résumé' contained within the 'fiche film' for *Olivia* at www.bifi.fr.

38. Christiane Jouve, '6ème festival de 'films de femmes à Sceaux: le triomphe d'"Olivia" ', *Lesbia*, May 1984, pp. 13–14 (13).

39. Jacques Baratier, 'L'arraignée de satin', *Le Monde*, 1 April 1986.

40. Louis Skorecki, 'Araignée et Renar vont au cinéma', *Libération*, 29 March 1986.

41. Frédéric Strauss, 'Entre les murs et l'affiche', *Cahiers du cinéma*, October 1988, p. 44.

42. Strauss, ibid.

43. Philippe Azoury, 'Carmen en boubou et vaudou', *Libération*, 27 June 2001.

44. Senegal's legal provisions vis-à-vis same-sex acts are incontrovertibly homophobic. Article 319 of the penal code provides for punishment of one to five years' emprisonment for 'immodest' or 'unnatural' acts with an individual of one's own sex. If the act is committed with a minor of 21 years or under, the maximum penalty will always be applied. (See Plein Sud Sénégal – B.P. 1532 – Mbour (Sénégal) – http://www.pleinsud.online.fr/conseils.htm.)

45. Claude Teuriau, 'Les orfèvres d'antan', *Lesbia*, December 1986, p. 33.

46. In Mauriac, the cycling scenes are nostalgically recalled by Thérèse as 'ces jours purs de sa vie – purs mais éclairés d'un frêle bonheur imprécis; et cette trouble lueur de joie, elle ne savait pas alors que ce devait être son unique part en ce monde' ['those pure days of her life – pure but enlightened by a frail, imprecise happiness, and she didn't then know that that shady glimmer of joy would be her only share in this world']. François Mauriac, *Thérèse Desqueyroux* (Paris: Grasset, 1927; Livre de poche, 1989), p. 27.

47. 'Ainsi leur semblait-il qu'un seul geste aurait fait fuir leur informe et chaste bonheur. Anne, la première, s'étirait – impatiente de tuer des alouettes au crepuscule; Thérèse, qui haïssait ce jeu, la suivait pourtant, *insatiable de sa presence*' [Thus it seemed to them that a single gesture would have banished their inchoate and chaste happiness. Anne was the first to stretch out – impatient

to kill the larks in the twilight; Thérèse, who hated this game, none the less followed her, insatiable for her presence]. See Mauriac, ibid., p. 29; my emphasis.

48. Mauriac, ibid., p. 31.
49. 'Le cinéma', *Europe*, 1 March 1963.
50. Just Jaeckin, *Emmanuelle* (France, 1974); Hubert Frank, *Melody in Love* (Germany, 1978).
51. Martin Pénet refers to Le Monocle, established in the 1930s in the boulevard Edgar-Quinet, Paris, as being 'réservé aux garçonnes' ['reserved for butches not femmes'], and to Le Moune as having been opened in the 1950s in Pigalle by Moune Carton (Pénet 2003: 88).
52. Danièle Dubroux, 'Simon Barbès ou la vertu', *Cahiers du cinéma*, March 1980, pp. 41–2 (41).
53. 'Simone Barbès ou la vertu. Entretien avec Marie-Claude Treilloux [*sic*]', *Masques: revue des homosexualités*, no. 5, été 1980, pp. 130–7.
54. Marie-Françoise Leclère, 'Les films-femmes', *Le Point*, 4 April 1983.
55. Jean Rochereau, 'Féminisme bien tempéré', *La Croix*, 7 April 1983.
56. Jean-Paul Grousset, 'Coup de foudre (Où est le mâle?)', *Le Canard enchaîné*, 13 April 1983.
57. There is no satisfactory English rendering of 'cons joints', which literally means 'joined cunts', but is also a homonym of 'conjoints', meaning 'spouses'.
58. 'Avec "Coup de foudre", Diane Kurys s'est exorcisée', *Le Provençal*, 10 April 1983.
59. Olivier Séguret, 'Coup de foudre: mariage de raison', *Libération*, 7 April 1983.
60. Dominique Jamet, 'Mais au café de Flore, y'avait déjà des folles . . .', *Le Quotidien de Paris*, 6 April 1983.
61. Patrick Thévenon, 'Ce que Sophie savait', *L'Express*, 8 April 1983.
62. Michel Pérez, 'Coup de foudre', *Le Matin*, 9 April 1983.
63. Fabienne Worth, 'Pour un cinéma des différences', *Lesbia Magazine*, June 1994, pp. 30–4 [31].
64. Suzanne Laverdière, 'Rencontre Léa Pool. Dire la dualité des êtres', *24 Images*, Autumn 1984–Winter 1985, nos 22–23, pp. 57–60.
65. Valérie Soria, 'J'enlève le bas!', *Lesbia*, November 1985, p. 39.
66. Michel Boue, 'Métamorphose mortelle', *L'Humanité*, 21 May 1985.
67. 'a young androgynous-looking girl': Jérôme Garcin, 'Téchiné modianesque', *L'Express*, 8 August 1996, p. 71.
68. Jérôme Garcin, 'Le porno, c'est du viol', *Le Nouvel observateur*, 22 June 2000, p. 4.
69. O.S., 'Sex shots', *Libération*, 28 June 2000.
70. *Le Monde*, 21 May 2003.
71. Philippe Pazo, 'François Ozon: "On se définit aussi par ses fantasmes"', *Le Monde*, 21 May 2003.

CHAPTER FIVE

Girls on Top: Sapphology

This chapter spotlights certain filmic moments which either resist the two stigmatising models of lesbianism discussed in Chapters 2 and 3, or transcend the encryptedness of those treated in Chapter 4. As such, and within the more gay-friendly (Western) episteme of the twenty-first century, these filmic moments may provide less limiting perspectives on inter-female desire – may, indeed, herald a new 'science' of lesbianism – what the present chapter's title archly alludes to as sapphology. This more upbeat agenda could, of course, be accused of pursuing a naïve positive images agenda. Ellis Hanson identifies one salient model of lesbian- and gay-oriented film criticism as 'a moralistic *politics of representation* that seeks to liberate us from damaging stereotypes', a model which he later equates with the provision of ' "positive" or "liberating" images of gay people' (Hanson 1991: 5–6). His statement that 'the very notion of an image that is inherently homophobic or inherently positive strikes me as naïve, since the political effects of an image are contingent upon the context of reception' (Hanson 1991: 8) has my complete assent. That said, it behoves us to recognise that the context of reception for most films is, by definition, mainstream and thus biased towards, if not always confined to, the heteronormative. In such a context, certain images that have the negative political effect of shoring up old stereotypes for the mainstream viewer may be invested with contrarily positive value for a lesbian spectator. To take one example: although a film celebrating (perhaps but not necessarily in camp mode) butch–femme couplings would do little to challenge hegemonic perceptions of lesbian couples, it might well have an empowering political effect within (at least certain sub-sections of) the lesbian community itself, even if only by dint of giving visibility (and thus, within mainstream purviews, granting ontological integrity) to a self-consciously stylised identitarian stance. Hanson's point is essentially that no filmic image can be pronounced positive or negative for all spectators, due to their differing social, gendered, classed and ethnic positionings and the way in which these positionings influence their responses to that image. But this point, while valid in itself, does not invalidate the use of the epithets 'positive' or 'negative' in relation to celluloid images of lesbian desire. I have deployed them above, and will continue to do so in the present chapter, where they appear appropriate to the probable majority response of most lesbians, with all due respect for the multiplicity of social and ideological identities that lesbians may inhabit beyond that of their sexuality. (Inevitably, the specificities of my own varied positionings will also play a role in that deployment.) Chapters 2 and 3 exemplify my point vis-à-vis the adjective 'negative': very few, if any, non-closeted lesbians would object to the use of that adjective to qualify mediations of lesbianism as criminal or sick. Perhaps less consensual is the term 'positive'. One example is filmic mediations of lesbian motherhood: for some lesbian spectators these will be inspiring, for others, negatively assimilationist in their co-opting of lesbians to *the* most primeval, and biologistically limiting, model of 'woman'.

The preceding chapters have adhered to principled resisting readings, and the present chapter in no sense denies the less uplifting and statistically more common images discussed in those chapters. In a genuinely heuristic spirit, and without indulging in mere wish-fulfilment, I will identify certain relatively lesbo-positive motifs to have emerged from the corpus. The chapter will acknowledge the fact that in some cases, these motifs both involve their own problems (again, the most obvious example is lesbian parenting) and may also be in conflict with other, more negative takes on lesbian desire within the same film. First, it will discuss scenarios which emphasise the problem not of lesbian desire, but of the socio-discursive barriers its subjects face, and usually surmount (including, prominently, the challenge of coming out to family members). Second, it will focus on scenes of erotic arousal and *jouissance* (albeit not always problem-free) between women. Third, moving from the inveterate, whether homo- or hetero-instantiated, ephemera of desire, it will turn to love between women and its possible issue. One type of issue is creation, and my attention will be to art as mediator of (lesboerotic) desire. Fourth, it will consider another type of issue: procreation. Self-evidently, a lesbian couple cannot jointly conceive a child biologically, but one of the two (or indeed, both, following separate medical procedures) may now have recourse to artificial insemination within a joint commitment to lesbian parenting, with the non-biological mother assuming the role of the 'social parent'. Fifth, and in refutation of what some readers may perceive as a teleological, utilitarian approach that seeks to justify lesbian desire through reference to its possible issue in the sense of products, I will foreground filmic mediations of inter-female desire as a simple, relatively unproblematic and self-sufficient factor in a woman's life. Throughout, close attention will be paid to reception of the films in question by both the lesbian and the mainstream press, thereby nuancing the reader's perception of these films as cultural artefacts whose (always already provisional) meanings have been unyoked from directorial intention and negotiated through the interaction of image, sound, their editing and patterning, and the spectator's response.

Our first area for analysis was filmic stress on the socio-discursive obstacles faced by a lesbian relationship. Nelly Kaplan's *Néa* (1976), set in Switzerland, narratively embodies such obstacles, but provides an empowering resolution exceptional for its time: no other French or francophone film of the 1970s featuring a lesbian relationship ends so affirmatively, to say the least. Sixteen-year-old Sibylle's surreptitious observation of clandestine sex between her mother, Helen, and her aunt, Judith, informs the writing of her eponymous erotic novel *Néa*, which is a runaway success, and to this extent her role could be viewed as exploitative. Yet this view belies two important points. First, her novel indirectly challenges stigmatising psychoanalytic theories of homosexuality. In conveying the fact that its first-person narrator, identified with Sibylle herself, began having sex with men at the age of ten but that her curiosity for women came later, her novel neatly reverses the normative Freudian-derived model whereby same-sex desire is minimised as fixation in or regression to an immature stage. Second, by urging her cowed mother to leave a bullying husband for her lover Judith 'sans regrets' ['with no regrets'], Sibylle is in effect the liberator and validator of her mother's lesbian desire and love. Her eloquent pleading occurs within a shot-reverse-shot conveying both the intensity of her own convictions and her mother's consequent sense of contented vindication.

The female solidarity is bilateral, for Helen supports Sibylle when the latter accuses her editor, Axel, of rape, believing in her daughter's victimisation and standing up to her husband's command that the whole affair be hushed up in order to protect the family's good name. Helen confronts her husband by saying that Sibylle will do as she wants, and that if he opposes this, she – his wife – will leave him, taking their daughter with her. When the husband mockingly queries 'Où ça? Chez la gouine?' ['Where's that? To the dyke's?'], Helen retorts 'Pourquoi pas?' ['Why not?'], and promptly comes out to her other daughter, Florence, saying it is time Florence knows that her mother loves Florence's aunt, Judith. Again through shot-reverse-shot, the camera emphasises Helen's new-found strength, dignity and pride in the face of a largely hostile heteronormative family.

No such maternal solidarity with a daughter is found in Philippe Faucon's *Muriel fait le désespoir de ses parents* (1995), whose very title highlights parental opprobrium. An early scene shows Muriel announcing to her mother, 'Je préfère les filles aux garçons' ['I prefer girls to boys'], followed by her shocked and censorious mother foreclosing revelation of any details by declaring that Muriel should not even have told her. Muriel holds firm, reiterating that she won't change and this time adding that she doesn't *want* to change, that her mother will have to accept her as she is. Shortly afterwards, her mother phones to admit that she had not reacted well to the revelation, and expresses simple parental affection. So, the mother is not demonised, but the difficulties of coming out to parents are not underplayed either. Towards the end of the film, however, the familiar litany is intoned when the mother self-righteously points to all they have done for her and to the 'fact' that all her friends are normal. Further, the familial network is seen fully to exclude Muriel when even her brother says sardonically that she could have spared their mother this 'histoire de lesbiennes' ['lesbian business']. The irony is that the straight relationship between Muriel's parents is conspicuously dysfunctional; but, importantly, it has the social armour of heteronormality in its defence. That defence was obliquely mobilised when *Libération* asked apropos the film, 'dans quelle mesure l'homosexualité ne peut être défendue qu'au regard d'une inexorable dévalorisation des couples hétérosexuels'[1] ['to what extent homosexuality can only be defended from the viewpoint of an inexorable devalorisation of heterosexual couples']. This is rather rich: historically, it is the homosexual couple that has been inexorably devalorised, yet lesbians and gays have not tended to claim that this has been the only way to defend heterosexuality. More basically, there has been a dearth of films which even dare to validate the homosexual couple, as *Lesbia Magazine* pithily remarked: 'Sans doute, il nous aurait été plus facile de vivre notre adolescence homosexuelle si nous avions pu voir en salle, à la cinémathèque du lycée ou même à la télé, le film de Philippe Faucon'[2] ['No doubt we'd have found our homosexual teen years easier if we'd been able to see Philippe Faucon's film at the cinema, at the school film library or even on TV'].

Coming out in the face of parental denial forms the thematic kernel of both *La Fête des mères* (1998) and *Que faisaient les femmes pendant que l'homme marchait sur la lune?* (1999) by Belgian director Chris Vander Stappen (scriptwriter of the hugely successful *Ma Vie en rose*,[3] which tackles the sensitive issue of trans-gender). The plot of Vander Stappen's short *La Fête des mères* is minimal: Sacha has taken her mother to a health-farm as a Mother's Day present, but tries to combine this conventional filial offering with a coming-out speech. Her repeated efforts to make the speech having been foiled, Sacha refers pointedly to an old acquaintance, Sophie, who now shares her life with a woman, as a preface to her (Sasha's) verbal leap into the dark: 'J'aime Odile et je m'installe avec elle. Voilà. Bonne fête, maman' ['I love Odile and I'm moving in with her. There. Happy Mother's Day, mum']. The contextual irony of the greeting generates comic relief from the tension governing the entire narrative; and the humour is accentuated by the incongruity between the discursive – the portentous performative act of coming out – and the visual: her mother being violently doused in health-giving water. The play on verbal/visual incongruity is reprised in the film's closing sequence, when the mother, reclining in her mud bath, tearfully but resignedly alludes to Sacha moving in with Odile, muttering clumsily but semi-acceptingly 'C'est . . . c'est . . . bien' ['That's . . . that's . . . good']. The humorous tenor of this short functions to de-dramatise the often extremely dramatic and fraught act of coming out to parents. Precisely because of this, it could be accused of trivialising the emotional and relational stakes of that act. Vander Stappen's next film on broadly the same theme negates that potential charge by nuancing and amplifying its treatment, whilst retaining a certain fey humour that helps the politico-discursive medicine go down for a much larger, and mainstream, audience.

So, *Que faisaient les femmes* fleshes out the bare bones of the short *La Fête des mères* into a full-length feature film. In interview, Vander Stappen elucidates the title by saying that she had thought everything would become possible on earth after human conquest of the moon in 1969, but that in fact, thirty years on, nothing has really changed in the private sphere: it is still very difficult to come out.[4] Whimsically fantastical elements periodically explode the largely realist framework of this film, which was warmly greeted by the French lesbian press:

> Quelle charmante et farfelue comédie où cependant des choses sérieuses et graves sont dites! Comment dire à ses parents qui ne veulent rien voir ni entendre que l'on est photographe et non pas médecin et que l'on aime une fille avec laquelle on veut vivre à l'étranger? Eh bien c'est impossible même quand l'homme est capable, en 1969, de marcher sur la lune! Alors c'est l'occasion pour une cinéaste et des acteurs inspirés d'inventer et de jouer des scènes qui vont, pour notre grand bonheur, dans tous les sens, avec leur part d'émotion, de cocasserie et de fantaisie. Le scénario est habilement ficelé. Chaque personnage vaut le détour par son originalité . . . Chris Vander Stappen, cinéaste belge, nous offre un joli film plein d'amour.[5]
> [What a charming and eccentric comedy! Yet it says serious and weighty things. How can you tell your parents who act blind and deaf that you're a photographer, not a doctor, and that you love a girl with whom you want to live abroad? Well it's impossible even when man is capable, in 1969, of walking on the moon! So, this is the opportunity for a director and her

inspired actors to invent and to act scenes that, to our great pleasure, go in all directions, with their share of emotion, funniness and imagination. The screenplay is skilfully put together. Each character is worth attention through their originality . . . Chris Vander Stappen, Belgian director, has given us a nice film that's full of love.]

The pre-film sequence plays with the viewer's expectations and credence. Sacha is shown rehearsing the coming-out speech she has promised her girlfriend Odile (who is fed up with being passed off as maid or distant cousin) she will make to her mother before man lands on the moon (timed for 20 July 1969): 'J'ai rencontré quelqu'un là-bas, et je l'aime, cette femme' [I've met someone over there, and I love her, this woman']. But her mother dies with shock at the news . . . at least in Sacha's over-heated imagination, with the fantasy patently projecting her own fears and moreover deceiving the viewer, albeit only momentarily. The same scenario is reprised much later in the film when her real attempt to come out has yet again been stymied by the mother, the only difference being the new, absurdist location of the coming-out: an aquarium.

Then the credits come up and the film proper begins, with a scene in Montreal where Odile gives her an ultimatum: either she comes out to her family or they separate. The following sequences are notable in their inscription of two forms of 'abnormality' sitting in isomorphism with the daughter's lesbianism in this petty bourgeois family: cancer and dwarfism. Back home in Belgium, Sacha attempts repeatedly to broach the subject of her secret sexuality, but finds that her family sedulously circumvents her efforts. The mother, however, is not as ignorant as she pretends to be. The hackneyed pathologising discourse on lesbianism is invoked as she covertly analogises her breast cancer with Sacha's lesbianism, without of course actually naming the latter: for the mother, both are a 'secret médical' ['medical secret'] which can be hidden and suppressed (for her part, she has burnt the X-rays confirming the cancer). Sacha finally succeeds in delivering her revelatory speech as the family watches the television coverage of man landing on the moon (thus, just before Odile's deadline expires). Here again, the director blurs the borderline between primary diegetic reality and ironic extra-diegetic commentary, for the mother comments, 'Dire qu'il y a des pauvres parents devant leur poste qui sont en train de découvrir des horreurs sur leurs enfants' ['To think that there are poor parents in front of their TV who are finding out horrible things about their children'], whereas no reference is made to Sacha's particular 'horreur' and the family's eyes remained glued to the television set. The viewer is left to ponder whether this is diegetic reality or, like the pre-credits scene, a projection of Sacha's fears. The fact that both this scene and the film's title refer to what in 1969 was an event (viz. human conquest of the moon) situated on the borderline of science fiction, a fantastical event embodying often utopian dreams of progress, serves to emphasise both the aspirational and the elusive quality of Sacha's far more mundane project: to come out as lesbian to her family, and for them to accept that previously inconceivable reality.

Interestingly, if somewhat improbably – but in keeping with the sometimes fantastical tenor of the film – Sacha's sister Elisa embodies another category of marginality which will ultimately form a tentative bridge between them, albeit not until much resentment has been cauterised. Elisa is a person of restricted growth, or as she herself urges Sacha to spit out, a 'naine' ['dwarf']. The exclusion she suffers due to her physical, visible abnormality parallels Sacha's exclusion due to her (potentially invisible, but in that case closeted) abnormality relative to sexual norms. The direct referent of Elisa's 'mot interdit, mot tabou' ['a forbidden, taboo word'] which she challenges Sacha to utter is 'naine', but through displacement it also refers along the signifying chain to 'gouine' ['dyke'].

The dénouement is prefigured by a comic misunderstanding which reverts to the topoi of mutual miscommunication and of hidden identities (the latter having featured in Odile's being passed off as Sacha's maid or 'chum'). Having mistaken Sacha's gay male friend (who has turned up unexpectedly along with Odile) as an applicant for the shop job she has been trying to fill, but wanting a female employee, the mother proclaims, 'Je préfère les femmes' ['I prefer women'] – a nice piece of ironic humour. The friend's reply, also misunderstood – 'Je savais pas que c'était hérédi-taire' ['I didn't know it was hereditary'] – serves humorously to send up one more homophobic discourse. Farcical overtones emerge from the mother's mistaken surmise that he is Sacha's fiancé. He and Odile initially go along with the pretence, but, while the truth is never fully articulated in unambiguous words, Sacha eventually gives her mother tacitly to understand it. The mother is at first profoundly perturbed (unlike the father), but by the closing sequences of the film has risen to the occasion. When the bailiffs turn up and confiscate goods from the shop (a sign of the times, a small family business is being squeezed out of existence by 'les grandes surfaces' ['supermarkets']), she retains her dignity and proposes that they all have lunch outside. Divesture of her material capital appears to promote a certain metaphysical lightness in this *petite bourgeoise* ('Je me sens légère' ['I feel light'] and a corresponding reinvestment in her emotional capital, which has been partially demoted or at least compromised over the years: she is able to tell *both* her 'abnormal' daughters (not just the family hope Sacha), 'Je t'aime les enfants. Je t'aime. Je t'aime tellement' ['I love you, children. I love you. I love you so much']. Finally, in an enormous gesture of goodwill and suspension of prejudice, she declares that Odile is married to her daughter.

Appearing on a different continent and of shorter duration, French Canadian Louise Archambault's *Atomic Saké* (1999) none the less bears certain marked similarities to *Que faisaient les femmes*. Both are francophone rather than French films, both make forays outside a basically realist framework, and both inscribe the difficulties of coming out. In *Atomic Saké*, however, the coming-out is to not to parents but to the desire-object herself. Archambault inserts into her fundamentally realist image-track hallucinatory images expressing anguish. Indeed, this experimental film opens with montage of disparate images, some of which allude to the title through their foregrounding of Japanese faces. One Japanese reference is obvious in the saké drunk by the three female friends (Mathilde, Ariane and Véro), but another may well be to Alain Resnais's *Hiroshima mon amour*.[6] Resnais's and Archambault's films are linked by the notion of atomic devastation (in *Atomic Saké*, a metaphor for the explosiveness of Mathilde's revelation) but also by the technique of poetic declaiming (see Archambault's opening sequence). *Atomic Saké*'s dominant and recurring image is that of Mathilde cycling furiously.[7] This image is accompanied by the soundtrack of her garbling equally furiously that there is something she has to say – as we deduce later on, that she is in love with a woman, and not just any old woman but one of her two best friends, Ariane. 'Je suis amoureuse. C'est con' ['I'm in love. It's fucking stupid'] is the most we get at this early point in terms of revelation, and the comment conveys the perceived untenability of lesbian love even in the relatively liberal social circle of her friends.

During after-dinner drinks (the eponymous saké) at Ariane's home, Mathilde's coming out to Ariane, her desire-object, is structurally identical to that found in Sylvia Calle's *Ô trouble* (1998) discussed in Chapter 4. However, Mathilde's attempt to reveal the identity of her desire-object – Ariane – is abortive; the hand-held camera, its characteristic shakiness reinforcing the emotional turbulence of the situation for Mathilde, focuses in close-up on her anguished face as she struggles but fails to make the love-declaration. Ellipsis operates at the end of the film, but the spectator is incited to infer that Mathilde's attempt to come out to Ariane remains a dead letter, since the close of the film sees Mathilde slipping away the following morning and Ariane finally waking up alone. The reasons why this apparently 'negative' film is included within the present chapter are that it was conceived for a lesbian audience (first being shown at the French lesbian film festival Cineffable) and mediates an important counter-example to the other coming-out paradigms discussed in this first section.

Returning to familial (as well as social) barriers to lesbian relations, the Belgian film director Dominique Baron's *Tous les papas ne font pas pipi debout* (2001)[8] centres on a 'lesbian family' comprising ten-year-old Simon, biological mother Zoe (whom he calls 'maman' ['mummy'/'mum']), and social mother Dan. (Despite a name that sounds masculine for an anglophone viewer, Dan is, in fact, like her partner Zoe, entirely feminine in appearance.) Set in a residential, family-oriented suburb of Brussels, the film initially focuses on a mother's difficulty in accepting her adult child's homosexuality.

Zoe's mother's warning that later on Simon will want to know about his father is, in retrospect, poignantly prescient. She is not exactly innocent in the process, however: at one point, a close-up shot pointedly draws our attention to her reading to Simon the strap line of a magazine: 'La chanteuse Marissa découvre son vrai père' ['Singer Marissa discovers her real father']. Further, the (grand-)mother superimposes a heterosexual model on what appears to be a fairly egalitarian relationship, claiming that Zoe does all the cooking and Dan all the gardening. It is true that Zoe's profession (school teaching) is more typically invested by the feminine than Dan's (medicine), but Dan hardly fits the butch stereotype. The only positive spin-off of the increasing tensions stemming from Simon's persecution by schoolmates is that the (grand-)mother ultimately stands up in public for the family – and it is indisputably a 'lesbian' family, however much the appellation sticks in her gullet. And later on, when Simon asks if they can buy a poster of the magazine running the story 'Marissa: un week-end avec son père retrouvé' ['Marissa: a week-end reunion with her father'], she dismisses it as 'des conneries' ['bullshit'], in contrast with her earlier references to it as a credible source of information.

An interlude between the dramatic events of Simon's rejecting his social mother Dan and its fallout, when Dan and her father talk whilst out on a country walk, presents the collocation of homosexuality and parenthood from a different perspective: that of a straight father coming to terms with his daughter's lesbianism. The conversation starts with Dan voicing her misery about Simon's rejection of her. Her father's lovingly supportive words encapsulate an interestingly hybrid discourse which blends existentialist voluntarism with social constructivism:

> Il faut pas avoir honte . . . tu as fait une petite entorse à la nature . . . L'homme et la nature c'est une guerre vieille comme le monde, tu sais . . . Ici c'est toi qui dois la gagner, cette guerre. Il faut te montrer digne de Simon. On doit mériter ce qu'on a engendré . . . Pour moi, tu étais . . . comme ce petit arbre que tu as tordu . . . on dirait un accident, et à force on ne peut pas s'empêcher d'admirer qu'il a le courage d'exister.

[You musn't be ashamed . . . You've just gone a bit against nature . . . Man and nature have always been at war, you know . . . Here it's you who has to win that war. You have to show yourself worthy of Simon. We have to deserve what we've created . . . For me, you were . . . like that little tree branch you twisted . . . you'd think it was an accident, and in the end you can't help admiring that it's brave enough to exist.]

Significantly, he adds that, finally, he was able to be proud of her in her difference, and the scene ends on a tender kiss between father and daughter.

In conclusion to the foregoing presentation of filmic scenarios which emphasise the problem not of lesbian desire but of the socio-discursive barriers its subjects face, I am struck by the fact that all of the films considered bar one – Archambault's – foreground familial obstacles to lesbian love, and that all, again bar Archambault's, document the overcoming of these obstacles. The fact that only in Archambault's narrative does the lesbian character fail to come out may well represent a crucial, if not exhaustive, hermeneutic tool: it would seem that, for full victory over these obstacles to be achieved, the closet must be fully vacated.

The second axis of analysis signposted above was explicit filmic mediation of erotic arousal and pleasure between women.[9] Chronologically, the first of these occurs in Guy Casaril's *Le Rempart des Béguines* (1972), which cumulatively increases the (lesbo)erotic tempo from scene to scene. The camera transforms what to other diegetic characters is the superficial gesture of shaking a stranger's hand into a significant linking of bodies: when schoolgirl Hélène is formally introduced to Tamara, the frame virtually freezes in a close-up of their hands, investing the contact with an import far outweighing its role in mere social protocol. After an intense exchange of gazes between the two, music is used for the first time in the film: a tense, aroused, expectant beat forming an aural correlate of the two women's mutual arousal. The camera details Tamara's hands responding to Hélène's gaze by sensuously feeling the arm of her chair, her fingers caressing it as if it were Hélène's flesh. Eventually, she reaches out towards Hélène's own fingers and Hélène takes her hand, her brushing of lips and forehead against it prompting a sharp intake of breath from Tamara which conveys the erotic impact of the gesture. Their intimacy, and the soundtrack which reinforces it, are interrupted by the arrival of Hélène's father: le Nom, but more particularly here, le Non du Père.

The next eroticised scene starts with Tamara in bed inviting the fully dressed Hélène to come closer. Hélène slowly approaches Tamara's hand, touching it as if it were magical, and again the camera provides an extreme close-up shot of their hands – as seen in the preceding chapters, a salient lesboerotic topos, indeed totem. With high-key lighting accentuating Hélène's sense of exposure and trepidation, the camera shows Tamara stroking Hélène's cheek, telling her to take off her shoes and skirt and come into bed beside her. On this first occasion, internalised censorship kicks in, but shortly afterwards the viewer is privy to an abandoned sex-scene in which the two women are shown rolling around in a whirlwind of kisses, with one of Tamara's breasts exposed. A shift to low-key lighting contrasts with the earlier more inhibited sequence; indeed, the lighting becomes so dim that eventually the viewer cannot distinguish anything save their rapid bodily movements. Music (from a slow string guitar piece) is again introduced, suggesting a profound emotional as well as erotic weight to the experience. Later on, a bird's-eye view camera angle shows the two locked in embrace kissing rapturously on the spiral staircase, with the latter reinforcing a sense of vertiginous exhilaration.

Two years later, the Belgian director Chantal Akerman released *Je, tu, il, elle* (1974), which contains what *Le Monde* qualified as the finest erotic scene in all cinema[10] – an astonishingly positive response from a mainstream, centrist newspaper in the mid-1970s. *Je, tu, il, elle* has a tripartite structure, with the three apparently discrete sections being linked by the central principle of desire. It is the third and final section of the film that is germane to our study. Julie (played by Akerman herself) turns up at the flat of a female friend whose verbal protest that she doesn't want Julie to stay is contradicted by her flirtatious body language and her not indifferent embrace. A long-held medium shot positions Julie in the foreground of the door frame, and we should, again, note that the door is the symbol *par excellence* of liminality (cf. Chapter 4): here, Julie is about to cross a threshold from straight to lesbian interaction. She stares at the other woman, who returns the stare, and the erotic tension between them escalates. Striking here are three points: the contrast with Julie's earlier refusal to return the stare of the male truck driver in section two; the fact that the main female character Julie is both the object and the subject of the desiring gaze here; and the fact that the desiring gaze is reciprocated by another female who is both object and subject of the gaze. Mutual 'mastery' of the desiring gaze is thus established outside the framework of masculine referents.

As Julie undoes the woman's buttons to reveal her breasts, she is told that she will have to leave the next day, whereupon the image-track briskly cuts to the two women in bed. The horizontally extended frame fully exposes their bodies locked in erotic wrestle while the soundtrack conveys intermittent gasps, pantings and the noise of their grappling bodies on the sheets. The suggestion is of erotic combat, but not, as yet, of genital sex.

The camera then cuts to a new frame of their kissing in which their heads and hands are foregrounded. While their facial expressions are often concealed by their long tousled hair (visual reinforcer of their joint femininity), the clear impression is of passion; at one point we see them both smiling, but by a curious camera effect they are upside-down, with their heads lowest in the frame (perhaps visually reinforcing the inversion of [hetero]norms). A further cut is effected to a third sequence, with Julie closest to us on the left-hand side of the frame and the other woman parting her legs to plunge her face between them. Julie's arousal is expressed very plainly by the soundtrack's registering of her sharp intake of breath. Then the other woman moves up and appears to enter a frenzy of tribadism; finally, she reverts to (implied) cunnilingus. The active and passive roles are seen to be interchangeable as Julie next assumes the former, but her own activity is visually foreclosed as the camera cuts to a shot of the two women asleep in bed together. Julie wakens, gets dressed and leaves; the last frame of the film shows the other woman still asleep, apparently unaware of Julie's departure. This 'open' ending does not promise any sort of lesbian future to the transient couple; but the structure of the film, which documents first absorption by the self, then interest in the opposite sex, and finally passionate attraction to the same sex, significantly inverts the old Freudian schema according to which the healthy psycho sexual subject passes from auto-eroticism to homosexuality to heterosexuality (with a few detours into more minor sub-phases). *Je, tu, il, elle* provides by far the most explicit mediation of lesbian sex in the whole of our corpus up until Sylvie Ballyot's *Alice* of 2002; and one cannot help but ponder the fact that it is the work not of a metropolitan French, but rather of a francophone Belgian, director.[11] The implications of this national specificity will be discussed in Chapter 6.

In comparison with *Je, tu, il, elle*, and with the stated exception of Ballyot's *Alice*, the remaining films to be considered are remarkably muted in their *mises en scènes* of erotic arousal and/or pleasure. Yet sexual explicitness is by no means my only yardstick, and the purpose of this overview is precisely to identify variety, nuance and range. The next text in chronological terms, Nelly Kaplan's *Néa* (1976), establishes a complicity between Sibylle and her cat Cumes which, in addition to connoting witchery (see Chapter 2), also serves as a conduit of female pleasures. When the cat licks itself, Sibylle masturbates; and it is the cat's preternaturally loud purring that leads her to the visual and aural spectacle of her mother Helen in bed with another woman, Judith, emitting moans of voluptuous pleasure. In a reversal of filmic cliché, the female viewer Sibylle assumes the classically masculine position of voyeur – a point visually and humorously reinforced by her donning of thick-rimmed black spectacles the better to observe. In point-of-view shots, we witness Sibylle sighting (initially in long shot) their outstretched naked bodies, resplendently and sumptuously feminine as in a classical painting: indeed, in a ludic *mise en abyme*, the frame includes just such a picture hanging above them, which obliquely mirrors, posits a historical continuity to and thus arguably validates erotic intimacy between women. This is succeeded by a medium point-of-view shot from Sibylle's perspective showing Judith kissing Helen, sucking her nipples, and smiling at her amorously. Sibylle's final observation is conveyed via a further medium-shot of their entwined legs, with Judith's hand caressing Helen's thighs then her genitals, and Helen's legs rising responsively, which lesboerotic idyll is curtailed by the eruption into this privileged space of the cuckolded husband (cf. Guy Casaril's *Le Rempart des Béguines* [1972], discussed above).

In his 1978 film *Messidor*, the Swiss director Alain Tanner is far less explicit than Akerman or even Kaplan. Framed rapt in the sunlit Swiss mountains, Jeanne warns her 'friend' Marie that opens spaces go to her head, declares that she feels like making love, strokes Marie's hair, then declares that she *will* make love to her. A long shot encompassing the two aroused women and the surrounding mountains visually reinforces the

10. *Messidor* (1978): Jeanne's warning to 'friend' Marie that open spaces go to her head begins to bear fruit (see Chapter 5). Action/Citel/Gaumont/The Kobal Collection

idyllic quality of the experience. However, whilst the viewer is privy to the build-up, s/he is denied visual access to its logical conclusion, which is only connoted by the cut which follows and its 'tasteful' elision. Tanner is good on atmosphere and suggestion – typically, lots of long shots portentously framing the two women together in isolated spots against spectacular rural landscapes – but seems to balk at providing a conclusion to such visual innuendo.[12]

Similarly delicate in touch, yet more engagingly *intimiste* is Geneviève Lefebvre's *Le Jupon rouge* (1986). Shortly after Manuela and Claude have met, the camera follows their car journey to Manuela's home in semi-darkness, amorous gazes and smiles passing between them, with the soundtrack evoking desire and heightened emotion. It then cuts to them at Manuela's flat, both still gazing at each other. When the younger Claude shows a gazelle-like timidity, Manuela tells her she shouldn't be frightened, that women are allowed to do anything. Is this lesbo-affirmative or, on the contrary, minimising, suggesting that women can do what they want together because it is trivial compared to straight relationships (to which both women have hitherto been limited)? The image-track details their touching of face and neck, the soundtrack a response of ecstatic moaning, then the image-track takes the relay by showing kissing on the lips and ecstatic smiles. To begin with, the viewer cannot see Claude because her head is facing us, but in the next shot she is on top of Manuela, taking the sexual initiative. Their positions are then reversed, recalling the interchangeability of inter-female active/passive roles mediated in Akerman's *Je, tu, il, elle*.

Press reception underscored the extreme delicacy with which *Le Jupon rouge* conveyed lesbian love and desire. *7 à Paris* remarked accurately that '[l]es gros plans de leurs visages ravis, où l'émerveillement vainc la timidité sans phrases, sont faits pour décourager les voyeurs et bouleverser les autres'[13] ['[t]he close-ups of their delighted faces, where wonder boldly overcomes shyness, are designed to discourage voyeurs and to deeply move others']. Such discouragement of male voyeurism is clearly a useful strategy for representations of lesbian desire which aim to transcend condemnation as soft porn. Similarly, *Les Echos* quite rightly noted that 'A vrai dire, "Le Jupon rouge", et son affiche osée, parle, certes, d'homosexualité féminine, mais autant le préciser . . . il n'est pas question, ici, d'images brûlantes, choquantes, ou même un peu provocantes'[14] ['To tell the truth, *Le Jupon rouge* and its daring poster admittedly refer to female homosexuality, but it might as well be made clear . . . you won't find here any passionate, shocking, or even mildly provocative images'].

However, the following sentence – 'L'amour est davantage traité en amitié amoureuse' ['Love is treated more as loving friendship'] – is woefully (and one cannot help but suspect, willfully) misleading. In casuist vein, this assertion cleverly tells the truth with respect to one inter-female relationship within the film, that between Manuela and the much older Bacha, but completely distorts the other inter-female relationship between Manuela and Claude. The effect is to edulcorate Lefebvre's thoughtful, earnest meditation on female intimacies which evokes the cinematic lesbian continuum (see Chapters 1 and 4).

Equally, the sexual love between two teenage girls depicted in Christine Lipinska's *Le Cahier volé* (1993) was trivialised by most mainstream press reviews. The right-wing *Le Quotidien de Paris*, for instance, averred that one eventually tires a little of what it patronisingly called tender love as flat as a little girl's chest, as boring as teenage acne;[15] *La Tribune des fosses* minimised the girls' sexual intimacy as consisting merely in little erotic games;[16] and even the usually less partisan *Le Monde* ridiculed this intimacy as young ladies fooling around, going so far as to impute a soft porn element to the film in its allusion to David Hamilton.[17] This united derisive front clearly derives from vulgarised Freudian notions of same-sex attraction as an immature phase on the royal road to heterosexual maturity. One doubts that the same treatment would have been meted out to a film portraying sexual love between a teenaged girl and boy.

Whilst genital sex between the two girls is not mediated visually – for obvious reasons: non-simulated sex in French film incurs an X-rating, and thus reduced profits – it is inaccurate to reduce their erotic exchanges to mere games or fooling around. In the resonantly named 'la grotte des résistants et des amoureux' ['the resisters' and lovers' cave'] (as well as denoting French resistance of the German occupation during the Second World War, in the direct aftermath of which the film is set, the title connotes resistance of sexual norms), Virginie caresses Anne's cheek to comfort her as she recounts her grim family history. Overcoming initial inhibitions, Anne kisses Virginie first on the hands, then on the lips. A close-up shot frames their head and shoulders; the filmic moment is infused by a delicate sensuality and mute intensity, the only sound being that of bird-song in the background. Virginie's hands – lesboerotic phallus – are foregrounded as they kiss. The voice-over conveying her diary account of the event reveals more than the spectator sees – that Anne put her tongue in Virginie's mouth, from which Virginie concludes that she has a lover. In a later scene, when Anne removes Virginie's nightjacket and Virginie undoes the front button of her corsage, voice-over narration from Virginie's diary again conveys a bolder sexual move than is visually mediated: 'elle m'a caressée entre les jambes et c'était doux. Après c'est moi qui ai mis ma main sous sa robe' ['she stroked me between my legs and it was lovely. Then I was the one to put my hand under her dress']. Hardly child's play, for although children may explore their own genitals and those of other children, they do not normally link such exploration with feelings of love and desire.

In Philippe Faucon's *Muriel fait le désespoir de ses parents* (1995), such explicit focus on lesbian sex gives way to scopic eroticisation of the female body by a female gaze. Filmed from Muriel's viewpoint, Nora's body as she dances winsomely becomes a potent desire-object. After splitting from the closeted Nora, Muriel relinquishes her former passivity and seeks out Caroline, with whom she had previously exchanged smiles at a party. Caroline looks surprised and pleased; Muriel alludes to her decision to leave Nora behind and to live for herself; and the camera provides a 'happy ending' by cutting to Muriel and Caroline naked in bed, detailing Muriel caressing Caroline's breasts, waist, hips, and their passionate kisses (if nothing more daring).

More ludic but no less potentially pleasurable is *L'Homme idéal* (1996), one of the short films in François Ozon's *Scènes de lit*. A conventionally attractive blonde, distressed by her boyfriend's lack of commitment, is being comforted by her dark-haired, less conventionally attractive friend (neither is named, in contrast with the absent boyfriend, designated Stéphane; arguably, this non-specificity lends a certain lesbo-universality to the female characters). The brunette proposes a little role-play in which the blonde will tell her what she cannot bring herself to tell Stéphane. Thus, simulation of a heterosexual scene is instigated by the brunette, who, it becomes clear, is sexually attracted to the blonde and gets a vicarious fantasised pleasure from her role as (fantasised masculine) object of desire – an interesting disloca-tion of conventional gaze theory. Visually, this is initiated by a close-up sequence framing the two women on the bed. Smiling enigmatically, the brunette, ostensibly acting Stéphane's role, asks the blonde what she feels for 'him', to which the blonde responds that she thinks she is in love with 'him'. The brunette now poses a leading question, encrypting her own desire for the blonde: is it really he with whom she is in love? The blonde insists that he is her ideal man (whence the title); in a strategic and discursively compact response, the brunette opines that, by definition, the ideal man only exists in thought, and not in reality. The scales begin to fall from the blonde's eyes as she wonders if she is maybe just projecting things onto Stéphane, and whether the person she thought he was does not in fact exist. The brunette's facial expression translates the erotic pleasure she is deriving from this exchange, in which she is ousting Stéphane from his masculine throne, but when the blonde bursts into tears she seems genuinely moved. She strokes the blonde's neck and face, then kisses her on the lips, a move shown in extreme close-up. The blonde asks what's going on, to which the brunette

replies, 'T'inquiète pas, c'est thérapeutique' ['Don't worry, it's therapeutic']. Thus reassured, the blonde's normative inhibitions are abandoned, and
she gets very much into the erotic exchange: their kissing becomes more
abandoned, they lick each other's mouths, their bodies move into each other.
This short film plays on the rhetorical structure of irony – viz. that the
blonde can only allow herself to experience lesboerotic pleasure once she has
conceptualised the situation in heteronormative terms (cf. Sara in Féret's
Mystère Alexina). However, Ozon also implicitly valorises the strategic wit
of the lesbian-oriented subject in turning to her advantage an ostensibly
hopeless situation. Foucault's relational virtualities are here interpreted
cannily, calculatingly, and – most importantly – empoweringly, for the
lesbian subject/viewer.

The French Canadian Jeanne Crépeau's *Revoir Julie* (1998), whilst
serious in its overt subject-matter – internalised lesbophobia, on the part
of Julie if not of Juliet, two old school-'friends' who meet up again after
fifteen years' estrangement – is also characterised by tongue-in-cheek
humour.[18] One example is the interpolation of old black-and-white documentary sequences which function as ludic allusions to lesbianism. The
first, ostensibly about rocks (Julie has just revealed she is a geological
researcher), stresses the structural difference of lesbians from the hetero-
environment surrounding them by referring to sectional lava veins
'appelées 'dykes' que l'on reconnaît facilement à la couleur foncée qu'elles
opposent au granit environnant' ['called "dykes", easily recognisable from
their dark colour contrasting with the surrounding granite']. In the bilin-
gual context of this French-Canadian film, the lesbian referent of the
anglophone word "dykes" is easily recognisable beyond its primary
meaning. The second such interpolation focuses on the production of
maple syrup, a subject so diegetically unmotivated as to license the
lesbian's viewer's interpretation of it as a comically risqué symbol for
female secretions. And when Julie's eventual surmounting of her own
repressions leads to lesbian love-making, humour is again deployed in a
charmingly fey, computer-manipulated montage (for details, see below).

Even more humorous, and certainly exceptional in its elected genre, is
Frédérique Joux's *Emma & Louise* (1998), whose title ineluctably evokes
upon the lesbian signifying chain the American hit *Thelma and Louise*.[19]
The only animated film in the entire corpus, *Emma & Louise* features plas-
ticine female characters who speak an incomprehensible language. They
meet at a disco, take a slow together and then chat flirtatiously at the bar.
The camera then cuts to a shot of their clothes strewn across the floor and
them in bed together, rubbing each other's buttocks and sucking each
other's nipples. But when one goes down upon the other, she is stopped by

her partner's fear of HIV. Significantly, this is virtually the only film in my entire corpus even to allude to this epidemic, presumably because lesbians are, erroneously, assumed to be immune from the condition: they are the least at risk, but certainly not immune. Graphic form is given to the various scenarios imagined by Emma and Louise, including a curious scene of straight sex complete with blow job. Bubbles representing dialogue, thought and apostrophes convey their earnest debate, along with its conclusion: the decision to use one hundred per cent latex to protect themselves from infection. This works a treat: the camera details an explosion in their sex life, with abundant cunnilingus and ecstatic moans accompanied by an upbeat jazzy soundtrack, then when things really hot up, by more mixed, vaguely techno-music. The visuals of this film are far more explicit about lesbian sex than anything that could escape censorship laws were the characters incarnated by real human beings. It would seem that cartoons can push the boundaries of on-screen depiction of genital sex between women further than conventional films wishing to elude classification as pornographic and the concomitant X-rating (under French law, pornographic films are essentially defined as those containing non-simulated sex-scenes, although there are other criteria).[20] Is this a function of their relatively trivialised status within filmic canons? If so, how might we explain the contrast with comic-strip *novels*? The *bande dessinée* enjoys respect in French reading culture; to take just one example beyond France, Art Spiegelman's graphic novel *Maus: A Survivor's Tale*[21] both mediated an eminently grave topic (his father's experience of the Holocaust, and his own experience of integrating that terrible heritage) and received great critical acclaim, being awarded the Pulitzer Prize for Letters in 1992.

Whilst touching deeply melancholic depths, Léa Pool's *Emporte-moi* (1998) is not entirely devoid of humour either, albeit of the attenuated, rueful type typifying adult response to adolescent fan-worship. Antecedents to thirteen-year-old Hanna's lesbian leanings are established in repeated shots of her at the cinema gazing adoringly at on-screen star Anna Karina. An early sequence forms a prototype of this recurring *mise en abyme*, of representation within representation: a close-up showing her smiling radiantly alternates with black-and-white film footage featuring her on-screen desire-object, Anna Karina in Godard's *Vivre sa vie*. (The intertextual network of lesbian connotation is rich here, for Karina as Godard's central protagonist Nana bears a striking resemblance to Louise Brooks, who herself played Lulu in Georg Wilhelm Pabst's *Pandora's Box* [Germany, 1929] – a woman involved in a lesbian relationship with the Countess Geschwitz, who attempts to make love to her in what has been hailed as the first ever lesbian sex-scene in cinema.) The lighting illuminates Hanna's face within the darkened cinema, imparting a fulgent quality to her desire, and her pleasure is conveyed by the rich, saturated colours. A shot-reverse-shot of Hanna's and Anna's faces, the former diegetical, the latter meta-diegetical, provides the wish-fulfilment illusion of their literally gazing at each other (cf. the realisation of this mutual 'mastery' of the gaze by two women in *Je, tu, il, elle* discussed above). Shot-reverse-shot, a technique frequently deployed in *Emporte-moi*, is central to the operation of suture. Suture may be defined as the means by which the imaginary completeness represented by the screen, akin to that represented by the mirror in Lacanian theory, is created, and also the means by which the spectator is 'stitched' into the diegetic fabric, making her/him believe that what s/he sees on the screen is, if not real, then at least what s/he wants to see. In *Emporte-moi*, the spectator is indeed stitched into the diegesis, believing, even if only temporarily, in a literal desirous exchange of looks between the diegetic spectator and her meta-diegetic screen idol. Indeed, we may even be stitched in so completely that we believe ourselves to be part of that visual desiring circuit – and our viewing pleasures may thus be further enhanced.

Hanna's schoolmistress closely resembles actress Anna Karina, and in one sequence the camera superimposes upon a shot of Hanna in the school playground black-and-white footage from *Vivre sa vie* showing Anna Karina smoking, then having sex with a man. The montage is telling, for this meta-diegetic footage is immediately succeeded by a framing of Hanna and her teacher finally making eye-contact in the diegesis; shot-reverse-shot is again deployed to convey their exchange of smiles and Hanna's consequent, though discreetly contained, rapture. Hanna returns to the cinema to see *Vivre sa vie* again, and once more, Pool alternates diegetic shots of her pleasure at watching her desire-object on screen with frames of Anna Karina in the Godard film. When Hanna later dances with joyous abandonment, the editing apprises the viewer that she is recalling and imitating Anna's own sensuous dancing: imitating but, importantly, also innovating by discovering her own female-oriented sexuality.

The connection between dance and desire, but here in negative obverse, is extended from fantasy into diegetic reality. At a teenagers' party, Hanna is clearly uncomfortable dancing a slow with a boy, and immediately cheers up once she has dispatched him with a shallow excuse. When she catches sight of another girl on her own (Laura), they exchange smiles. A close-up shot of their two faces conveys flirtatious visual clues; and when another would-be male suitor takes her hand, Hanna portentously drops it in favour of Laura's, a linking emphasised in close-up shot. The camera then cuts to the two outside in the moonlight, standard signifier of romance, with a medium close-up shot showing their kissing on the lips and caressing.

Altogether darker in tone is Jean-Pierre Denis's *Les Blessures assassines* (1999), for obvious reasons: its basis in the real-life case of the Papin sisters, who worked as maids in the same bourgeois household and ultimately butchered their employer and her daughter (see Chapter 2). Yet certain scenes are none the less ripe for the lesbian viewer's delectation (for discussion of the incestuous dimensions which may compromise such delectation, see Chapter 3). At the age of about fourteen, Léa asks if she can stay in Christine's bed. In a point-of-view shot, we watch Christine desirously watching Léa undress; the camera highlights her naked back in an eroticising, female-agentic gaze. When Léa innocently tickles Christine in bed, Christine strokes her face and looks serious, then, as normative taboos click into place, tells her to go to her own bed. After this sequence the soundtrack reveals Christine's masturbating in the dark as her younger sister sleeps, oblivious to her role as sexual stimulant. In the next bedroom scene, the same pattern recurs, but is developed: Christine and Léa are playfully tussling on the bed when suddenly Christine, still pinioning her arms down, gazes intensely at Léa, who in turn becomes serious. The camera's attention to their facial expressions signifies their tacit awareness of having transgressed a certain limit. The taboo broken, Léa takes the lead: in a subsequent bedroom scene, comprising mainly close-up or medium close-up shots, Léa caresses one of Christine's breasts, circling her sister's nipple. In response, Christine touches Léa's thigh, then her genitals. Léa looks startled but starts to get aroused; Christine kisses her; both begin to breathe deeply. Christine strips off, and when Léa expresses moral reservations, Christine pithily riposte that it would be worse if they were whores. Ironically, the viewer clearly discerns within one frame a conspicuous crucifix on the bedroom wall behind the sisters as Léa visibly derives intense voluptuous pleasure from Christine's kissing of her body. The consummation of their very explicit sexual desire is mediated via filmic codes which, without actually showing genital sex, leave the spectator in no doubt. The point made by *Les Inrockuptibles*, cited in Chapter 3, is well judged (for the original French, see Chapter 3):

> Some of the best scenes are those of sex between the two sisters, the gradual taming of their bodies . . . But one can't help thinking that there were seeds here of a radical form of representation that the director doesn't quite dare to see through to completion.[22]

Following these sex-scenes through to their logical conclusion would indeed have required a radicalism of filmic representation. Whether Denis wished to focus on the bare facts of the historic case rather than the sisters' rumoured lesbianism, or else simply feared alienating mainstream audiences – or even risking an X-rating – is a moot point.

Although Catherine Corsini's *La Nouvelle Ève* (1999) also interpellates a mainstream audience, one of its more interesting features is a brief interlude in which the gaze is lesbianised, if only momentarily. When chief protagonist Camille passes out from alcoholic excess, her old friend Louise and Louise's female partner Solveig try to undress her and put her to bed. As they gaze at the unconscious female body, Louise's apparently jocular proposal 'On se la fait?' ['Shall we shag her?'] generates an erotic ambiguity which is exacerbated by Louise's consequent confession that she had long ago had a sexual relationship with (the now unsuccessfully straight) Camille. Yet no sooner is the lesbian gaze instantiated than it is usurped by a different, exploitative (and impliedly if unsubtly masculine-connoted) gaze: all three women are framed together from the back, with their backsides prominent and vulnerable.

Sylvie Ballyot's *Alice* (2002) is altogether differently conceived. Whilst longer than most shorts at forty-eight minutes, it is not a feature-length film aimed at mainstream audiences; rather, its implied viewer[23] is lesbian, and thus the sort of risks declined by directors such as Denis become opportunities: indeed, *Alice* won the 'Prix du public ex-aequo' at the lesbian film festival Cineffable of 2003 (as well as the Prix du Public at the Créteil women's film festival of the same year). In the long tracking shot forming the prologue, two young women are seen approaching each other on a beach, first smiling, then embracing; the slow-motion filming of their caresses and the silence broken only by the muted sound of the sea impart to this prequel a diffusely erotic quality. Thus the tone is set for the film proper, in which the lesboerotic ante is increasingly upped. One long sequence particularly invites comment.

As Alice sleeps, girlfriend Elsa strokes her hand and whispers her name. When Alice awakens and appears in the bathroom, the swaying, hand-held camera conveys their two smiling faces next to each other in close-up. The female hand again assumes centre-screen – Elsa's hand on Alice's face and neck. The soundtrack conveying their deep breathing intensifies the erotic tempo of the scene, and indeed they proceed to undress and kiss passionately. The camera lurches between various bodily parts and acts – a back, a kiss, a stomach, even an underarm – and infringes conventional visual codes of female propriety by showing sweat beads glistening. This could incur an old-style feminist charge of atomising female corporeal integrity, but frankly that charge strikes me as aesthetically reductive and puritanically limiting. What ensues is the most authentic and the least airbrushed mediation of lesbian sex in the entire filmic corpus treated by this book. The image-track details Elsa's hand pumping between Alice's upper thighs, the soundtrack Alice panting and reaching a climax, then the image-track takes the relay again by showing her falling back in post-coital exhaustion whilst Elsa gazes at her, smiling, and stroking her breasts. The verbal exchange between the two at this point also merits attention: Elsa says that she loves being inside Alice, that she feels everything, to which Alice responds, 'Tu sens quoi?' ['What do you feel?'], and Elsa explains, 'Bouger . . . vibrer . . . et une petite bosse toute sensuelle au bout . . . J'ai encore envie . . .' ['Movement . . . vibration . . . and a little hump that's really sensual at the tip . . . I still want it . . . ']. Two points are striking in this dialogue: first, that the clitoris is referred to directly, desirously but non-pruriently and non-exploitatively; second, that it is the more feminine-looking, and thus in traditional binary thought, the more passive, of the sexual partners who is in fact ascribed the more active role normatively associated with the masculine. For all her long, curly-girly hair, Elsa is sexually insatiable with the more androgynous-looking Alice, who eventually has to admit defeat. This prompts a transitory sulk which is dissolved by Alice tickling her, thus combining the erotic and the playfully childlike, rather than positing the two as mutually exclusive or, more perniciously, associating the latter with lesbian sexuality as regressive/immature.

Finally, a scene towards the end of the film confirms Alice's eventual success in psychically separating her sexual experiences as an adult with a loved and desired woman from those of childhood rape by a male cousin. As she caresses Elsa's naked body, kissing her stomach, nipples and then cradling her in her arms, the viewer witnesses Alice's new ability to trust and to give sexually as well as to lie back and receive (or endure). Later still, at the very close of play, we have a close-up of Elsa's outstretched body with Alice touching her pubic hair, kissing her belly and laying her head on it. This scene is suffused with light, contrasting positively with earlier sex scenes which had tended to involve dim, low lighting, especially in mediation of rape and incest. This closing technical effect, together with the narrative closure consisting in Alice's decision to move out of the family home, jointly suggest a note of hope for a future in which Alice has been able to move on both literally and figuratively.

Contrapuntally, rather than being visually mediated, lesboeroticism in Claire Simon's *Mimi* (2002) is filtered through the verbalised memories of Simon's eponymous interviewee. Appearing in the same year as *Alice*, but reaching a far wider audience by virtue of its general release, *Mimi* adopts a documentary reportage style via which Simon encourages Mimi to recount significant events, feelings and stages in her life. Thus, Simon appears to grant more agency to her object than in fact turns out to be the case. The first mention of lesbian desire comes when Mimi recalls being in love in her early teens with a neighbour's daughter, an African woman whom she would watch playing tennis for hours. In an interestingly synaesthetic memory, Mimi evokes the exoticism of the woman's smell and skin colour ('caramélisé' ['caramel-coated']) contrasting with her western white tennis-skirt. Two further elements to the sensory cocktail are added by the recollection that the woman would always give her a little bottle of perfume before departing and would run her fingers through Mimi's hair, appearing to be 'troublée' ['aroused']; Mimi's remark that she doesn't know if the women made these gestures maternally or not preserves ambiguity, but the strong suggestion is that there was a lesboerotic current between this age-asymmetrical female couple.

Towards the end of the film, in explication of the term 'femmes fontaines' [literally, 'fountain women'], Mimi talks to her friend Diego about female ejaculation, remarking that when they reached orgasm some women spurted this vaginal secretion which could amount to as much as half a litre (!). Discretion is exercised, however: she assures him that there certainly are women like that, but that she will say no more on the subject. In interview with *Lesbia Magazine*, the reaction of director Simon, who anxiously stressed her own heterosexuality by insisting that she does not share Mimi's sexual tendencies, expresses a certain ambivalence about gender fluidity:

> J'aime beaucoup quand elle raconte des choses de l'amour et du désir des femmes. Aucun homme ne le raconterait comme ça et pourtant c'est quelque chose que beaucoup d'entre eux partagent avec Mimi. Dans sa façon de décrire ses amours, elle peut être par moments assez macho. On ne supporterait pas tellement d'entendre ça d'un homme, mais dit par une femme, ça devient très beau.[24]
> [I really like it when she tells us about love and desire for women. No man would tell it like that and yet it's something that many of them share with Mimi. She can sometimes be a bit macho in the way she describes her relationships. We wouldn't really put up with hearing that from a man, but said by a woman, it becomes beautiful.]

Such ambivalence, historically common in old-guard straight feminist women, is largely uninformed by queer theory's authorisation of the manipulations of gender. In all intellectual honesty, I must also acknowledge that resistance to queer is also common in many older French *lesbians*, for whom the concept is at best exotically alien, at worst an anglophone aberration which dissolves lesbian specificity within an erotic melting-pot invariably benefiting men (specifically, gay men).[25] Yet it could also be argued that one of those manipulations of gender, viz. transsexuality, is a legitimate, if unintended, reference-point for Simon's film: 'ça a été un grand plaisir pour moi de filmer une femme qui est une femme et en même temps se voit, se rêve en homme. Elle m'offrait une espèce d'accès aux hommes que je n'avais jamais pu avoir' ['it was a real pleasure for me to film a woman who is a woman and at the same time sees herself, dreams of herself as being a man. She gave me a kind of access to men that I could never have had']. The question of transsexuality will be revisited in the concluding paragraphs of this chapter.

From this brief overview of explicit filmic mediations of erotic arousal or pleasure between women, two points emerge. First, female directors distinctly outnumber male directors: the ratio is roughly ten to five.[26] This is encouraging in that it suggests women's increasing enfranchisement in the creation of images inscribing inter-female desire. Second, there is frequent focus on stroking of the female face, sometimes mutual, sometimes not. I am loath to draw hasty and clichéd conclusions here. Attributing priority to the face, that primary locus of affective expression, rather than to other, more conventionally eroticised bodily parts, dovetails all too easily with traditional, simplistic and limiting binarisms consigning women to emotion and men to sex. What invalidates these binarisms in this context is the fact that the focus on the face is only one among many other foci on those other bodily parts. Yet the fact that it acquires a greater significance than in straight-oriented erotic scenes in film cannot and should not be ignored.

The third area for analysis signposted above was creation: art – in the widest of senses, including performance – as mediator of lesboerotic desire. In ultimately inverted misogynous articulation of that motif is Michel Wichard's *Le Quatrième sexe* (1961). The viewer first sees an American artist, Sand, moodily sketching a naked woman, Myriam, who codedly solicits her sexual attention. When Sand is later introduced to a certain Caroline the two compliment each other; their verbal language is mirrored by their body-language (thrusting forward of hips, flirtatious fiddling with fingers), and the camera lens focuses portentously on their longer than socially necessary handshake. The operation of shot-reverse-shot first conveys Sand's intense gaze then Caroline's rather startled response to being invited to her fancy-dress party (supreme forum for queer performances of non-conventional sexual identities), and finally returns to Sand's now unambiguously seductive gaze. Significantly, Sand's trump seduction card is the declaration that she wants to paint a portrait of Caroline, and that she is the long-awaited ideal. Immediately after the party, Sand asks Caroline to start posing for her, to which request she complies, naked save for the drape placed loosely over her genitals. However, the idyll (emphasised by the comment of another of Sand's girls that Sand has never looked so happy) is literally dispersed by male invasion in the form of Michel. He denigrates Sand by saying she has no artistic talent, that painting is just a pretext for her to get acquainted with the girls she keeps. Implausibly, and for the lesbian viewer frustratingly, she defers to his judgement. Similarly, Guy Casaril's *Emilienne et Nicole* (1970) features two artistic women who connect sexually, but ultimately capitulate to (hetero) male hegemony. It is not insignificant that art student Nouky's pretext for meeting her male lover's wife Emilienne, an art-gallery owner, is to show her lesboerotic drawings (suggesting an isomorphism of lesbian desire and art). When Emilienne looks at the drawings, Nouky suggestively touches her own breasts, hips and lips as Emilienne's fascinated gaze follows her autoerotic movements. The seduction-fascination schema is conveyed via shot-reverse-shot, aided by a resonant soundtrack. The exhibition of Nouky's lesboerotic drawings is, alas, a flop, and it is revealing that Emilienne blames Claude for having deliberately urged Nouky to exhibit too early on in her career – a *sabotage amoureux*?

Le Quatrième sexe and *Emilienne et Nicole* converge in minimising both lesbian desire and the artistic creation with which it is metonymic. (For discussion of this metonym, see the conclusion to this section below.) In contrast, five further films mediate an isomorphism of lesbian desire and artistic creation uncompromised by such masculine-authored trivialisation. In three cases, the form of artistic creation is specifically painterly/drawerly; chronologically, the first of the three is Geneviève Lefebvre's *Le Jupon rouge* (1986). Claude's fascination with Manuela is paralleled by fascination with her drawings, as is visually registered by the intense mutual gaze following Claude's scrutiny of them. In a subsequent scene the camera emphasises the amorous quality to Manuela's sketching of Claude's body, naked from the waist up and clad in the eponymous pink petticoat from the waist down, with the emotional transcendence of the moment being amplified by the soundtrack. Also appearing in 1986 was Léa Pool's *Anne Trister* (1986), of which press reviews, both mainstream but more particularly lesbian-authored, emphasised the imbrication of creativity and lesbian desire. *Télérama* noted that the eponymous character 'peint en trompe-l'œil les murs d'un grand loft pour, dit-elle, en repousser les limites. Comme elle voudrait faire éclater les limites de l'amour en vivant jusqu'au bout sa passion pour Alix'[27] ['paints the walls of a big loft in *trompe-l'œil* style in order, she says, to push back its boundaries. Just as she would like to make the boundaries of love explode by living out fully her passion for Alix']. And *Lesbia Magazine* situates a moment of amorous rapture between the two women within aesthetic exaltation: 'Certaines scenes sont d'une intensité jubilatoire; entre Alix et

Sarah. . . . Ou lorsque Alix rend visite à Anne à l'atelier et découvre son travail superbe au pochoir. Elles se parlent sans que leurs lèvres ne bougent'[28] ['Certain scenes are exhilaratingly intense; between Alix and Sarah. . . . Or when Alix visits Anne at the studio and discovers her superb stencil work. They talk to each other without their lips moving'].

Only a year later, Claudie Lesselier's *Portrait d'Hélène Azenor* (1987) also spotlights a lesbian painter, but within a very different genre. As its title suggests, this video documentary provides a portrait, or rather a snapshot (it lasts only twenty-one minutes), of Hélène Azenor, and its structure has elements of a collage. Interview sequences with Azenor filmed in her studio are interspersed by shots outside that confined space as well as by photographs showing areas of Paris associated with her personal trajectory and with lesbian topographies of inter-war Paris: for example, bohemian Montparnasse in the 1930s and the pioneering lesbian nightclubs Le Sélect and Le Monocle (where there was a distinct butch–femme demarcation). The documentary also registers the cultural impact of certain lesbian cult-figures like Suzy Solidor and also singer Damia, whose lyrics were gender-neutral. Hélène recalls how in 1931 a female model who posed nude in her art classes took her to a 'bal d'homosexuels' in the Latin Quarter, in the rue de la Sainte Geneviève. The illustrating photo, Gyula Halász Brassaï's *Le Bal des invertis de la montagne Sainte-Geneviève*,[29] has subsequently become iconic of the lesbian and gay scene of 1930s Paris, showing both women and men heavily made up and dancing with same-sex partners. Here it was that Hélène met her first love, a young woman who took her back to the young women's hostel where she was living and taught her, as she coyly puts it, many things of which she had been completely ignorant.

The creative element in the lesbianism-creation metonymy changes from the image-based to the written in André Téchiné's *Les Voleurs* (1996). Philosophy teacher Marie plans to publish a book based on recordings of her former lover Juliette narrating her life (but not without Juliette's consent). Before committing suicide, Marie sends policeman Alex, Juliette's ex, tapes and a manuscript on Juliette's life. Why? Because she knows Alex is the only other person linked to Juliette with sufficient emotional investment and cultural capital to seek the conferment of aesthetic form on Juliette's hitherto pitiful life. The mainstream weekly *Le Point* obliquely referred to the literary dimension, or rather heritage, of the lesbian relationship, ascribing to it a redemptive influence on the previously delinquent Juliette: 'J'aime beaucoup la transformation physique de Juliette à la fin. . . . La voleuse doit sa rédemption au professeur, et ce n'est pas un hasard si on la retrouve, radieuse, au milieu d'une librairie. C'est l'héritage de Marie'[30] ['I really like the physical transformation of Juliette at the end. . . . The thief owes her redemption to the teacher, and it's no coincidence that we find her looking radiant in the middle of a bookshop. This is Marie's legacy'].

The painterly and the literary are fused in the lesbian nexus inscribed by French Canadian Jeanne Crépeau's *Revoir Julie* (1998). *Revoir Julie* is a highly artistic text in the sense of being saturated by allusions to other artistic works, mainly of literature but also of painting. The first of these takes the form of an intertitle quoting Gabrielle Roy to the effect that will always be a way of finding an old friend if the will to do so is there – paralleling Juliet's desire to find her old 'friend' Julie again. Most remarkable, however, is a sequence towards the end of the film in which sex between the two women is implied via artistic intertexts. Chantal Nadeau's underwhelmed remark about the two so-called friends' final assumption of mutual desire – 'Un peu "granola", pas vraiment osé, ni sexy, quelques becs de sœurs et hop! On est compagnes'[31] ['A bit "wholesome", not really daring, nor sexy, a few sisterly pecks and hey presto! They're partners'] – is mistaken in implying an erotic void in *Revoir Julie*. Sex between the two women is not visually represented but, rather, imaginatively conveyed via allusion to artistic artefacts. When Juliet and Julie eventually make it to bed together, Crépeau surprises and teases in her fade-out to a feyly charming interpolation of various lesboerotic paintings. Some of these, such as *Gabrielle d'Estrée et l'une de ses sœurs*, are part of the Western artistic canon; their computer-manipulated montage – coy raising of the pictured women's eyebrows – invites a comedic complicity in the creation of a lesbian visual space, which is complemented by a soundtrack of singing female voices.

The obvious question to be addressed in concluding this section is: why do lesbianism and art often stand in a metonymic relationship? Historically, a heterosexual couple has been likely to procreate; indeed, that has been the chief rationale for marriage and the only legitimation of sexual intercourse. Whilst an increasing number of lesbians are choosing to bear children (see below), the majority do not. It may be that lesbians who have chosen to decline reproduction and who are still relatively resistant to social norms find a 'natural' home in the contestatory arena of art marked by evolutionary gratuitousness.

Moving from creation to *pro*creation as the possible 'issue' or 'product' of lesbian love, I turn to the fourth area for analysis identified above: lesbian parenting. Léonard Keigel's *Une Femme, un jour* (1974) foregrounds the obstacles such parenting faced in 1970s France. Despite the so-called sexual revolution following 1968, attitudes to female sexuality and women's right to dispose of their own body were hardly liberal in France at this historical juncture: contraception had only been legalised in 1967, while abortion was not to be legalised until 1975 – and then only on a trial basis of five years. Caroline, who enters into a lesbian relationship with Nicky after deciding to divorce her husband, has a five-year-old son. The young Patrick's precocious disillusionment with the heteronormative family unit is powerfully conveyed when, having crudely sketched on the toilet wall a female and a male figure whom he labels 'maman et papa' ['mummy and daddy'], he urinates on them. It is Caroline rather than the child who has problems in integrating Nicky's role as social parent: when Nicky gives her money to buy Patrick clothes, Caroline asks what it is she wants – to be his 'papa?', to which Nicky replies no, but that she earns enough to help bring Patrick up. Keigel clearly conveys Caroline's inability to think outside the oedipal nucleus, and equally clearly, Nicky's conviction that her relation to Patrick does not have to be problematised. However, when Patrick has an accident and his biological parents are unavailable, Keigel's editing constructs her as a paternal substitute, for it is after a shot relaying the father's refusal to go to the hospital that he cuts to the frame of Nicky alone at the child's hospital bed.

One of the few trouble-free moments of happiness in the lesbian family – indeed, and this is signally important, in the entire film – occurs when the two women have picked Patrick up to go to the seaside and all three are singing during the journey, whereupon he spontaneously expresses both his joy and Nicky's part in it with the statement, 'C'est chouette Nicky quand on va à la mer tous les trois' ['It's great Nicky when all three of us go to the seaside']. Ironically, it is Caroline's inability verbally to explain her relationship with Nicky to her biological son – who has shown as much affection to Nicky as to her – that destroys the lesbian couple and thus the lesbian family. When Patrick wakes up one night and finds Caroline and Nicky naked in bed having sex, his comically naïve but narratively pivotal question 'Qu'est-ce que vous faites?' ['What are you doing?'] throws Caroline into social, moral and ontological panic. It is directly after this episode that she withdraws from Nicky, saying in mitigation, 'C'est pas de ma faute. Je suis pas vraiment comme ça' ['It's not my fault. I'm not really like that']. Nicky's response adroitly acknowledges Caroline's refusal of lesbian agency whilst ignoring her denial of lesbian attraction: 'C'est vrai, tu n'y peux rien' ['You're right, you can't help it']. Biological mother and son are framed walking away from the car, with social mother Nicky framed in isolation, left in the car on her own. As L'Express commented, 'Caroline, à la fin, préférera pour son fils un nouveau père, un père "normal", le dentiste de la famille (Jean-Luc Bideau), qui n'osera se déclarer à sa patiente qu'une paire de tenailles à la main . . . Inquiétante symbole'[32] ['Caroline, at the end, will favour a new father for her son, a "normal" father, the family dentist (Jean-Luc Bideau), who will only

dare to declare his love to his patient with a pair of pincers in his hand . . .
A worrying symbol']. Keigel drives home the point that it is Caroline's bad
faith rather than her son's reaction to lesbian intimacy that destroys the
nascent lesbian family: in a poignant scene after their rupture, he shows
Patrick taking the metro alone to track down Nicky, whom he hugs
affectionately, blissfully unaware of the discursive forces driving a wedge
between them.

In structural contrast but in ideological sympathy is the ending of Diane
Kurys's *Coup de foudre* (1982), which sees the constitution of a lesbian
family comprising the lesbian couple and their children from marriage, but
inflects it with a highly negative charge by framing the whole sequence
through the eyes of one of the children (who turns out to be Kurys as a
child) mourning the loss of her father. *Le Quotidien de Paris* adopts the tone
of heteronormative stricture:

> A la fin, quand elle dit à Michel: 'Tu dormiras sur le canapé et tu partiras
> demain matin, sans réveiller personne', Léna sait-elle seulement qu'elle
> casse cet homme en deux, qu'elle lui vole ses enfants, que les enfants en
> souffriront peut-être. 'J'avais cinq ans quand mon père est parti', rappelle
> Diane Kurys, 'la seule chose que je n'ai jamais compris, c'est pourquoi il n'est
> jamais revenu. J'ai fait ce film, sans doute, pour les remettre ensemble'.[33]
> [At the end, when she says to Michel: 'You'll sleep on the sofa and you'll
> leave tomorrow morning, without waking anyone up', does Léna have any
> idea that she's breaking this man apart, stealing his children from him, that
> his children will perhaps suffer from this? 'I was five when my father left',
> remembers Diane Kurys, 'and the only thing I've never understood is why
> he never came back. No doubt I made this film to bring them back together'.]

With respect to lesbian parenting, Josiane Balasko's *Gazon maudit* (1995)
provides a superficially more upbeat ending, but the key word here is
'superficially'. *Lesbia Magazine* wittily registered strong reservations:

> pas facile de casser les stéréotypes et les tabous, n'est-ce pas?! Surtout dans
> un film grand public! Voilà que Marijo décide de faire un môme. Non pas
> par insémination artificielle comme n'importe quelle goudou qui lit *Lesbia
> Magazine* depuis douze ans mais avec le mec de la Loli, histoire déjà de se
> risquer un sida vu le nombre de nanas que celui-ci a déjà collectionnées et de
> compliquer un peu plus la vie. Enfin bref et pour nous résumer, voilà une
> goudou bien libre au volant de son bahut dans les premières images que l'on
> retrouve au lit avec un bébé regardant partir le père au travail à la fin de l'his-
> toire . . . Bien sûr elle partage toujours Loli, bien sûr on peut même sup-
> poser, si l'on en croit les dernières images, que ledit père va peut-être
> terminer dans le lit d'un bel hidalgo, mais ouf, la morale patriarcale est bien

sauve . . . même dans la 'camionneuse' la plus aguerrie sommeille une mère
attendrie, qui pour une partie de jambes en l'air régulière avec sa dulcinée
est d'accord pour supporter le macho, la coupure avec ses meilleures copines,
et surtout de perdre son autonomie financière!!! . . . La Marijo, vierge
effarouchée, avec son bébé ne peut pas faire peur au grand public . . . [34]
[it's not easy to break stereotypes and taboos, is it?! Particularly in a film for
the general public! So, Marijo decides to make a kid. Not by artificial insemination like any old dyke who's been reading *Lesbia Magazine* for twelve years,
but with Loli's guy, which is already a good way of risking getting AIDS given
the number of chicks that he's already collected, and a good way too of com-
plicating life. Anyway in brief, here we have a dyke with real freedom at the
wheel of her truck in the first images who by the end of the story we find in
bed with a baby watching the father leave for work . . . Of course she still
shares Loli, of course we might even suppose, if we're to believe the last
images, that the said father may end up in the bed of a handsome hidalgo, but
phew, patriarchal morality remains intact . . . even in the most hardened of
butch-dykes lies dormant a melting mother, who for a regular shag with her
lady-love agrees to put up with the macho, with breaking from her best
friends, and above all with losing her financial autonomy!!! . . . Shy virgin
Marijo with her baby can't scare the general public . . .]

To put it bluntly, and to avoid duplicating my previous analyses (see Cairns
1998), suffice it to say that motherhood edulcorates Marijo by neutralising
the threat she had previously posed to the heteronormative family unit,
and that, moreover, her maternal yearnings strike at least this viewer as an
unconvincingly patched-on narrative device to achieve the saccharine and
profit-making harmony of *Gazon maudit*'s 'happy ending'.

Gabriel Aghion's *Belle maman* (1998) etches in sub-plot the long-term,
stable partnership between two women who conform to the stereotypical
butch–femme model. Yet contrary to stereotype, it is the more masculine
of the two women, Nicou, who became a mother, and from the daughter
Léa's account a very successful one despite her mother's 'lack' of a male
appendage to complete the classic parenting unit. Léa's song pays homage
to her lesbian mother's courage and strength in assuming both the maternal and paternal role. Léa is living proof that this non-normative upbring-
ing has been successful: she is beautiful, intelligent, desirable, and . . .
heterosexual. Herein lies the ambiguity of Aghion's sexual politics. On the
one hand, one of the implied criteria for the success of this lesbian mothering is the (hetero)normative sexual development of the child. On the
other hand, Aghion's camera-work betrays no discomfiture on Léa's part
with her mother's sexuality; indeed, he even chooses to have the daughter
mention in her song Nicou's risqué remark to a young male suitor 'Je

préfère les gazons' ['I prefer bushes']. Further, one cannot fault Johnston's analysis:

> Nicou's homosexuality [is] treated simply as part of her character without becoming a problematic issue to be dealt with. On the contrary, Aghion seems keen to use Nicou as a means of affirming the potential positive results of gay parenting. . . . From the outset, Aghion presents us with an older lesbian character, not as a desexualized figure, but rather as a woman who has lived, who chose a male partner because she wanted a child and then raised the child herself and whose long-term stable relationship is rendered unhappy only by the failing health of her partner. The mother–daughter relationship described in the lyrics of Léa's song can only be seen as displaying the merits of gay parenting. (Johnston 2002: 28)

And finally, the film ends upon commentary from the various young offspring of the extended family: Nicou's granddaughter refers non-judgementally to her grandmother's 'fiancée', and another child to his father having concluded a *Pacs* (see Chapter 1) with his male partner. The device of placing wisdom in the mouth of children is heavy-handed, but the fact that the message being conveyed – viz. that prejudice is the result of acculturation rather than any objective moral truth – reaches a mainstream audience carries considerable political weight.

Less directorially hetero-centred was Baron's *Tous les papas ne font pas pipi debout* (2001) (see above). Baron's scriptwriter Vander Stappen, a director in her own right, is also a lesbian parent. In an interview accompanying the DVD copy of the film, Vander Stappen remarks that she and partner Fabienne, who also features in the interview and is the biological mother of their two children, were able to benefit from Belgium's state provision of artificial insemination, in striking contrast with the situation in France. Baron's film examines the topos of gay parenting from various perspectives. In politically correct if not time-honoured tradition, I will privilege the child's optic, without entirely occluding that of the lesbian parents. The latter optic, for instance, demonstrates how ambient homophobia filtered through children can adversely affect a lesbian couple. Further, through their rows, it is revealed that since Dan is from Belgium, Zoé (herself from France) could have had artificial insemination, but that Zoé insisted on conceiving through sex with a man, against Dan's wishes. And penultimately, such homophobia causes the break-up of the lesbian couple, for Dan leaves in despair.

But what of the child's experience of lesbian parenting? Simon's question to his parents about the meaning of an expression heard at school, 'un vrai mec' ['a real guy'], is met by a naïve attempt to combat the tyranny of gender normativity by simply ignoring it; unsatisfied with Dan and Zoé's claims that a man is 'une femme avec des trucs en plus' ['a woman with some extra things'] and a woman 'un homme avec des trucs en plus' ['a man with some extra things'], he resolves to ask Papy ['grandad']. In an interesting twist, Papy is the father not of his biological mother Zoé but rather of his social mother, Dan, and is both a loving and a solid, stable presence in the life of his non-biological grandson.

Yet family is only one factor in the equation; the wider social environment is shown in this film to be equally influential. Hearing that Dan is Simon's 'papa' ['dad'], new boy on the block Max tells his family that Simon is a 'fils de gouines' ['son of dykes'] with no father. His remarkably liberal sister Jennifer objects that this is none of his business, but their father counters such enlightenment with the truism that all children have a father. Meanwhile, Max's mother insists with crushingly ironic goodwill, 'Il ne faut pas voir le mal partout' ['You shouldn't see bad in everything'], suggesting that Dan and Zoé may be two sisters or two friends; again, Jennifer's Socratic question challenges such heterocratic thinking – 'Pourquoi ce sera mal?' ['Why would that be a bad thing?'] – whilst her mother simply shores it up by explaining that 'it' (the word 'lesbianisme' is so far assiduously eschewed) 'est un peu comme une maladie, c'est pas normal' ['is a bit like an illness, it's not normal']. The two older brothers, less mealy-mouthed in voicing prejudice, chip in with 'Moi, lesbienne, ça me coupe l'appétit' – 'Ouais, c'est dégueulasse' ['Lesbians, they put me off my food' – 'Yeah, it's disgusting']. (Later on, they engage in paranoid masculine braggadocio when Zoé thinks they are about to offer help with her broken-down car: 'Pour une fois qu'on est content d'avoir un mec sous la main, hein, pas vrai Bob?' – Ouais t'as raison, un mec peut encore servir – à démarrer une bagnole, par exemple. – Ou à donner du sperme tout frais pour des gousses . . . ' ['For once they're glad to have a guy handy, eh, ain't that right Bob?' – 'Yeah you're right, a guy still has some uses – getting a car started, for instance.' – 'Or giving nice fresh sperm for dykes . . .']. The father intones that they should have been warned, that it's not a good example (Zoé teaches at the local school). In reply, the mother shows a glimmer of tolerance: 'On ne va pas leur mettre une pancarte, quand même' ['Come on, you're not going to stick a label on them']. And her thinking is also challenged more obliquely by Lise, the only truly non-judgemental member of the neighbourhood community, who, being infertile herself, can understand that a woman would want a child 'quelle que soit sa vie' ['whatever kind of life she has'], and stresses that Zoé and Dan 'aiment leur gosse' ['love their kid'].

Another absurdity of homophobic thought, viz. the illogical amalgamation of a gay male child with lesbian parents (which is also indirectly refuted by Marie Mandy's *Nos Parents sont gays et c'est pas triste*, 2003), is mediated when, in paranoid reaction to the fear that Simon has humiliated him in front of their peers, Max flings the insult 'pédé de gouines' ['poofter son of dykes']. Other boys defend Dan and Zoé, saying they like them, with one even valorising their difference: 'Dan c'est comme un père et une mére . . . c'est encore plus fort' ['Dan's like a father *and* a mother . . . it's even stronger']. Significantly, the same boy is later accused by Simon's enemies of being a 'collabo' ['collaborator'] merely for talking to Simon – in the French context at least if less in the Belgian, a pernicious conflation of homosexuality with fascism.[35] This is all to no avail: smarting from public humiliation, Simon starts to resent and to reject Dan.

Eventually, a contrived plot mechanism allows Dan's rehabilitation in the eyes of Simon's arch-enemy and tormentor Max, for she saves Max from drowning. The event also allows a telling comparison in Dan's favour between her as ersatz/false 'father' and Max's 'natural', biological father, when the latter is told by his wife that if he had spurned their son Max a little less, the boy would not have felt he had to act the fool in order to get attention. Dan comes out of the episode redeemed in the eyes of the straight community, but alas, to add poignancy to the unfolding dénouement, she has already left home in despair by this point. The next sequence conveys the fact that Simon is missing her via visual clues such as his pensive staring into space, his insomnias, and his wistful expression when he wins a swimming competition and his trainer is named as being Dan. However, the viewer is led to infer that it is only a matter of time before Dan returns; and indeed, by the final sequence of the film, Dan is shown walking through the park in the direction of their home bearing flowers. The film's title is now clarified by a frame in which we see Dan in a point-of-view shot from the perspective of Max and Simon: she has been asked to hold a hose pipe by the park gardener while he takes a phone-call, but the visual configuration – her with back to us, a large jet of water appearing to surge from her body – humorously gives the illusion of her peeing standing up. The two boys are momentarily taken in but end up laughing in friendly complicity; and discursively, the whole issue of gendered linguistic labels is neatly glossed over – Dan remains a 'papa' with different toilet habits from men. The happy ending thus provided is banal in the genre of feature films aimed at a mainstream audience, but is probably unique within Baron's particular sub-set of that genre, viz. the lesbian-family romance.

Marie Mandy's *Nos parents sont gays et c'est pas triste* (2003) adopts a different genre and a different, that is, univocal, perspective: it is a thirty-minute documentary film giving voice exclusively to four teenaged children of lesbian mothers. The children are, on the whole, extremely upbeat about their alternative families, without being implausibly positive: they refer, for instance, to keeping their familial status a secret to schoolfriends unless they can truly trust them, through apprehension of prejudice. Interestingly, when questioned on their sexual orientation, all four (two sets of brothers and sisters) profess a preference for the opposite sex, although the possibility of change in the future is acknowledged by some. Further, the hetero-centric anxiety that homosexuality may somehow be transmitted from parent to child, whether by genes or lifestyle, is discredited not just by this empirical, and inevitably limited, sample, but also by the wry comment of one of the children that if the heredity theory were to be taken seriously, no straight couple could produce a gay child – a conceptual non-starter in this context (cf. Gide's *Corydon* for a similar point made in a literary context as early as 1924).[36] One detail of historic import should be noted: one of the four, a girl, was conceived through artificial insemination in France, and far from being traumatised by 'lack' of a traceable father figure, she expresses the positive sense of being a pioneer.

Finally, I turn to the fifth area identified in my introduction: filmic mediations of lesbian desire as an unproblematic and self-sufficient factor in a woman's life. In French Canadian Manon Briand's *2 Secondes* (1998), Laurie's lesbian desire is quite simply not an issue, and forms only one part of a complex identity. Laurie is a champion cyclist who is forced to retire by her boss after she hesitated for two seconds (hence Briand's choice of title) at the start of an important match. Back in Montreal working as a bike courier, she calls at a photographic studio for a delivery and falls instantly for the female photographer, who asks her to hang on for 'deux secondes' (reprising the title) before turning round and being assimilated, in Laurie's imagination, to the woman she had vividly imagined during her friend Lorenzo's evocation of his lost love. The epistemological key to the title seems to hinge on hesitation: Laurie ruined her career by hesitating for two seconds, but it is subsequently a hesitation of two seconds that leads her to emotional and erotic fulfilment. The two smile at each other intensely; the tension is emphasised by the soundtrack conveying a deep heart-beat; then we witness burn-out whilst the soundtrack conveys a loud explosion, metaphorically implying the explosion of their desire for each other, which is confirmed by their radiant appearance together as an obvious romantic item in the scene to which the camera then cuts (the start of the bike couriers' race). Remembering Lorenzo's loss when he carried on with his cycling race and never saw his love-at-first-sight desire-object again, Laurie takes a couple of seconds after the start of the race to get off her bike and kiss her girlfriend rapturously on the lips. Thus she symbolises the main priority in her life – but in fact winner takes all, for she soon catches up with the other cyclists, getting to the front line. The film ends with a freeze on her joyous face as she cycles on. This happy ending, so rare in our corpus, is in fact unique here in being totally uncompromised.

Happiness is rarely conducive to or the subject of great art, or indeed of art full stop, and the eponymous protagonist's basic contentment in her sexuality as conveyed by director Claire Simon in *Mimi* (2002) is fairly barren ground for analysis. One of the very rare elements of the film foregrounding 'pure' lesbianism unadulterated by potential lesbophobia in its myriad forms is a cameo shot of a rose bush which a woman with whom Mimi had lived in the 1960s had had planted for her in a public garden. An extreme close-up shot of one of the roses emphasises the singularity of this memory as, while narrating it to Claire Simon, she states, 'On s'était juré de vivre ensemble . . . J'y croyais toujours' ['We'd sworn each other we would live together for always . . . I still believed in that']. Whilst tinged with the ruefulness of worldly experience, the remark amplifies the emotional investment in this relationship, which has found permanent commemoration in a living organism. Such purity is rare; beyond its fleeting imprint, what does merit attention is Simon's documentation of relatively positive reactions by others to Mimi's lesbianism, and, less positively, the fact that Simon *herself* does, even if only extra-textually, manage to problematise that sexuality. Mimi, a real-life personage whose life Simon traces, is filmed talking about how, at the age of twenty, she had needed considerable courage to go to a church: although she herself did not consider her lesbian desire to be a sin and did not want to be confessed, she asserts that she was very lucky indeed, because the monk to whom she confessed her lesbian love averred that, while she had chosen a difficult path and would never have children, everyone needed to live at peace with themselves. She reports having left the church feeling very happy, and declares that this was when her life truly began, as if she had needed some kind of 'autorisation au bonheur' ['permission to be happy']. Such a concession from the Catholic Church is remarkable for its historical context (one assumes the early 1960s), but perhaps the key to this is its location within a monk's rather than a priest's discourse: the former has less of an obviously proselytising role. Similarly, it is worth noting the good grace with which Etienne, her neighbour, had taken her refusal of his marriage proposal ('Tu sais Etienne je ne me marierai jamais' ['You know Etienne I'll never get married']): acceptance without demand for explanation, which she adjudges to have been 'formidable' ['brilliant'].

French reception of *Mimi* was on the whole extremely laudatory. The lesbian press drew attention to Mimi's complete sense of ease with her lesbianism:

> l'on suit pas à pas Mimi qui nous livre peu à peu et avec beaucoup de pudeur certains événements de sa vie. Événements qui nous persuadent que Mimi est une femme libre qui s'assume totalement. Elle . . . parvient à parler de son homosexualité et de sa sexualité avec le plus grand naturel.[37]
> [step by step, we follow Mimi who little by little and with great modesty tells us about certain events in her life. Events which persuade us that Mimi is a free woman who is completely at ease with herself. She . . . manages to talk about her homosexuality and her sexuality with total naturalness.]

The mainstream press adopted a more assimilatory stance, arguing for the universality of Mimi's life-experiences and of her character: to take just one example, 'Ce n'est pas qu'on s'identifie à Mimi. Tout le dispositif ciné-matographique de Claire Simon, entre théâtralité et mise à nu, tient l'ego de son héroïne à distance. Pourtant, ce que dit Mimi nous touche, nous revigore. Parce que le cinéaste réussit à en faire un personnage familier, universel'[38] ['It's not that we identify with Mimi. Claire Simon's whole cinematic system, between theatricality and stripping bare, keeps her heroine's ego at a distance. Yet what Mimi says touches and invigorates us. Because the director manages to make of her a familiar, universal charac-ter']. Even in the comments of the director herself, the word 'universel' recurs, but here in service of a contentious argument which flagrantly ignores the self-positioning of her real-life character Mimi:

> *Contrairement à ce qu'elle dit* elle est à la fois fille et garçon. C'est ce double point de vue qui me touche. . . . Dans son désir d'être un homme, il y a chez Mimi une admiration folle des hommes. Et une certaine jalousie. Cela a dû guider nos rencontres finalement puisque je n'ai filmé que des hommes, à part Mimi. Elle rêvait d'être un jeune ouvrier niçois, ou un marin, ou un mauvais garçon. Je trouve que ce désir de ressembler aux hommes est certes sexuel mais aussi très enfantin et *assez universel*. C'est quelque chose qui me gênait avant et que je reconnais aujourd'hui comme plutôt charmant et pas du tout honteux. Et partagé par beaucoup de femmes qu'elles soient homos ou hétéros.[39]
> [*Contrary to what she says* she is at one and the same time a girl and a boy. It's this double perspective that I find touching. . . . In her desire to be a man, there is in Mimi a tremendous admiration for men. And a certain jealousy. That must have ended up guiding our meetings because apart from Mimi, I filmed only men. She dreamed about being a young male worker from Nice, or a sailor, or a bad boy. I find that this wish to resemble men is certainly

sexual but also very childish and *fairly universal*. It's something that both-
ered me before and that I now recognise as being rather charming and not at
all shameful. And something shared by a lot of women, be they gay or
straight.]

Of course, from one point of view, a contented lesbian constructed as a
universal figure is hardly cause for complaint, but what one must question
is the process of that construction and its political implications. From a
different angle, it should be noted that some spectators might take Simon
to be presenting Mimi as transsexual, a positionality which would find an
honourable place in the contemporary pantheon of queer practices and
affinities. Frankly, however, this reading does not convince me, precisely
because queer positionalities represent resistance to sexual norms, whereas
Simon is basically positing Mimi as a hypostatised version of a supposedly
universal, and normative, penis envy on the part of women. I aver that, in
emphasising one lesbian's emulation of masculinity, Simon skirts dangerously close to reinforcing the old solecism that conflates on the one hand
gender-identification, and on the other, sexual orientation (conceived
according to strict hetero-binaries). In classical if unconsciously pathologising mode, she reverts to the classic *Zwischenstufen* theory, vulgarised
inter alia by Marcel Proust and Radclyffe Hall, according to which a lesbian
is a man trapped inside a woman's body (and a male homosexual the con-
verse).[40] Of course, this model of what we now call homosexuality could be
construed, rather, as an early avatar of the category transsexuality.

A more charitable view would be that Simon is in fact queering those two
notoriously confused categories of gender identification and sexual desire.
In this more indulgent interpretation, she finds touching the double viewpoint which she perceives, rightly or wrongly, to result from Mimi's simultaneously 'masculine' and 'feminine' subjecthood, and to this extent is
attenuating rather than defending the oppressive binaries of gender. Yet her
blindspot is egregious with regard to sexual orientation, for she implies a
causal link between Mimi's espousal of masculinity and her desire for
women. Further, whilst one might applaud Denis's inchoate sensitivity to
queer – her admission and generalising of the impulse to transgress one's
socially assigned feminine identity – I for one find suspect its unilateral
nature: there is no suggestion that such openness to the other gender is an
aspiration shared by men, and this absence once again leads to a devalorisation of 'the feminine': the socially constructed, but also biologically instantiated, category of woman. As Monique Wittig would have argued, the
fundamental problem lies in the instantiation and upholding of those culturally (over-)determined terms and concepts 'masculine', 'feminine', and

even 'man' or 'woman'. But for the moment, those terms and concepts look as if they are here to stay, and one can only regret Simon's (I am sure unintentional) travesty of Mimi's lesbian self-positioning.

This chapter began by refuting the possible charge of pursuing a naïve positive-images agenda. Ironically, it ends with the observation that filmic images which at face value appear positive – lesbians defying the epistemology of the closet (often through humour and/or forays into the fantastic), enjoying sex, creating and procreating, and even (though rarely) appearing immune to lesbophobia – have, when subjected to critical scrutiny, often been shown to contain a negative obverse. Perversely, this lamination of the negative to the positive forms a second, discrete avatar of the spectral metaphor so common in debates on cultural mediations of lesbianism: it is the ghostly shadow of regression haunting the more visible lesbian presence in recent French and francophone cinemas. If this statement strikes the reader as politically vapid lyricism, she will be relieved to find that the sixth and final chapter of my study returns to hard material synthesis and assessment of lesbianism's evolving status in those cinemas.

Notes

1. D.P., '"Muriel", homo consensuelle', *Libération*, 17 December 1997.
2. Catherine Gonnard, 'Muriel rentre "au club"', *Lesbia Magazine*, December 1997, p. 26.
3. Alain Berliner, *Ma Vie en rose* (1997). See Cairns 2001.
4. This interview with Vander Stappen is included in the DVD version of the film.
5. Jacqueline Pasquier, 'Cinéma', *Lesbia Magazine*, September 2001, p. 33.
6. Alain Resnais, *Hiroshima mon amour* (1959); screenplay by Marguerite Duras, whose literary *œuvre* is not devoid of lesboerotic content: see the highly sensual evocation of Hélène Lagonelle's body by the female narrator in *L'Amant* (Paris: Éditions de Minuit, 1984).
7. Cf. Manon Briand's *2 Secondes*, also discussed in the present chapter.
8. First shown as a TV film on M6 in December 1998.
9. I use the words 'arousal' and 'pleasure' advisedly here because they are affects to be distinguished from desire.
10. L. M., '"*Je, tu, il, elle*" de Chantal Akerman', *Le Monde*, 22 November 1976.
11. Censorship of films is very rare in Belgium, and would only result from the decision of a tribunal in response to official complaints once the film had been distributed, rather than being an *a priori* judgement imposed to *prevent* distribution in the first place.
12. Censorship regulations in Switzerland are devolved to the various cantons. One of the most salient bodies is the Commission cantonale de contrôle de

films du Canton de Vaud, which is linked to the Geneva Commission with which its provisions are aligned. Films adjudged purely pornographic are banned to the under-eighteens; those with arguably pornographic elements generally escape this rating. Thus it is clear that Tanner could have been far more explicit in mediating lesbian desire and its physical consummation without compromising his potential viewing numbers.

13. Sophie Cherer, 'Attention une femme peut en cacher une autre!', *7 à Paris*, 24 June 1987.
14. A.C., 'Le Jupon rouge', *Les Echos*, 26 June 1987.
15. Anne de Gasperi, 'Dans le blé en herbe', *Le Quotidien de Paris*, 28 April 1993.
16. *La Tribune des fossés*, 28 April 1993.
17. J.-M.F., 'Cahier des charges', *Le Monde*, 3 May 1993.
18. I am grateful to Durham Modern Languages Series for permission to reproduce here certain comments on *Revoir Julie* from my chapter in Günther and Michallat (eds) 2006.
19. Ridley Scott, *Thelma and Louise* (US, 1991).
20. Since 1916, in order to be distributed in France, a film has had to obtain a distribution number, granted by the Minister of Culture upon recommendation of the Commission de Classification. Currently, the Commission may recommend one of the following for a given film: that it be authorised for all viewers; that it be banned to the under-twelves (usually because of violent or sexual content); that it be banned to under-sixteens (usually because it depicts suicide or drugtaking); since 1975, that it be granted an X-certificate if it is pornographic or incites violence; finally, but very rarely since the introduction of the X-rating, that it be banned altogether. The criterion of non-simulated sex is important for the Commission, serving as a distinction between a ban for the under-sixteens, a ban for the under-eighteens, or an X-rating. The explicit representation of genitals does not in itself entail an X-rating. A film is deemed pornographic if it contains non-simulated sex that is unmitigated by artistic concerns; but authorial intention, the topic treated and the quality of the directing may all enable a film to escape an X-rating. Thus, Nagisa Oshima's *L'Empire des sens* avoided an X-rating because of its artistic value. By contrast, *Baise-moi*'s distribution number was cancelled by the Conseil d'État because it considered that the film was essentially composed of a succession of extremely violent scenes and of non-simulated sex-scenes, without the other sequences expressing a deliberate intention on the part of the director to denounce violence against women. A film may also be X-rated on the grounds that it presents a succession of highly violent scenes which must usually be associated with pornographic scenes to justify this rating.
21. Art Spiegelman, *Maus: A Survivor's Tale* (New York: Pantheon Books, 1986 [vol. 1] and 1991 [vol. 2]). It should be noted that by no means all critics would agree with this blunt designation 'graphic novel', but to my mind it is the least inaccurate of the various possibilities.

22. 'Sœurs Papin, films frères', *Les Inrockuptibles*, 21 November 2000.

23. See Chapter 4, note 12.

24. Claire Vassé, 'Entretien avec Claire Simon', *Lesbia Magazine*, April 2003, pp. 36–9.

25. This point is difficult to prove by reference to written texts: since the view is generally more common among non-academic French lesbians, it axiomatically receives little published expression. But a deep scepticism for queer was verbally articulated in no uncertain terms by several of the older conference delegates at the colloquium entitled 'Autour de l'œuvre théorique, politique et littéraire de Monique Wittig', which was held in 2001 at Columbia University in Paris. Anecdotal evidence suggests that this was not a unique resistance: I personally have witnessed it in several community-based rather than academic lesbian fora in France and Belgium. One of the reasons underlying such resistance may well be the perception that it is an anglophone, and particularly an American, discursive import: France at least has a tradition of anti-Americanism which should not be ignored. The irony is, of course, that queer theory often extrapolates from the insights of certain French thinkers such as Deleuze, Derrida, Foucault, Guattari and Hocquenghem.

26. The female directors concerned are Akerman, Ballyot, Corsini, Crépeau, Joux, Kaplan, Lefebvre, Lipinska, Pool and Simon; the male, Casaril, Denis, Faucon, Ozon and Tanner.

27. Claude-Marie Trémois, 'Anne Trister . . . et Louise Marleau', *Télérama*, 30 July 1986.

28. 'Cinéma: De la main gauche', *Lesbia*, October 1986, pp. 34–5 (p. 35).

29. Included in Gyula Halász Brassaï, *Le Paris secret des années 30* (Paris: Gallimard, 1976).

30. Michel Pascal, 'Entretien avec André Téchiné', *Le Point*, 17 August 1996.

31. Chantal Nadeau, 'Copines et compagnes à la campagne: réflexions "queer" sur Revoir Julie', *Nouvelles vues sur le cinema québécois*, no. 2, été–automne 2004, 2. Pagination on net version of article: 1–8 (4).

32. Danièle Heymann, 'Léonard Keigel: Nicky et Caroline', *L'Express*, 7 September 1977.

33. Anne de Gasperi, 'Kurys, Miou-Miou, Huppert . . . Femmes entre elles', *Le Quotidien de Paris*, 8 April 1983.

34. Catherine Gonnard, 'Au ras du gazon', *Lesbia Magazine*, March 1995, pp. 33–4.

35. Whilst homosexuality, like Jewishness, has been injuriously conflated with both extremes of the political spectrum, communism and fascism, in the French context it is the latter which is the more sensitive charge historically, evoking as it does France's right-wing collaborationist Vichy regime during the Second World War and the now-reviled activities of those who collaborated with Nazi Germany.

36. In André Gide's *Corydon* (1924), the eponymous chief protagonist wryly observes that homosexuality can hardly be hereditary because the very act that

would transmit it is necessarily an act of heterosexuality (Gide 1924: in 1991 edition, 39).

37. Jacqueline Pasquier, 'Mimi', *Lesbia Magazine*, April 2003.
38. Isabelle Fajardo, 'Mimi', *Télérama*, 9 April 2003. Another example of this universalising tendency is contained in 'A propos d'une Niçoise', *L'Humanité*, 9 April 2003.
39. Claire Vassé, 'Entretien avec Claire Simon', *Lesbia Magazine*, April 2003, pp. 36–9 (p. 39); my emphases.
40. See Chapter 3, note 4.

CHAPTER SIX

Conclusion

This brief concluding chapter has three aims. The first is to provide for the corpus an overview which locates broad shifts in French/francophone cinematic mediations of lesbian desire from 1936 to 2002. The second is to consider to what extent national specificities have emerged: that is, differences between films from metropolitan France and from francophone Belgium, Canada, Switzerland and Africa. The third is to tease out the implications of the predominance of *femme* as opposed to butch lesbian configurations within the corpus as a whole.

Quantitative surveys are usually regarded as the methodological preserve not of cinema studies, but rather of the human sciences. However, as my introductory chapter emphasised, the present study is a contribution not so much to French cinema studies as to lesbian/gay/queer cultural studies *within a French-language cinematic context*. Of course (and indeed this is one of its strengths), lesbian/gay/queer cultural studies straddles a variety of academic disciplines; in the following two sections of this chapter, the quantitative analyses of the filmic corpus will supply empirical data complementing and amplifying the more text-based analyses of the foregoing chapters.

This study covers the work of forty-eight male and forty-one female directors. From 1936 to 1979 inclusive, male-directed vastly outnumbered female-directed French-language films representing lesbian desire. Jacqueline Audry, Nelly Kaplan and Chantal Akerman were the only women to explore sapphism on screen prior to 1980; none, it should be stressed, ventured into this marginalised territory before having positioned herself more or less in the cinematic centre. Of course, male directors outnumbered female directors generally in French and francophone cinema until the 1980s, so in itself this gender imbalance is probably unremarkable. What *is* of interest is the growing domination of female over male directors treating lesbian desire from the 1980s: ten to nine in the 1980s, eleven to nine in the 1990s, and, from 2000 to 2002, eight to four. The obvious fulcrum in female directors' appropriation of an exclusively female experience was the rise of second-wave feminism from the 1970s onwards and the upsurge of female-authored creativity which it fostered in the West generally.

A useful snapshot of the cinematic climate in late 1970s France is provided by a lesbian reviewer's critique of Léonard Keigel's *Une femme, un jour* (1977):

> Un film sur l'homosexualité féminine, même fait par un homme, lorsqu'on est soi-même lesbienne, on y court, que dis-je on y vole, même si c'est sans croire au miracle et prête au pire, les films sur les homosexuelles étant dans la majorité des cas: ou des histoires porno, ou de tristes mélos avec jeunes filles de pensionnat qui grandiront et redeviendront normales ou de petites bourgeoises frustrées qui vont chercher pour un temps (celui de se retaper) un amour différent, havre de tendresse après ou avant le cyclone dévastateur de l'amour mâle.
>
> Dans les deux cas, l'homosexualité n'est qu'un passage, une entorse vécue et montrée comme telle, c'est-à-dire superficiellement, en référence continuelle à l'amour 'normal' sans analyse sérieuse de ce qu'est vraiment le lesbianisme si ce n'est sous la forme des poncifs habituels.[1]
>
> [When there's a film on female homosexuality, even if it's made by a man, when you are lesbian yourself, you run to see it, what am I saying, you fly to see it, even if you don't believe in miracles and are prepared for the worst, since films on homosexual women are in most cases: either porn stories, or sad melodramas with young girls at boarding school who'll grow up and become normal again, or frustrated little bourgeois women who will look a bit (enough to get back on their feet) for a different kind of love, a haven of affection after the devastating whirlwind of male love.
>
> In both cases, homosexuality is only a passage to something else, an infringement lived as such and shown to be thus, that is to say superficially, with continual reference to 'normal' love with no serious analysis of what lesbianism really is apart from the usual clichés.]

Twenty-four years on, if we are to believe the triumphalist argument of Dina Sherzer, the situation had changed radically for the better:

> [W]hereas French mainstream cinema previously offered representations of desire that were mainly heterosexual and addressed desire between French-French men and women, New New Wave films offer a *mise en scène* of sexual diversity. Spectators are exposed to a panorama of sexual orientations and arrangements. These include heterosexual, interreligious and interracial couplings, and various forms of homosexuality, involving bisexual and

transvestite characters. Contemporary French cinema no longer works as the medium of a restricted sexual code, but is instead open to difference(s). (Sherzer 2001: 232)

Sherzer's argument is true of one particular movement in recent French cinema, namely the New New Wave. Stéphane Giusti's *Pourquoi pas moi?* (1999) provides a good exemplar for Sherzer in staging a panoply of sexual identifications, including straight, which are all held to be equally valid. But it is hardly representative of the entire corpus, and its message is somewhat clunking, as *Le Monde*'s review implied:

Une maladresse certaine dans l'exposition des personnages, une déclinaison convenue du communautarisme (c'est la majorité qui a des problèmes avec sa marge), une morale gentillette (il suffit d'être soi-même) concourent à faire de *Pourquoi pas moi?* une variation homosexuelle de la traditionnelle comédie sentimentale de groupe.[2]
[A definite awkwardness in the exposition of the characters, a conventional declension of communitarianism (it's the majority that has problems with its marginal elements), a nice-enough morality (it's enough just to be yourself) combine to make of *Pourquoi pas moi?* a homosexual variant on the traditional romantic group comedy.]

This assimilation of *Pourquoi pas moi?* to the 'traditionnelle comédie sentimentale de groupe' is very telling within the universalist discourse of French Republicanism, which is hostile to the *différencialisme* [differentialism] of *communautarisme* [communitarianism]. Interestingly, assimilation, albeit of a different sort, also characterises the synecdochical move by which Sherzer comes to equate 'New New Wave films' with contemporary French cinema in general. To state the obvious, contemporary French cinema is no cultural monolith: its forms are pluralistic, and the majority of those forms are above all commercially driven, thus axiomatically designed to appeal to the mainstream, and *a fortiori* to heterosexually positioned viewers. That said, it would be both churlish and misleading to deny the significant growth in French films breaking the heteronormative mould. Two caveats apply here. First, breaking the heteronormative mould is more frequently to the advantage of gay men than gay women – for various reasons, chief amongst which is the greater economic benefit to be derived from plugging the gay male market. Second, in a comparativist perspective, it should be noted that although the same economic inferiority of gay women compared to gay men obtains in the UK and the US also, proportionally fewer lesbian-themed films have emerged from France than from those anglophone countries. Again, this is a function of the all-pervasive influence of the Republican model, to which identity politics are inimical; and identity politics form the perceived linchpin of any filmic body purporting to portray lesbian (as indeed gay) sexuality. While queer theory attempts to exceed, indeed to refute, identity politics, its impact on French culture is only just nascent.

The second stated aim of this chapter is to consider to what extent national specificities have emerged from the preceding chapters.[3] Eighteen films from the total corpus of eighty-nine (20.22 per cent) come from francophone countries as opposed to France. Of those eighteen, 5.55 per cent are African, 5.55 per cent Swiss, 38.9 per cent Belgian, and 50 per cent Canadian. Among the eighteen, only four (22.22 per cent) are male-directed: Paul Carrière's *Maman et Ève* (1996) from Canada, Harry Kümel's *Les Lèvres rouges* (1971) from Belgium, Joseph Gaï Ramaka's *Karmen Geï* (2001) from Senegal, and Alain Tanner's *Messidor* (1978) from Switzerland. However, these data should be set aside the fact that no female-directed film treating lesbian desire has yet emerged from francophone Africa or Switzerland.

The Belgian Kümel's vampire movie reflects and perpetuates a demonising cultural mythology according to which lesbianism is synonymous with at best danger, at worst death. The Swiss Tanner's film mediates lesbian desire as ethically neutral, but subordinates it to wider existential preoccupations. Significantly, despite strenuous efforts, I have been unable to locate a copy of the Canadian Carrière text, so am unable to comment on it. The African Ramaka's *Karmen Gei*, for its part, is something of a cultural hapax, for it is the only film to be set in a non-Western country (which, moreover, strongly condemns homosexuality: see Chapter 4, note 44). In terms of style and ideology, it depicts lesboeroticism openly and sensuously, but represents the only genuinely lesbian character – Angélique, the prison governor who falls for bisexual Karmen – as doomed, and, moreover, uses the old chestnut of her suicide to underwrite this negative fate.

Amongst the fourteen female-directed non-metropolitan French films in our corpus, six (42.85 per cent) emanate from Belgium, and eight (57.15 per cent) from Canada. Three of the six Belgian products (50 per cent) are the work of a single director, Chantal Akerman, whose resistance to co-option by lesbian as well as by feminist identity-politics is well known. Yet these three films are exceptional within the entire corpus in being the work of an acclaimed *auteur* whose richly textured filmic *œuvre* has successfully borne the weight of a minoritarian element. *Je, tu, il, elle* (1974) was a truly groundbreaking work in filmic mediations of lesbian sex, and has acquired an iconic status within both lesbian ('imagined') communities and in more heterosexually-oriented avant-garde film circles. Akerman's *Les Rendez-vous d'Anna* (1978) elided the sexual explicitness of its predecessor, but placed at its enigmatic emotional centre the literal absence of Anna's desired female Other. In Akerman's *La Captive* (2000), an extremely loose adaptation of Proust's literary monument *La Prisonnière*, lesbian desire is the elusive, damaging yet compulsive conundrum haunting the Marcel-figure. The other three Belgian films – Dominique Baron's *Tous les papas ne font pas pipi debout* (2001), and Chris Vander Stappen's *La Fête des mères* (1998) and *Que faisaient les femmes pendant que l'homme marchait sur la lune?* (1999) – all foreground questions of lesbian kinship/family, be it relations between lesbian daughter and straight mother (*La Fête des mères*), lesbian daughter and petty-bourgeois blinkered family (*Que faisaient les femmes pendant que l'homme marchait sur la lune?*), or lesbian mother(s) and child (*Tous les papas ne font pas pipi debout*).

In the French-Canadian films, the issue of lesbian kinship is quite simply absent. Extreme diversity marks the foci of these eight films. Only one feature provides a link, and a tenuous one at that, between four of them (*Anne Trister* [1986], *Revoir Julie* [1998], *Emporte-moi* [1998] and *Atomic Saké* [1999]): the tensions generated by a lesbian woman's (or in the case of *Emporte-moi*, girl's) attraction to a straight, or seemingly straight, female friend. Otherwise, there is no thematic continuity between the eight films. Briand's *2 Secondes* (1998) is refreshingly robust: in it, lesbian attraction is entirely unproblematised and figures as a healthy and unremarkable part of a complex subjecthood, reversing the common synecdochal operation by which lesbian-identified subjects are perceived above all in terms of their sexual orientation – an impoverishing and repressive operation. Crépeau's *L'Usure* (1986), an eight-minute short, centres on the efforts of two women to end their long-term but flagging relationship; and her *Le Film de Justine* (1989), a medium-length film at forty-five minutes, traces a young woman's effort to wean herself off love after a painful break-up from her girlfriend, ending in failure when she falls for another woman. Finally, Pool's *La Femme de l'hôtel* (1984) explores liminal lesbian attraction, overlaid by questions of creativity and the stealing of subjecthood.

One important observation to be made in concluding this inevitably limited and broad-brush overview is the generally more upbeat, lesbo-affirmative take of the female-directed French-Belgian and French-Canadian films as compared to the metropolitan French films. Yet this observation may be misleading in the absence of a thoroughgoing comparative analysis with the totalities of French-Belgian and French-Canadian cinemas, as may be inferred from the following statement on Québécois lesbian-themed cinema:

> Les films québécois francophones eux – Surprise! Surprise! – ont fait peu de cas de ... la lesbienne tout court, tout occupés qu'ils sont à nous montrer le mâle hétéro de preference en perpetuelle crise d'adolescence, avec une imagination sexuelle à peine plus grosse qu'une crotte de pigeon et une fascination morbide pour un post mortem national. (Nadeau 2004: 4)
> [As for francophone Quebec films – Surprise Surprise! – little importance is attached to ... lesbians full stop, they're so busy showing us the male, preferably straight, in a perpetual adolescent crisis, with a sexual imagination not much bigger than a pigeon turd and a morbid fascination for a national post mortem.]

Wholescale analysis of French-Belgian and French-Canadian cinemas lies outside the purview of the present study:[4] I have proceeded within inevitably limited parameters, endeavouring to identify and analyse French-language lesbian-themed films. Acutely aware of the narrowness of these parameters, I can only stress the need for future studies which will provide more finely-honed comparativist perspectives. The one tentative hypothesis I would like to advance is that, when lesbian-themed films do get made in francophone Belgium and Canada, the lesbian content tends to be more overt, less encrypted and less problematic in itself than in metropolitan French films; if problems there are, these tend to be situated in heteronormativity rather than posited as immanent in lesbian sexuality *per se*.

By contrast, the majority of metropolitan French films over the period under scrutiny (1936–2002) have tended to connote rather than to denote lesbianism: to mediate it as a liminal eventuality rather than a centred reality. Simultaneously, they have tended to figure characters invested with this potentiality as canonically feminine in appearance: to use the lesbian vernacular, as *femme* (or 'fem') rather than butch. One could argue that this is merely a function of the wider interpellation of French women generally into hyper-normative femininity, which is but the counterpart of a French male chauvinism needing a strongly differentiated feminine Other against which to define itself positively. It may be that the francophone Belgian and Canadian films differ here because of the influence on them of other linguistic and cultural traditions: the Flemish in Belgium, the anglophone in Canada, both of which are marked by their tolerance of diverse linguistic communities (and where languages proliferate, cultures and ideologies do also – though which precedes which is moot).

I would like, however, to approach the phenomenon from a different and deliberately speculative angle. As Clare Whatling observes, Lisa Walker, in her article 'How to Recognise a Lesbian: The Politics of Looking Like What You Are', contends that 'there is a tendency in lesbian critics to theorise largely from the position of the butch, conferring upon her the position of active, instigative desirer, whilst confining the femme to the role of passive recipient of her desire' (Whatling 1997: 666). Walker, however, identifies the pitfalls of a politics of the predominantly visual:

> While privileging visibility can be politically and rhetorically effective, it is not without its problems. Within the constructs of a given identity that invests certain signifiers with political value, figures that do not present these signifiers are often neglected. Because subjects who can 'pass' exceed the categories of visibility that establish identity, they tend to be regarded as peripheral to the understanding of marginalization. (Walker 1993: 868)

Metropolitan-French filmic lesbians certainly 'pass' in the sense of often not revealing their lesbianism overtly according to stereotypical visual codes based on the butch/*femme* binarism; in fact, there are very few butch lesbian characters indeed in metropolitan French film. But many of them also 'pass' in the sense of exceeding that other tenacious binarism, homosexual/heterosexual. By far the longest chapter in this study, Chapter 4, has focused on liminal lesbianism in French film, and its length is a function of this configuration's stronghold within the corpus. For the perhaps not so 'ideal'[5] lesbian reader, this apparent depoliticisation will provoke frustration. For the more queer-oriented ideal reader, along with non-metropolitan French mainstream readers, it will comfortably support embedded cultural myths of French subtlety, wit and contestation of all norms. Gallic gaiety, after all, takes many forms.

Notes

1. Stéphanie, 'De la difficulté de parler de ce qu'on ne vit pas', *Rouge*, 23 February 1977.
2. J. M., '*Pourquoi pas moi?*', *Le Monde*, 7 January 1999.
3. I am grateful to Durham Modern Languages Series for permission to reproduce here certain comments on national differences between films from my chapter in Günther and Michallat (eds) 2006.
4. Bill Marshall's *Quebec National Cinema* (2001) is highly recommended reading for greater knowledge of French Canadian cinema generally.
5. See Chapter 4, note 12, for an explanation of the term 'ideal reader'.

Annotated Filmography

This appendix seeks not to summarise the films in their entirety, but briefly to indicate their lesbian content and, where appropriate, to indicate thematic intersections with anglophone films. Whilst this study has largely addressed a research constituency, this supplement may have more appeal to a popular readership, which is reflected in its lighter style. None the less, I hope my annotations will provide a useful resource both for scholars and for university teachers wishing to work on gender and sexuality in French and francophone cinemas. To facilitate the location of the films, I indicate in brackets where they are available for consultation at the following Paris-based institutions.

BiFi: Bibliothèque du Film, 51, rue de Bercy, 75012 Paris (www.bifi.fr)
BN: Bibliothèque Nationale de France, Quai François-Mauriac, 75706 Paris Cedex 13 (www.bnf.fr)
FDI: Forum des Images, Forum des Halles 75001 Paris (www.forumdes-images.net/fr)
IRIS: IRIS Centre de documentation et d'information, Maison des Arts – Place Salvador Allende, 94000 Creteil (iris@filmsdefemmes.com)

Names of actresses are supplied parenthetically in two cases: first, where the actress enjoys something of a cult status in (imagined) lesbian communities; second, where she has appeared fairly regularly, though not necessarily in leading roles, in lesbian-themed movies – the two cases in point being Pascale Bussières and Marie-France Pisier. This onomastic extra is my modest contribution to the rising (sub-) genre of star studies within the broader discipline of film studies.

Finally, it should be noted that six of the films listed in this filmography have proved unobtainable either at the research holdings listed above or through commercial outlets: *La Garçonne* (Audry's version), *Maman et Ève*, *Le Film de Justine*, *La Pirate*, *Simone* and *Valérie*. However, as an aid to future researchers for whom these films might subsequently become available on DVD or through private loans, they have been included.

Aghion, Gabriel, *Belle maman* (France, 1999) (BN)
A rare example of an older lesbian couple, Nicou and Brigitte, in a long-term relationship and of successful lesbian parenting (on Nicou's part).

Akerman, Chantal, *Je, tu, il, elle* (Belgium, 1974)
The third part of this film contains the most explicit lesbian sex sequence ever in French or francophone cinema before 1974; it has scarcely been rivalled. Akerman plays one of the lovers.

Akerman, Chantal, *Les Rendez-vous d'Anna* (Belgium/France, 1978)
Anna travels, meets many people, but is preoccupied by an absent female lover. Ambiguous coming-out scene featuring mother and daughter lying next to each other in bed.

Akerman, Chantal, *La Captive* (Belgium/France, 2000) (BN)
Simon is obsessed with the suspected lesbian attraction of his girlfriend Ariane (Sylvie Testud) to her 'friend' Andrée.

Albicocco, Jean-Gabriel, *La Fille aux yeux d'or* (France, 1961) (BN)
Eléonore attempts to wean the girl with the golden eyes (Marie Laforêt) off her straight love; failure to do so prompts a fatal stabbing.

Archambault, Louise, *Atomic Saké* (Canada, 1999) (IRIS)
Mathilde tries unsuccessfully to come out to Ariane, with whom she is in love. Humorously wistful and stylistically experimental.

Assayas, Olivier, *Irma Vep* (France, 1996)
Supposedly bisexual wardrobe mistress Zoé courts classically beautiful actress Maggie Cheung. Her efforts fail and she turns ever more to drugs.

Audry, Jacqueline, *Huis clos* (France, 1954) (BN)
Film adaptation of Sartre's famous play. Inès (Arletty) is one of three dead souls condemned to hell, her crime being the murder of the man to whom her female lover had turned.

Audry, Jacqueline, *La Garçonne* (France, 1957)
Based on Victor Margueritte's 'scandalous' novel of 1922. After betrayal by her fiancé, Monique gets a career and a more varied love life, including

a relationship with a woman. The so-called tomboy eventually marries old chum Georges.

Audry, Jacqueline, *Olivia* **(France, 1951) (BN)**
Set in girls' boarding school. Pupil Olivia falls in love with Mlle Julie, one of the two lesbian headmistresses; the other, Mlle Cara, commits suicide. Mlle Julie leaves with her devoted young Italian (school-) mistress.

Balasko, Josiane, *Gazon maudit* **(France, 1995) (BN)**
Fed up with philandering husband Laurent, Loli (Victoria Abril), mother of two, has an affair with butch Marijo (Josiane Balasko). The ensuing *ménage à trois* is destroyed by Loli's jealousy. Mari-Jo gets Laurent to sire a baby. They all end up living together, whilst Laurent discovers his own homoerotic potential.

Ballyot, Sylvie, *Alice* **(France, 2002) (IRIS)**
With loving support from partner Elsa, Alice overcomes the trauma of childhood rape by a male cousin and incestuous love for her sister. Contains the most explicit lesbian sex-scene of the entire corpus bar that in Akerman's *Je, tu, il,elle*.

Baratier, Jacques, *L'Araignée de satin* **(France, 1984) (BN)**
Gothic movie set in a girls' boarding school where, along with black magic and diabolism, lesbianism runs rife.

Baron, Dominique, *Tous les papas ne font pas pipi debout* **(Belgium, 2001) (BN)**
Only film in corpus featuring a lesbian couple bringing up a child. Both the parents' and the child's considerable problems are foregrounded, but a happy ending ensues.

Birot, Anne-Sophie, *Les Filles ne savent pas nager* **(France, 1999)**
Teenager Lise becomes jealous when her life-long 'friend' Gwen starts seeing boys. Ends in murder, but with a twist. Cf. *All Over Me* for teenaged girls' 'friendship'. (Pascale Bussières plays Gwen's mother.)

Briand, Manon, *2 Secondes* **(Canada, 1998)**
Laurie finds lesbian love: period. For once, no problems with the lesbianism; the problems lie elsewhere.

Buñuel, Luis, *Belle de Jour* **(France, 1967) (BN and BiFi)**
Bored middle-class housewife Séverine (Catherine Deneuve) turns to high-class prostitution for diversion. Her madame has a soft spot for her.

Calef, Henri, *Féminin-Féminin* (France, 1973) (BN)
Cécile secretly desires daughter-in-law Françoise (Marie-France Pisier), who spurns her overly subtle attentions in favour of Marie-Hélène; their apparently perfect happiness eventually alarms Marie-Hélène, who goes back to her boyfriend.

Calle, Sylvia, *Ô trouble* (France, 1998)
Egged on by gay male friends, Inès eventually confesses to flatmate Laura that she loves her; Laura knew all along, but doesn't return the compliment.

Carrière, Paul, *Maman et Ève* (Canada, 1996)
One of only two male-directed films from Quebec with any lesbian element. Four married women with children decide to embark on sexual experimentation, and dally with lesbianism.

Casaril, Guy, *Emilienne et Nicole* (France, 1970) (BN)
Nicole, Claude's mistress, seduces Claude's wife Emilienne. Various improbable elements including lesbian witches, but ends in a fatuous *ménage à trois* and a baby to bind them all together.

Casaril, Guy, *Le Rempart des Béguines* (France, 1972) (BN)
Schoolgirl Hélène falls passionately in love with her father's mistress Tamara, secretly of s/m bent. It ends in marriage for the latter two and tears for Hélène.

Chabrol, Claude, *Les Biches* (France, 1968) (BN and BiFi)
Frédérique (Stéphane Audran) seduces young female artist Why; Why has sex with Paul; Frédérique steals Paul; Why ingratiates herself with the straight couple, then eventually stabs Frédérique and steals the dead woman's identity. Cf. Barbet Schroeder's *Single White Female* (US, 1992).

Chabrol, Claude, *La Cérémonie* (France, 1995) (BN and BiFi)
Jeanne (played by Isabelle Huppert, of *Coup de foudre* 'lesbian' fame) and Sophie form an ambiguously close relationship and end up killing the bourgeois family for which Sophie works as maid. Lesbian desire is potential rather than overt.

Chabrol, Claude, *Marie-Chantal contre le Docteur Kha* (France, 1965) (BN)
Very slight 'lesbian' content, better described as potentially lesboerotic: Olga (Stéphane Audran) sensuously divests Marie-Chantal (Marie

Laforêt) of her stockings. But included in Philbert's early study of homo-sexuality in cinema.

Clouzot, Henri-Georges, *Les Diaboliques* (France, 1954) (BN and BiFi)
Coded lesbian desire permeates the relationship between Nicole (Simone Signoret) and Christina. Implausible heterosexualised ending which tra-duces the novel on which it is based. Cf. Jeremiah Chechik's *Diabolique* (US, 1996).

Clouzot, Henri-Georges, *Quai des orfèvres* (France, 1947) (BN and BiFi)
Photographer Dora (Simone Renant) harbours an undeclared and unre-quited passion for singer Jenny. Her passion prompts her to acts of high heroism.

Corsini, Catherine, *La Nouvelle Ève* (France, 1999) (BN)
Vignette role for a lesbian couple in a largely straight-oriented film. Only mention of gay marriage in the whole corpus, and only representation of a mixed-race lesbian couple.

Corsini, Catherine, *La Répétition* (France, 2000)
Best 'friends' Nathalie (Emmanuelle Béart) and Louise (Pascale Bussières) split after a jealous outburst by the latter, who slashes her wrists in despair. Ten years on they meet, and the infernal spiral is repeated.

Crépeau, Jeanne, *L'Usure* (Canada, 1986)
Two women meet up in an effort to end a lesbian relationship eroded by time.

Crépeau, Jeanne, *Le Film de Justine* (Canada, 1989)
A young woman tries to turn her back on love after a messy split from her girlfriend, but fails by falling in love with another woman.

Crépeau, Jeanne, *Revoir Julie* (Canada, 1998)
Two old 'friends' from school days meet after a fifteen-year gap. Julie even-tually overcomes her internalised lesbophobia. Stylistically innovative evo-cation of lesbian love-making.

Denis, Jean-Pierre, *Les Blessures assassines* (France, 2000) (BN)
Based on the infamous case of the Papin sisters, Christine (Sylvie Testud) and Léa, who shot to notoriety by butchering their employer and her

daughter in 1933. Includes (incestous) lesbian sex-scenes. Cf. Nancy Mekler's *Sister, My Sister* (UK/US, 1994).

Despentes, Virginie and Trinh Thi, Coralie, *Baise-moi* (France, 2000) (BN)
A borderline case: lesboerotic potential rather than realisation marks the relationship between serial killers Manu (Raffaëla Anderson) and Nadine (Karen Bach). Cf. Ridley Scott's *Thelma and Louise* (US, 1991) and Alan Rudolph's *Mortal Thoughts* (US, 1991).

Deval, Jacques, *Club de femmes* (France, 1936)
Set in a young women's hostel. Alice's doomed love for Juliette leads to murder of Juliette's male abuser. Dyke-encoded house doctor Gabrielle covers up the crime, but sends Alice away to nurse in a leper colony.

Doillon, Jacques, *La Pirate* (France, 1984)
Alma (Jane Birkin) is caught in a triangular trap, torn between love for her husband Andrew and passion for her 'friend' Carole. Carole's child finally kills Alma.

Ehm, Christine, *Simone* (France, 1984)
Plunged into suicidal depression, Françoise regains the will to live when she meets enigmatic stranger Simone and the two explore their fantasies together.

Faucon, Philippe, *Muriel fait le désespoir de ses parents* (France, 1995)
Teenager Muriel steadfastly ignores her parents' and sibling's disapproval of her lesbian identification, and progresses from fixation on the flirtatious but closeted Nora to happiness with the out Caroline.

Féret, René, *Mystère Alexina* (France, 1985)
True story of a nineteenth-century hermaphrodite. Lesbian-connoted in so far as it depicts love and sex between a 'real' woman and a person whose civil status was female at the time of the relationship.

Fleury, Joy, *Tristesse et beauté* (France, 1985) (BN)
The inaptly named Prudence attempts to avenge her sculpture teacher and desire-object Léa (Charlotte Rampling) of betrayal by Hugo twenty years ago, with fatal consequences – though not for the primary female relationship.

Franju, Georges, *Thérèse Desqueyroux* **(France, 1962)**
A fairly faithful adaptation of Mauriac's famous novel, in which Thérèse harbours a doomed love for her sister-in-law Anne.

Girod, Francis, *La Banquière* **(France, 1980) (BN)**
Based on the life of successful financier Marthe Hannau (here re-named Emma) who fell (literally) fatally foul of the phallocratic financial fraternity of the inter-war period, and had relationships with women as well as men. Includes Marie-France Pisier as Colette, one of Emma's seductees.

Giusti, Stéphane, *Pourquoi pas moi?* **(France, 1999) (BN)**
A comedy of manners in which a group of young lesbians and gays, along with their parents, meet at a country house for the weekend with the aim of coming out to their respective family members.

Granier-Deferre, Pierre, *Cours privé* **(France, 1987) (BN)**
Blackmail leads high-school teacher Jeanne to regret her lesbian relationship with pupil Agnès, but by close of play she is surreptitiously eying up the pupils at her new, all-girls school.

Héroux, Denis, *Valérie* **(Canada, 1968)**
One of only two male-directed films from Quebec with even a token role for lesbianism, *Valérie* at one point shows its eponymous heroine rebuffing the advances of a minor lesbian character.

Joux, Frédérique, *Emma & Louise* **(France, 1998)**
The only animated film in the corpus, humorously featuring explicit lesbian sex but also stressing the need for lesbians to practise safe sex.

Kaplan, Nelly, *La Fiancée du pirate* **(France, 1969) (BN)**
Butch farmer Irène extracts sexual services from servant Marie, who eventually gets her revenge on both Irène and her (Marie's) male clientèle.

Kaplan, Nelly, *Néa* **(France, 1976)**
Sixteen-year-old Sibylle successfully encourages her mother Helen to leave her abusive husband for the woman she loves and desires – sister-in-law Judith.

Keigel, Léonard, *Une Femme, un jour* **(France, 1974) (FDI)**
Mother of a five-year-old son and engaged in divorce proceedings, Caroline begins a relationship with out lesbian Nicky, which founders on Caroline's bad faith.

Klapisch, Cédric, *Chacun cherche son chat* (France, 1996)
Chloé lives with a gay male flatmate whom she attempts to seduce, but skittishly rejects the advances of barmaid Blanche who had defended her against intimidating male lechery.

Kümel, Harry, *Les Lèvres rouges* (Belgium, 1971; originally entitled *Le Rouge aux lèvres*)
Glamorous vampire Elisabeth (Delphine Seyrig) seduces Valérie and they rid themselves of the latter's vicious husband but, true to formula, it all ends rather darkly. Cf. Tony Scott's *The Hunger* (1983).

Kurys, Diane, *À la folie* (France, 1993) (BN)
The possessive, invasive and potentially sexual love of Elsa for her sister Alice threatens the latter's very identity. Cf. Barbet Schroeder's *Single White Female* (US, 1992).

Kurys, Diane, *Coup de foudre* (France, 1982) (BN)
Critical debate has raged about whether the bond between Léna (Isabelle Huppert) and Madeleine (Miou-Miou) is lesbian or not, but when in the 1950s two wives and mothers leave their husbands to set up business and home together, incidentally taking the children into a recomposed family, one has to wonder.

Lefebvre, Geneviève, *Le Jupon rouge* (France, 1986) (BN)
Bacha's perception that her 'friendship' with Manuela is threatened by the latter's lesbian relationship with Claude leads to the older woman trying to sabotage that love.

Lesselier, C. et Vanbemburghe, J., *Portrait d'Hélène Azenor* (France, 1987) (FDI)
Documentary about the life, lesbian loves and creations of Hélène Azenor, a painter born in 1910 whose youth coincided with Paris's bohemian *Belle Époque* period.

Limur, Jean de, *La Garçonne* (France, 1936) (FDI)
Like Audry's film of the same name, based on Victor Margueritte's 'scandalous' novel of 1922. Arletty plays Niquette, one of Monique's admirers. Also features Edith Piaff in a minor role.

Lipinska, Christine, *Le Cahier volé* (France, 1992) (BN and BiFi)
Teenager Virginie has three erotic foci, two of whom are male and one female – with the latter assuming a far greater, and ultimately tragic, weight.

Malle, Louis, *Milou en mai* **(France, 1989) (BN and BiFi)**
Vignette role for literally lame lesbian Claire, who indulges in mild sado-masochism with her flighty young lover Marie-Laure, and humiliates the straight bravado of lorry driver Grimaldi.

Mandy, Marie, *Filmer le désir* **(Belgium and France, 2000)**
Documentary on women directors' mediation of desire, including its lesbian avatars.

Marshall, Tonie, *Pas très catholique* **(France, 1994) (BN and BiFi)**
While denying lesbian identification, Maxime (Anémone) enjoys sex with Florence, who for her part supplies a compelling apologia of female genitalia.

Mizrahi, Moshe, *Les Stances à Sophie* **(France, 1970)**
Based on the novel by Christiane Rochefort. Young bourgeois housewives Cécile and Julia enter into an amorous and sexual relationship. Their relationship is cut tragically short.

Mulot, Claude, *L'Immorale* **(France, 1980)**
Soft-core pornographic film in which Carole, a high-class prostitute, rather enjoys servicing her one female client.

Ozon, François, *Huit femmes* **(France, 2001) (BN and BiFi)**
Parodic mystery spoof featuring one unashamed lesbian (significantly, a trebly marginalised character in that she is black, working-class and lesbian: played by Firmine Richard), one white, working-class woman who adores her previous female employer (Emmanuelle Béart), and two white bourgeois women (Catherine Deneuve and Fanny Ardant) who pass as straight but betray distinct lesbian temptations.

Ozon, François, *L'Homme idéal* **(France, 1996)**
One unnamed woman encourages her 'friend', worried about her boyfriend's lack of commitment, to pretend she is with him, for therapeutic reasons. The so-called therapy turns into lesbian sex.

Ozon, François, *Regarde la mer* **(France, 1997) (BN, under title** *Scènes de lit***)**
Wife and mother Sacha is fascinated by vagrant Tamara, masturbating while watching the tent in which Tamara is sleeping. The fascination has literally fatal results.

Ozon, François, *Swimming Pool* (France, 2002)
The initially disapproving gaze of Sarah (Charlotte Rampling) sexualises the sumptuous forms of a much younger woman, Sarah, with whom she develops an ambiguously complicitous relationship.

Papatakis, Nico, *Les Abysses* (France, 1963)
First film in the corpus to be based, albeit loosely, on the infamous real-life case of the Papin sisters. Development of another lesbian character, Elisabeth, who unlike the sisters belongs to the bourgeoisie. Cf. Nancy Mekler's *Sister, My Sister* (UK/US, 1994).

Plessy, Armand du, *La Garçonne* (France, 1923)
First French film based on Victor Margueritte's novel of 1922, and first to feature a lesbian relationship. Was banned, and has proven unobtainable in all my searches.

Poligny, Serge de, *Claudine à l'école* (France, 1937)
Based on Colette's famous 1900 novel about passionate friendships and games of seduction between girls (and occasionally mistresses) at a girls' boarding school.

Pool, Léa, *Anne Trister* (Canada, 1986) (BN and IRIS)
Artist Anne falls in love with straight-identified psychotherapist Alix, who initially resists but ultimately realises the amorous strength of her feelings for Anne after the latter suffers a serious accident.

Pool, Léa, *Emporte-moi* (Canada, 1998)
Thirteen-year-old Hanna adores actress Anna Karina on screen, and becomes aware of her nascent lesbian feelings in real life when she kisses teenager Laura. Hanna's equally adored mother is played by Pascale Bussières.

Pool, Léa, *La Femme de l'hôtel* (Canada, 1984) (IRIS)
Director Andréa becomes obsessed with a woman in the hotel where she is staying. Their relationship is charged with the unspoken potential of lesbian desire. For recourse to male character as courier of unavowed lesbian desire, cf. Bob Rafelson's *Black Widow* (US, 1986).

Ramaka, Joseph Gaï, *Karmen Geï* (Senegal, 2001)
Only African film in the entire corpus. Bizet's Carmen becomes a black bisexual with whom stern prison governess Angélique falls hopelessly and fatally in love.

Rivette, Jacques, *Céline et Julie vont en bateau* **(France, 1973) (BN and BiFi)**
Lesbian desire is hinted at but never made explicit; what is clear is an intimacy, complicity and periodic fusion of identities that is often, if problematically, equated with lesbianism.

Rivette, Jacques, *Suzanne Simonin, La Religieuse de Diderot* **(France, 1965) (BN)**
Based on Diderot's canonical eighteenth-century novel *La Religieuse*, this once-banned film includes the lesbian advances made by a Mother Superior upon novice Suzanne.

Rollin, Jean, *Le Viol du Vampire* **(France, 1967) (BN)**
The second part of the film features 'la reine des vampires', a black s/m dominatrix surrounded by devoted female vampires.

Rollin, Jean, *Le Frisson des vampires* **(France, 1970) (BN)**
S/m-encoded vampire Isolde bewitches newly married Yse with her 'evil' sexual advances and bites the nipples of Isabelle in reaction to the latter's caresses.

Rollin, Jean, *Vierges et vampires* **(France, 1971) [also known as** *Requiem pour un vampire*] **(BN)**
Two precocious schoolgirls stumble on an old castle, which turns out to be the lair of the last ever vampire. They are shown naked in bed together, and vampire Erica's arousal at watching women being raped may either excite or horrify.

Rollin, Jean, *Fascination* **(France, 1979) (BN)**
The male intruder in the lesbian relationship between vampires Elisabeth and Eva is murdered by Elisabeth, along with Eva, who had unwisely had sex with him. A lesbian vampire community sucks the life-blood from the dying Eva.

Rollin, Jean, *La Morte vivante* **(France, 1982) (BN)**
Hélène provides a gory supply of fresh blood from human beings to living-dead lover Catherine.

Silvera, Charlotte, *Prisonnières* **(France, 1988) (BN)**
Set in a women's prison, where one (sub-)plot among others is the lesbian relationship that develops between the younger Sabine and the older Lucie.

Simon, Claire, *Mimi* **(France, 2002) (BiFi)**
Documentary in which Mimi evokes among other aspects of her life her lesbian relationships. Singularly uncontaminated by angst.

Tanner, Alain, *Messidor* **(Switzerland, 1980)**
A 'road movie' involving crimes committed by Marie and Jeanne, who form a lesbian relationship in their existential adventure. Cf. Ridley Scott's *Thelma and Louise* (US, 1991) and Alan Rudolph's *Mortal Thoughts* (US, 1991).

Téchiné, André, *Les Voleurs* **(France, 1995)**
Features as a sub-plot the lesbian love of philosophy lecturer (and wife and grandmother) Marie (Catherine Deneuve) for petty criminal Juliette, who eventually goes on the run to escape arrest. Marie commits suicide.

Treilhou, Marie-Claude, *Simone Barbès ou la vertu* **(France, 1980) (BN, BiFi and FDI)**
Features an ambiguous relationship between Simone and her 'friend' Minouche. The second of the film's three sections is set in a famous lesbian nightclub in Paris.

Vander Stappen, Chris, *La Fête des mères* **(Belgium, 1998)**
As a Mother's Day present, Sacha takes her mother to a health farm, where she attempts to come out to her as lesbian.

Vander Stappen, Chris, *Que faisaient les femmes pendant que l'homme marchait sur la lune?* **(Belgium, 1999)**
Development of *La Fête des mères*, including parallel with another marginalised identity: that of dwarfism, incarnated by Sacha's sister. A whimsical film with a feel-good ending.

Wichard, Michel, *Le Quatrième sexe* **(France, 1961)**
Misogynous movie tracing the psycho-sexual trajectory of Sand, a rich American painter in Paris, from lesboeroticism to virtually parodic heteronormativity. Cf. David Butler's *Calamity Jane* (US, 1953) and Rouben Mamoulian's *Queen Christina* (US, 1933).

Yedaya, Keren, *Les Dessous* **(France, 2001)**
Marie gets aroused when trying on underwear and overhearing a couple of women doing the same in the adjacent cabin.

Bibliography

Barthes, Roland (1970) *S/Z*, Paris: Éditions du Seuil.
Cairns, Lucille (2002a) *Lesbian Desire in Post-1968 French Literature*, New York/Ontario/Lampeter: The Edwin Mellen Press.
Castle, Terry (1993) *The Apparitional Lesbian: Female Homosexuality and Modern Culture*, New York: Columbia University Press.
Deleuze, Gilles (1967) *Présentation de Sacher Masoch*, Paris: Éditions de Minuit.
Dyer, Richard (1990) *Now you See It: Studies on Lesbian and Gay Film*, London: Routledge.
Edwards, Rachel and Reader, Keith (2001) *The Papin Sisters*, Oxford: Oxford University Press.
Foucault, Michel (1978) *Herculine Barbin, dite Alexina B.: Mes souvenirs*, Paris: Gallimard.
Fuss, Diana (ed.) (1991) *Inside/Out: Lesbian Theories, Gay Theories*, New York: Routledge.
Gide, André (1924) *Corydon*, Paris: Gallimard. Reproduced in Folio edition, 1991.
Günther, Renate and Michallat, Wendy (eds) (2006) *Lesbian Inscriptions in Francophone Society and Culture*, Durham: Durham Modern Languages Series.
Hanson, Ellis (ed.) (1999) *Out Takes: Essays on Queer Theory and Film*, Durham, NC and London: Duke University Press.
Hart, Lynda (1994) *Fatal Women: Lesbian Sexuality and the Mark of Aggression*, Princeton, NJ: Princeton University Press.
Hughes, Alex and Williams, James (eds) (2001) *Gender and French Cinema*, Oxford/New York: Berg.
Irigaray, Luce (1977) *Ce sexe qui n'en est pas un*, Paris: Éditions de Minuit.
Irigarary, Luce (1985) *Parler n'est jamais neutre*, Paris: Éditions de Minuit.
Irigaray, Luce (1987) *Sexes et parentés*, Paris: Éditions de Minuit.
Jagose, Annamarie (1994) *Lesbian Utopics*, London: Routledge.
Kabir, Shameem (1998) *Daughters of Desire: Lesbian Representations in Film*, London and Washington: Cassell.
Kristeva, Julia (1980) *Pouvoirs de l'horreur. Essai sur l'abjection*, Paris: Éditions du Seuil.

Kristeva, Julia (1983) *Histoires d'amour*, Paris: Éditions Denoël.

Lacan, Jacques (1994) *La Relation d'objet*, Paris: Seuil.

Lauretis, Teresa de (1994) *The Practice of Love: Lesbian Sexuality and Perverse Desire*, Bloomington and Indianapolis: Indiana University Press.

Marshall, Bill (2001) *Quebec National Cinema*, Montreal and Kingston: McGill-Queen's University Press.

Mayne, Judith (2000) *Framed: Lesbians, Feminists and Media Culture*, Minneapolis: University of Minnesota Press.

Metz, Christian (1983) *Psychoanalysis and Cinema: The Imaginary Signifier*, London: Macmillan.

Nilson, Herman (1998) *Michel Foucault and the Games of Truth*, trans. by Rachel Clark, New York: St. Martin's Press; London: Macmillan Press.

Oliver, Kelly (1993) *Reading Kristeva: Unravelling the Double-bind*, Bloomington and Indianapolis: Indiana University Press.

Peary, Gerald and Shatzkin, Roger (1977) *The Classic American Novel and the Movies: Exploring the Link between Literature and Film*, New York: Frederic Ungar Publishing.

Penley, Constance (ed.) (1988) *Feminism and Film Theory*, New York and London: Routledge.

Philbert, Bertrand (1984) *L'Homosexualité à l'écran*, Paris: Henri Veyrier.

Reader, Keith (2006) *The Abject Object: Avatars of the Phallus in Contemporary French Theory, Literature and Film*, Amsterdam: Rodopi.

Roof, Judith (1991) *A Lure of Knowledge: Lesbian Sexuality and Theory*, New York: Columbia University Press.

Russo, Vito (1981) *The Celluloid Closet*, New York: Harper & Row.

Sedgwick, Eve Kosofsky (1990) *Epistemology of the Closet*, London: Harvester Wheatsheaf.

Stacey, Jackie (1994) *Star Gazing: Hollywood Cinema and Female Spectatorship*, London: Routledge.

Stein, Edward (ed.) (1992) *Forms of Desire: Sexual Orientation and Social Constructionist Controversy*, London: Routledge.

Tarr, Carrie with Rollet, Brigitte (2001) *Cinema and the Second Sex: Women's Filmmaking in France in the 1980s and 1990s*, London/New York: Continuum.

Weiss, Andrea (1992) *Vampires and Violets: Lesbians in the Cinema*, London: Jonathan Cape.

Whatling, Clare (1997) *Screen Dreams: Fantasizing Lesbians in Film*, Manchester and New York: Manchester University Press.

White, Patricia (1999) *Uninvited: Classical Hollywood Cinema and Lesbian Representability*, Bloomington and Indianapolis: Indiana University Press.

Wilton, Tamsin (1995) *Immortal, Invisible: Lesbians and the Moving Image*, London and New York: Routledge.

Wollen, Peter (1969) *Signs and Meaning in the Cinema*, 2nd edn, London: Thames and Hudson.

Academic Journal Articles and Chapters in Edited Works

Argote, Joël (2002) 'Plus ça change: Screening Difference in French Film', in Martine Antle and Dominique Fisher (eds), *The Rhetoric of the Other: Lesbian and Gay Strategies of Resistance in French and Francophone Contexts*, New Orleans: University Press of the South, pp. 143–50.

Butler, Judith (Winter 1989) 'The Body Politics of Julia Kristeva', *Hypatia* 3, no. 3, pp. 104–18.

Butler, Judith (1991) 'Imitation and Gender Insubordination', in Diana Fuss (ed.), *Inside/Out: Lesbian Theories, Gay Theories*, New York: Routledge, pp. 13–31.

Cairns, Lucille (June 1998) '*Gazon maudit*: French National and Sexual Identities', *French Cultural Studies*, vol. 9 part 2, no. 26, pp. 225–37.

Cairns, Lucille (2000) 'Sexual Fault Lines: Sex and Gender in the Cultural Context', in William Kidd and Siân Reynolds (eds), *Contemporary French Cultural Studies*, London: Arnold, pp. 81–94.

Cairns, Lucille (2001) 'Gender Trouble in *Ma Vie en rose*', in Lucy Mazdon (ed.), *France on Film: Reflections on Popular French Cinema*, London: Wallflower Press, pp. 119–31.

Cairns, Lucille (2002b) 'Identity or Difference? The Ontology of Lesbianism in Contemporary French Realist Fiction', in Lucille Cairns (ed.), *Gay and Lesbian Cultures in France*, Oxford: Peter Lang, pp. 157–71.

Cairns, Lucille (2002c) 'Le Phallus Lesbien (Bis): Lesbo-Erotic French Writing of the Late 1990s', *Nottingham French Studies*, vol. 41, no. 1, pp. 89–101.

Cairns, Lucille (2006) 'Lesbian Desire in Recent French and Francophone Cinema', in Renate Günther Renate and Wendy Michallat (eds), *Lesbian Inscriptions in Francophone Society and Culture*, Durham: Durham Modern Languages Series.

Creed, Barbara (1995) 'Lesbian Bodies: Tribades, Tomboys and Tarts', in Elizabeth Grosz and Elspeth Probyn (eds), *Sexy Bodies: The Strange Carnalities of Feminism*, London and New York: Routledge, pp. 86–103.

Doane, Mary Anne (September/October 1982) 'Film and the Masquerade: Theorizing the Female Spectator', *Screen*, 23.3–4, pp. 74–87.

Erhart, Julia (1997) 'She Must Be Theorizing Things: Fifteen Years of Lesbian Film Criticism, 1981–96', in Gabriele Griffin and Sonya Andermahr (eds), *Straight Studies Modified: Lesbian Interventions in the Academy*, London and Washington: Cassell, pp. 86–101.

Evans, Caroline and Gamman, Lorraine (1995) 'The Gaze Revisited, or Reviewing Queer Viewing', in Paul Burston and Colin Richardson (eds), *A Queer Romance: Lesbians, Gay Men and Popular Culture*, London: Routledge, pp. 13–56.

Hayward, Susan (1995) 'Simone Signoret 1921–1985: The Star as Sign – the Sign as Scar', in Diana Knight and Judith Still (eds), *Women and Representation*, Nottingham: WIF Publications, 1995, pp. 57–74.

Hayward, Susan (2003) 'Literary Adaptations of the 1950s *Thérèse Raquin* (1953) and *Les Diaboliques* (1955)', *Studies in French Cinema*, vol. 3, no. 1, pp. 5–14.

Holmlund, Christine (1991) 'When is a Lesbian not a Lesbian? The Lesbian Continuum and the Mainstream Femme Film', *Camera Obscura*, no. 25, pp. 144–79.

Irigaray, Luce (October 1977) 'Misère de la psychanalyse', *Critique*, 365, pp. 879–903.

Johnston, Cristina (2002) 'Representations of Homosexuality in 1990s Mainstream French Cinema', *Studies in French Cinema*, vol. 2, no. 1, pp. 23–31.

Johnston, Claire (1976) 'Women's Cinema as Counter-cinema', in Bill Nichols (ed.), *Movies and Methods: an Anthology*, Berkeley: University of California Press, pp. 208–17.

Jousse, Thierry (October 1994) 'A la folie', *Cahiers du cinéma*, no. 484, pp. 68–9.

Kast, Pierre (1953) 'Il est minuit, docteur Kinsey . . .', *Cahiers du cinéma*, no. 30, tome V, Noël, p. 51.

Mayne, Judith (2004) 'Dora the Image-maker, and Henri-Georges Clouzot's *Quai des orfèvres*', *Studies in French Cinema* 4:1, pp. 41–52.

Mulvey, Laura (1975) 'Visual Pleasure and Narrative Cinema', *Screen* 16, pp. 6–18.

Mulvey, Laura (1981) 'Afterthoughts on "Visual Pleasure and Narrative Cinema" inspired by *Duel in the Sun*', *Framework* 6, nos 15–17. Reproduced in Constance Penley (ed.) (1988) *Feminism and Film Theory*, New York and London: Routledge, pp. 69–79.

Nadeau, Chantal (1995) 'Girls on a Wired Screen: Cavani's Cinema and Lesbian s/m', in Elizabeth Grosz and Elspeth Probyn (eds), *Sexy Bodies: The Strange Carnalities of Feminism*, London and New York: Routledge, pp. 211–30.

Nadeau, Chantal (Summer/Autumn 2004) 'Copines et compagnes à la campagne: réflexions "queer" sur *Revoir Julie*', *Nouvelles vues sur le cinema québécois*, no. 2, 2. Pagination on net version of article: pp. 1–8.

Pénet, Martin (2003) 'Cabarets', in Didier Eribon (ed.), *Dictionnaire des cultures gays et lesbiennes*, Paris: Larousse, pp. 87–90.

Reader, Keith (2001) ' "Mon cul est intersexuel?": Arletty's Performance of Gender', in Alex Hughes and James Williams (eds), *Gender and French Cinema*, Oxford and New York: Berg, pp. 63–76.

Rich, Adrienne (1980) 'Compulsory Heterosexuality and Lesbian Existence', *Signs: Journal of Women in Culture and Society*, 5, no. 4, pp. 631–60. Reproduced in A. Snitow, C. Stansell and S. Thompson (eds) (1983) *Powers of Desire: the Politics of Sexuality*, New York: New Feminist Library, Monthly Review Press, pp. 177–205.

Sherzer, Dina (2001) 'Gender and Sexuality in New New Wave Cinema', in Alex Hughes and James Williams (eds), *Gender and French Cinema*, Oxford and New York: Berg, pp. 227–39.

Tarr, Carrie (1993) 'Ambivalent Desires in Jacqueline Audry's *Olivia*', *Nottingham French Studies*, vol. 32, part 1, pp. 32–42.

Traub, Valerie (1991) 'The Ambiguities of "Lesbian" Viewing Pleasure: The (Dis)articulations of *Black Widow*', in J. Epstein and K. Straub (eds), *Body Guards: The Cultural Politics of Gender Ambiguity*, London: Routledge, pp. 305–28.

Walker, Lisa (1993) 'How to recognise a Lesbian: The Politics of Looking Like What You Are', *Signs*, 18:4, pp. 866–90.

White, Patricia (1995) 'Governing Lesbian Desire: *Nocturne*'s Oedipal Fantasy', in Laura Pietropaulo and Ada Testaferri (eds), *Feminism in the Cinema*, Bloomington: Indiana University Press, pp. 86–105.

Worth, Fabienne (1993) 'Toward Alternative Film Histories: Lesbian Films, Spectators, Filmmakers and the French Cinematic/Cultural Apparatus', *Quarterly Review of Film and Video*, vol. 15 (1), pp. 55–77.

Index

215